HOW TO RESTORE

Ford Tractors

The Ultimate Guide to Rebuilding and Restoring
N-Series and Later Tractors 1939-1962

Tharran E. Gaines

Voyageur Press

First published in 2008 by Voyageur Press, an imprint of MBI Publishing Company, 400 First Avenue North, Suite 300, Minneapolis, MN 55401 USA

Copyright © 2008 by Tharran E. Gaines

All rights reserved. With the exception of quoting brief passages for the purposes of review, no part of this publication may be reproduced without prior written permission from the Publisher.

The information in this book is true and complete to the best of our knowledge. All recommendations are made without any guarantee on the part of the author or Publisher, who also disclaim any liability incurred in connection with the use of this data or specific details.

This publication has not been prepared, approved, or licensed by CNH Case New Holland. We recognize, further, that some words, model names, and designations mentioned herein are the property of the trademark holder. We use them for identification purposes only. This is not an official publication.

Voyageur Press titles are also available at discounts in bulk quantity for industrial or sales-promotional use. For details write to Special Sales Manager at MBI Publishing Company, 400 First Avenue North, Suite 300, Minneapolis, MN 55401 USA.

To find out more about our books, join us online at www.voyageurpress.com.

ISBN-13: 978-0-7603-2620-6

Editor: Amy Glaser

Designer: Greg Nettles

Printed in Singapore

On the cover: This beautifully restored Ford 8N, owned by Chris Mercer of Excelsior Springs, Missouri, easily explains why the 8N became one of the company's most popular models. As a refinement of the 9N and 2N, it featured 30 PTO horsepower, a four-speed transmission, and position control, in addition to automatic depth control on the three-point hitch system. It was also the first model built after the split between Ford and Ferguson, hence the new color scheme.

On the frontispiece: Light kits were a dealer-installed option for several years on Ford tractors. Ford used two types of mounts over the years. The wing-style mounts, shown here, were used up until mid-1950 when they were replaced in the kits with the stamped-steel round mounts.

On the title pages: Tractor cruises, which can cover distances of 30 to 40 miles, have become an annual highlight for a number of Ford vintage tractor owners. In fact, most tractor cruises require that the tractor must be over a certain age to be registered for the cruise.

On the back cover 1: You'll need one or more sturdy jacks to support the chassis, since the tractor has to be split in order to work on the engine or transmission.

On the back cover 2: Steel wheels were only used on the 1942 and some early 1943 Model 2N tractors built at the beginning of World War II. They were available on 9N tractors as a special order option. Note the steel front and rear wheels attach to the standard hubs and rear wheel discs.

On the back cover 3: Replace all valve assemblies, springs jets, and needle assemblies as necessary.

Contents

Acknowledgments

Despite more than 30 years of agricultural writing experience, I'll be the first to admit that I could not have written and illustrated this book without the generous help of numerous people. Even after writing three other books on classic tractor restoration, there are still a vast number of things I don't know about different models, especially when it comes to a brand like Ford. Having grown up on a farm in north central Kansas, where wheat was the predominant crop, I didn't get much exposure to Ford tractors. In fact, I can't think of anybody in the area who owned one. Moreover, I didn't drive one myself until I was in college and working part-time for a tree farm. Consequently, I had to rely heavily on a few people for help.

To begin with, I owe a great deal of appreciation to my wife, Barb. Not only was she overly patient while I tried to fit this book in between all my other projects, she spent several hours proofreading the copy and the photo captions for typographical and grammatical errors.

There is another group of people who deserve a special thank you. Without their help, I literally would not have been able to put this book together. Even though I don't have any antique tractors myself and have a limited amount of experience working on tractors, I have approached tractor restoration in much the same way I did when I was a technical writer for companies like Sundstrand, Hesston, Winnebago, and Kinze. My job with those companies was to glean information from a variety of sources in marketing, engineering, product service, and the test lab and turn it into manuals that could be used by the customer to assemble, service, or repair the machine he or she had purchased from my employer.

I figure the people I have talked to and photographed while preparing this manuscript have forgotten more than I could ever learn about Ford tractor restoration. So in reality, this book is their story, not mine. With that in mind,

I want to express my sincere appreciation to three people in particular. One of them is John Smith, a Ford tractor enthusiast from Peoria, Illinois. John not only provided a wealth of information through emails and his website, www.8nford.com or www.oldfordtractors.com, but he helped review much of the copy in this book for technical errors. I also owe a debt of gratitude to Tom Armstrong, owner of N-Complete in Wilkinson, Indiana, and Dallas Mercer, owner of Mercer Restoration in Excelsior Springs, Missouri. Tom and his staff generously allowed me to take a number of photographs of tractors being remanufactured in their shop. As Tom would tell you, N-Complete doesn't restore tractors, but instead tears them down to the bare frames and remanufactures the units from the ground up. As a Ford tractor restorer in his spare time, Dallas Mercer was also very generous with his time and knowledge, not to mention a few photographs that he allowed me to use in this book.

Two more people who provided tremendous assistance were Chris and Kim Pratt, who write and edit the *Yesterday's Tractors* online magazine found at www.ytmag.com. Not only is their website an excellent source of tips and advice on restoration, but they also offer a variety of parts, kits, and manuals. Others who have provided resources, illustrations, or information include Paul Cummings, a tractor collector from Amsterdam, Missouri; the capable staff at Dennis Carpenter Ford Tractor Restoration Parts in Concord, North Carolina; and Paul Jensen and his staff with Jensales Inc. in Manchester, Minnesota.

I want to thank the staff at O'Reilly Auto Parts in Savannah, Missouri; Bill Briner and his staff at Bill's Auto Electric in Savannah; Gary Ledford, a technician at Auto Body Color, Inc., in St. Joseph, Missouri; and B. J. Rosmolen, owner of BJ's Auto Collision and Restoration, also in St. Joseph, for their help with photos and technical information on paint, electronics, and supplies.

Most of all, though, I want to thank Amy Glaser with Voyageur Press for her editorial guidance and direction on this project, not to mention her extreme patience every time I asked for an extended deadline. She and her boss, Michael Dregni, have been a pleasure to work with over the past couple of years.

CHAPTER 1

Ford Tractor History

If you're already the proud owner of a Ford tractor or if you have your heart set on finding one and restoring it, you already know that there is nothing quite like a Ford model—particularly if you're talking about a 9N, a 2N, or an 8N. Compared with other tractors of the time, the Ford 9N, which was the first model introduced, was already far ahead of the competition upon its release in 1939.

Although this book is designed to start with the N Series and carry through the first of the "blue" Ford tractors that were introduced in the 1960s, the N Series tractors weren't the first to carry the Ford name.

Testing the Waters

Having grown up on a farm, Henry Ford had an interest in tractors that rivaled his interest in automobiles. In fact, before he ever became famous for his Model T, Henry Ford built what he called his Automobile Plow in 1906. It was propelled by a four-cylinder engine and transmission taken from his Model B touring car.

Ironically, Ford's Model T even saw duty as a farm tractor, not through Ford's efforts, but from other companies like Smith Form-A-Tractor, Staude Mak-A-Tractor, the Auto Pull Company, the Pullford Company, and even Sears Roebuck. All of them built kits that could be used to convert a used or new, more affordable Model T into a field machine that was "guaranteed to do the work of four horses" when disking, plowing, mowing, drilling, and hauling crops.

By 1917, however, Henry Ford was ready to enter the tractor market in earnest with a new brand and a new design. Built by a separate division called Henry Ford and Son, the tractor was simply named the Fordson. There was at least one reason, and possibly two, why Ford settled on the Fordson name rather than the name previously made famous on his automobiles. For one, the name "Ford" was already being used on a tractor built in Minneapolis, Minnesota.

Perhaps realizing the Ford name was a valuable commodity, a group led by financier W. Baer Ewing rushed to incorporate the Ford Tractor Company in 1916. Although the company roster did include one person named Ford, neither he nor the company had any relationship with Henry Ford. Unfortunately,

that soon became obvious to anyone who bought one of the Minneapolis Ford tractors. They were poorly designed and engineered and had reliability problems from the start, which prompted one unhappy owner to do something about it. As a Nebraska state legislator, Wilmot F. Crozier used his unpleasant experience with a (Minneapolis) Ford tractor to initiate legislation that would require all tractors sold in Nebraska to undergo testing at the University of Nebraska to guard against false claims by tractor manufacturers, which marked the beginning of the Nebraska Tractor Tests.

If the Minneapolis company had visions of Henry Ford paying top dollar for the Ford tractor name, that didn't work either. Some theorize that Ford thought the Fordson name was best from the beginning since

This beautifully restored Ford 8N, owned by Chris Mercer of Excelsior Springs, Missouri, easily explains why the 8N became one of the company's most popular models. As a refinement of the 9N and 2N, it featured 30 PTO horsepower, a four-speed transmission, and position control, in addition to automatic depth control on the three-point hitch system. It was also the first model built after the split between Ford and Ferguson; hence the new color scheme.

The Fordson Model F, introduced in 1917, was Henry Ford's first attempt at marketing a farm tractor in North America. The Fordson name, which was a shortened form of the Henry Ford & Son Company, was chosen for a couple of reasons, one of which was the fact that there was already another tractor using the Ford name.

some Ford Motor Company shareholders didn't approve of tractor production. At any rate, the Fordson F was introduced in 1917, with a four-cylinder engine that delivered 20 horsepower at the drawbar.

Not only was the Fordson F smaller than most other tractors, which made it more affordable and easier to produce, but it also lacked a conventional frame. The engine, transmission, and axle housings were all bolted together to form the basic structure of the tractor. That practice started a trend that would carry on through the N Series Ford tractors and most of Ford tractor history. The Fordson market took a turn during the Great Depression when sales for all tractors began to fall in the United States. Consequently, Henry Ford ceased production in the United States and transferred Fordson production to Great Britain.

Due to the high cost of shipping Fordson farm tractors to the United States from Britain, not to mention competition from a growing number of American companies, Fordson's market share among American consumers slipped to a low of only

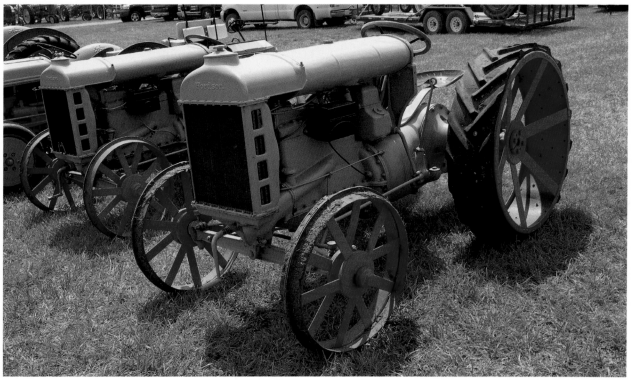

Although manufacturing was soon relegated to factories in Ireland, and later Britain, Fordson tractors were still marketed in the United States through the 1930s. Unfortunately, the high cost of importing the tractors and the development of newer models by American competitors, which made the Fordson look obsolete, eventually caused Ford's market share to slip to a low of 5 percent.

5 percent, even though a new, more powerful Model N had been introduced. Ford even tried to revive the market with a row-crop version of the N called the Fordson All-Around but had little success. Introduced in 1937, it was the first and only Fordson with a tricycle-style wheel arrangement.

Ford N Series: A New Direction

Even though Fordson tractors would go on to be successful in Great Britain and Europe for the next 25 years, the poor acceptance of the Fordson line in the United States was unacceptable to Henry Ford. As a result, he had already commissioned development work on a new model by the time he met Harry Ferguson in the late 1930s.

Ferguson had several unique ideas of his own about tractor production. He had already been working on building an implement hitch for the Fordson but it had proved unsuccessful. He was eventually introduced to Ford and convinced him to look at one of his concepts via a demonstration of his British-built Ferguson-Brown tractor. The rest, they say, is history.

There probably isn't a Ford enthusiast alive who hasn't heard of the famous handshake agreement between Henry Ford and Harry Ferguson to join forces on a new tractor to be built in the United States. According to the agreement, Ford would manufacture the tractors using Ferguson's patents and Ferguson would market the machines. Often referred to as Ford-Ferguson, the venture released its first tractor in 1939 and named it the 9N after the year of its release.

From the very start, the Ford 9N represented a true revolution compared with other tractors on the market. While other brands were moving away from wide front axles to a tricycle configuration, the Ford design embraced the wide front axle, or utility axle, along with a wide, low profile that was extremely stable yet very maneuverable. Mounting a cultivator on the rear of the tractor instead of on a high-clearance tricycle design would also permit a lower operator station that was ahead of the axle for a smoother ride.

In the meantime, the 9N had the talents of the Ford design department behind it, which resulted in stylish sheet metal that not only enclosed the grille,

This 1942 model, owned by Wayne and Joyce McGuire of Parker City, Indiana, is a nicely restored example of the Ford 9N introduced in 1939. The 9N was rated at 28 PTO horsepower and was the result of a verbal agreement between Henry Ford and Harry Ferguson to build a revolutionary new tractor.

As a result of World War II and the shortage of certain raw materials, Ford replaced the 9N with the 2N in 1942. It was basically the same tractor as the 9N, except the 2N featured steel wheels in place of rubber tires and the generator and battery were replaced with a magneto. This rare 1942 golf course model is a prime example of a restored 2N model. By 1943, most of the 2N models were shipped with rubber tires and an electrical system.

but also provided a hint of art deco. In contrast, John Deere and Farmall were just beginning to look at tractor styling and each hired a designer to streamline their designs.

Ford was ahead of most tractors in that it had a complete electrical system as standard equipment. That included a starter, battery, generator, and a direct-drive distributor with an integral coil. Rubber tires and a power take-off (PTO) were also standard. Most important, the 9N boasted all of Ferguson's revolutionary features, including a three-point hitch system that changed the entire tractor industry, and automatic depth control. The three-point hitch allowed implements to be easily attached and removed, while the draft control system automatically regulated the working depth of the implement, which particularly helped on steep slopes.

For power, the 9N featured a 28-horsepower, 119.7-cubic-inch displacement four-cylinder engine that was actually based on one-half of the 239-cubic-inch

Ford/Mercury V-8 truck engine. Consequently, it used the same pistons, rings, valves, connecting rods, and bearings. The parts commonality, combined with the benefits of mass production, which was actually a Henry Ford innovation, helped make the Ford 9N one of the most affordable tractors on the market. At a launch price of $585, it was priced much lower than tractors offered by any of the competitors. Ironically, Henry Ford's challenge to the engineering department was to build a tractor that would cost no more than the combined cost of a team of horses or mules, the harness, and the 10 acres of land required to produce enough feed for the team. At an estimated cost of $590 for the latter, the engineering team came out with $5 left over.

If the 9N had any shortcomings, it was the fact that it was fairly light for a field tractor. In fact, the weight of the 9N was approximately 2,500 pounds compared with 3,800 pounds for the average competitive tractor. As a result, it didn't have much traction

This Ford 9N, owned by Paul Cummings of Amsterdam, Missouri, is a mixture of eras. Although the tractor itself is a 1939 Model 9N, Cummings has it outfitted with steel wheels reminiscent of the early 2N models. The tractor was purchased by Cummings' father as a used model in 1950 to replace the family's team of horses. Cummings says another unusual fact about the tractor is that it probably spent more time on the road than it did in the field, as he hauled hay and often made round trips of up to 64 miles.

without the weight-transferring force of a three-point implement, which meant that the rear tires on a lot of Ford tractors were filled with calcium chloride for added weight.

The Ford 2N

In many respects, Ford was lucky to be producing tractors in 1942, let alone coming out with a new model, as many factories were converted to the production of war supplies. The problem for everyone, however, was that the war efforts required a vast amount of raw materials, chief among them being rubber and copper. Hence, Ford introduced the 2N, which was basically a revised version of the tractor designed to use materials that were not as scarce. The 2N was essentially the same tractor as the 9N in terms of specifications but featured steel wheels, a magneto, and hand-crank in place of the generator, battery, and starter.

It has been said that the change in model designation was also a way of getting a price increase past the

A remanufactured Ford 8N graces the office/reception area at N-Complete in Wilkerson, Indiana. The company, which also stocks a vast inventory of Ford reproduction parts, rebuilds vintage Ford tractors from the frame up.

The Ford NAA was first introduced in 1953 as the Ford Golden Jubilee model to celebrate the 50th anniversary of the Ford Motor Company.

U.S. War Production Board. At any rate, the 2N was produced until mid-1947. In the meantime, it didn't take long for Henry Ford to convince the government that the tractor was as important to food production back home as the other products were to the war effort. As a result, material restrictions were relaxed within a year and tractors could again be built with starters and batteries and rubber tires. Unless steel wheels were used, 10x28 rear tires were standard.

The Famous 8N

It's hard to know whether Harry Ferguson saw the handwriting on the wall in 1945 when Henry Ford stepped aside in favor of his grandson, Henry Ford II, but a change seemed certain when the Ford patriarch died in April 1947 at the age of 83. Henry Ford II and the new team he had hired immediately saw a problem.

The 1954 Ford model was known as the NAA. In addition to having more horsepower from a new overhead-valve engine, the Jubilee and NAA models featured changes in the hydraulic system to conform to stipulations set forth in the settlement of Ferguson's lawsuit.

This Ford Model 740 was one of several new models introduced in 1954. It was the first time Ford offered more than one model. The new line included the 600 Series, which was very similar to the NAA, and the 800 Series, which featured a similar design with a larger engine. The 700 and 900 Series were row-crop tricycle versions of the 600 and 800 Series. The second number specified the transmission and presence of a PTO and/or three-point hitch. The 740 was a row-crop version of the former NAA with a four-speed transmission, PTO, and three-point hitch.

Even though Ford was building a product that had become widely popular, the company had no marketing control over the business since the marketing and distribution were handled by Ferguson, per the original agreement.

Following Henry's death, Ford soon announced that the handshake agreement was null and void and that the company would establish its own marketing and distribution company to handle a new and improved version of the Ford tractor. Again named for the first year of full production, the 8N made its debut in late 1947. In an effort to distinguish the 8N from

Ferguson's tractors, Ford changed the colors of the 8N to the familiar red frame and chassis covered by a lighter shade of gray sheet metal.

Ford also incorporated a four-speed transmission for more flexibility and an improved braking system that positioned both brake pedals on the right side. In addition, the company raised the steering wheel, installed running boards, and added a position control to the three-point hitch system. A small lever on the right side, located under the seat, switched the system between position and draft control. To Ferguson's dismay, the 8N still used the same Ferguson system that had been used in the 9N/2N line. That, of course, led to a bitter lawsuit that cost Ford millions of dollars to settle and millions more in legal fees. The lawsuit forced Ford to develop a new hydraulic control system and make other changes to avoid using patents that were owned by Ferguson.

A New Look for an Anniversary Year

The Ford NAA, which was introduced in 1953, represented a major change in the Ford line for a number of reasons. For one thing, it was a way to introduce new features that got around Ferguson's patent, even though Ford had planned an improved tractor before the lawsuit was settled in 1952. Among those changes was a new vane-type hydraulic pump that was powered off

In 1958, Ford introduced an expanded lineup renamed the 01 Series. These included the 501 (offset), 601, 701, 801, and 901 Series tractors. In addition to more horsepower and various improvements, the 01 Series offered new options, such as power steering. The 501, 601, and 701 Series became known as the Workmaster tractors, while the 801 and 901 were introduced as the Powermaster models.

the engine. This also meant the advent of live hydraulics since hydraulic power no longer depended on engagement of the PTO. The new styling also gave the Ford NAA a look that differed from the previous N Series tractors, as well as the Ferguson TO Series tractors that Ferguson continued to build.

The NAA allowed Ford to market a larger, more advanced tractor than the 8N. For starters, it was four inches taller, four inches longer, and around 100 pounds heavier than the 8N it replaced. It was also equipped with a larger, more powerful overhead-valve Red Tiger engine. The new inline four-cylinder engine featured a 134-cubic-inch displacement that had a rating of 31 horsepower.

Finally, the NAA, which has most often been referred to as the Jubilee, was used to celebrate Ford's 50th anniversary as a company. In fact, the first year's models carried a circular emblem on the grille that read, "Golden Jubilee Model 1903–1953." The nose emblem on the 1954 model had a similar appearance but the words were replaced with stars that circled the outside border.

Among the NAA's other improvements, beyond the extra power and hydraulics, were a better governor and a temperature gauge on the instrument panel. The NAA also had the muffler relocated under the hood alongside the engine, where it reduced the chance of a fire in hay fields and stubble.

The Hundred Series

Throughout the history of Ford tractors to this point, the company had only built one model at a time. In the meantime, competitors like Farmall offered several models, including the C, H, M, and W-6 Letter Series, followed by the 200, 300, 400, and W-400. John Deere had almost always had a full line and moved from the A, B, H, G, L, M, and R models to the 40, 50, 60, 70, and 80.

Ford obviously felt the need to expand its lineup if it was to compete in the agricultural tractor market—particularly as farms continued to increase in size. Although the new Hundred Series included four new models, the line basically consisted of numerous configurations.

The first was the Model 600, which had the same 134-cubic-inch engine as the Jubilee and a very similar appearance. Unlike the Jubilee, however, the 600

This pair of Ford 961 models is representative of the choices customers had between 1957 and 1962. The model in the foreground is equipped with a 172-cubic-inch gasoline engine, whereas the one in the background is equipped with a diesel engine of the same size. According to the number code, both have a five-speed transmission, a three-point hitch, and live PTO.

came in different variations. The 640, for example, had a four-speed transmission and a non-live PTO. The 650 had a new five-speed transmission and the non-live PTO, and the 660 had the five-speed transmission with a live PTO.

Ford also released the Model 800, which became Ford's first three-plow tractor. While it was basically the same tractor as the 600 with the same four-cylinder engine, it did have a larger rear end/differential to handle the extra power from the engine, which was now bored out to 173 cubic inches to offer a rating of around 46 horsepower. The hood was also mounted two inches higher to accommodate a larger fuel tank. Like the 600, it was offered in several configurations that provided a choice of transmissions, live PTO, and three-point hitch.

In 1956, Ford added the 700 and 900 Series, which were essentially the same tractors as the 600 and 800 Series, except they each featured a tricycle-style

While American farmers were seeing new models in the 01 Series, Ford was continuing to build and market Fordson tractors in Britain and other parts of Europe, including this Fordson Dextra diesel model introduced in 1957.

row-crop configuration. This represented the first tricycle frame tractors offered by Ford since the Fordson All-Around was built in 1937. Both models were offered in several different configurations to meet the needs of farmers in different parts of the country.

Although there were several modifications between the two series, it's easy to see the similarities between a Model 960 and a Model 981.

In late 1957, Ford introduced another expanded lineup renamed the "01" series for 1958. This included the 601, 701, 801, and 901 Series tractors. Although the models were very similar to their predecessors, they did include several new improvements and options, such as power steering and liquefied petroleum gas (LPG) variations of each engine. Horsepower also increased across the full line and new grilles were used to designate the different models.

The 501, 601, and 701 Series models powered by the 134-cubic-inch gas or 144-cubic-inch diesel engine were labeled as the Workmaster tractors and retained the earlier NAA-600-style grille. The 801 and 901 Series models with the 172-cubic-inch gas or diesel engine were known as the Powermaster tractors, which were identified by a new egg-crate-style grille.

In 1959, Ford introduced its new Select-O-Speed power-shift transmission that offered ten forward and two reverse gears with the use of hydraulic clutch packs,

Although American- and British-built tractors were starting to share some common features, this tricycle-style Fordson still looked dramatically different from its U.S. counterparts.

This Ford 4000 Industrial model with an Elenco power front axle was one of the new models introduced in 1963, when Ford changed the color scheme to blue and white. The industrial models were painted blue and cream.

bands, and planetary gears. The transmission also allowed shifting up or down on the fly with no clutch.

Around the same time, Ford changed the color scheme and gave the Workmaster an all-red hood with gray only on the grille, fenders, and wheels. The Powermaster tractors retained the red cast iron and gray sheet metal, except for a red grille and a red stripe added down the center of the hood.

Ford also issued a number of gold tractors at this time, even though they were never intended to be customer tractors. As part of one of the biggest advertising campaigns ever conducted by the company, Ford required each of its dealers to have at least one Select-O-Speed demonstrator tractor on hand as a sales tool. They were painted gold to draw attention, which has made them very collectible today.

The Move to a World Tractor

Although the factory in Dagenham, England, continued to build Fordsons throughout the reign of Ford tractors in North America, it wasn't until 1956 that U.S. tractor production actually fell below that of the British Ford plant. Sales continued to slide for Ford through the end of the 1950s and early 1960s to prompt Ford to merge the two operations into the new Ford Tractor Operations in 1961. It was the first step in a plan to develop and market a single line of products for worldwide distribution.

Ford introduced the first Thousand Series tractors in 1962. The 2000 and 4000 Series tractors were basically the same as the 601 and 801 Series, except for an updated grille that ended 10 years of the cyclops front emblem. The 6000 Series was an all-new row-crop tractor that featured a six-cylinder engine that was available in gasoline, diesel, and LPG versions. It was also available with either a wide-front or tricycle-style front wheels. In a move toward unification, Ford also imported the Fordson Super Dexta for sale in America as the Ford 2000 Diesel, and the Fordson Super Major was imported as the Ford 5000.

The Hundred Series

To decode the three-digit model numbers on Hundred Series and 01 Series tractors, refer to the following numbers:

First Number

5: One-row offset tractor with 134-cubic-inch gas or LPG, or 144-cubic-inch diesel engine.

6: Four-wheel utility-type with adjustable front axle, 134-cubic-inch gas or LPG, or 144-cubic-inch diesel engine.

7: High-clearance row crop with 134-cubic-inch gas or LPG, or 144-cubic-inch diesel engine.

8: Four-wheel utility-type with adjustable front axle, 172-cubic-inch gas or LPG, or diesel engine.

9: High-clearance row-crop type, 172-cubic-inch gas, LPG, or diesel engine.

Second Number

1: Select-O-Speed transmission, no PTO.

2: Four-speed transmission, no PTO or three-point lift.

3: Four-speed transmission, no PTO.

4: Four-speed transmission with PTO and three-point lift.

5: Five-speed transmission with three-point lift and non-live PTO.

6: Five-speed transmission with three-point lift and live PTO.

7: Select-O-Speed transmission with single speed PTO and three-point lift.

8: Select-O-Speed transmission with dual and ground speed PTO and three-point lift.

Third Number

0: Hundred Series 1955–1958

1: 01 Series 1958–1961

Suffixes

1: Tricycle with single front wheel.

4: High-clearance with wide front.

L: LP gas engine.

D: Diesel engine.

The Ford Model 4000 was one of the first to carry the new blue and gray paint scheme introduced in 1964.

A Permanent Change in Color

In essence, the 2000, 4000, and 6000 Series introduced in the traditional gray and red paint scheme in 1962 were just a stop-gap until the real World Tractors could be introduced. The U.S. market wasn't the only one on hold. In Europe, the Fordson Super Major was given the Ford 5000 designation and the Super Dexta was called the Ford 2000. The European tractors were also painted in different versions of blue and gray, rather than the previous blue and orange.

By October 1964, the World Tractor line was finally ready. Ironically, about the only thing that didn't change about the tractors was the numbers. Except for the row-crop 6000, the new tractors were more like the British Dextra and Super Major models than the earlier Jubilee or 600 models. The new models also sported a new paint coat. For the first time, blue paint replaced red, which meant the familiar red and gray paint scheme long associated with Ford was gone forever. Naturally, the same paint scheme and numbers were used in Britain and the rest of Europe.

New three-cylinder engines also replaced the four-cylinder models used in the previous 2000, 3000, and 4000 Series tractors. The Model 5000 received a new four-cylinder version of the new engine and the 6000 was essentially unchanged and renamed the Commander 6000.

Despite the model number difference, it's easy to see the similarities between this 541 offset model and the Model 2000, which immediately followed the 541.

A Changing of the Guard

The Ford tractor line took even more turns in the 1980s, starting with the purchase of Sperry New Holland by Ford in 1986. The name Ford New Holland soon replaced the Ford name. The following year, Ford purchased the Versatile Tractor Company in Winnipeg, Manitoba, and merged it into the Ford New Holland line.

In 1993, Ford Motor Company completed the sale of its tractor division to Fiat Agri, which had earlier purchased a controlling share in New Holland. For a while thereafter, the New Holland tractors continued to carry the Ford name in smaller type through the introduction of New Holland's new Genesis tractors. The Ford name was eventually dropped, which left New Holland to carry on the legacy started by Henry Ford more than 80 years earlier.

With the merger of the American and British models and the introduction of a new color scheme, Ford finally had its world tractor. This Model 3000 was one of the new models that followed.

CHAPTER 2

Shopping for a Tractor

One of the first things you'll discover when shopping for a Ford tractor to restore is that they hold their value well. That's due in part to the fact that Ford models have always been popular with hobby farmers and agricultural producers who need a tough, reliable tractor that is stable in a variety of field conditions. Expect to pay more than you would for most vintage farm tractors of the same year and horsepower class. The good news is that there are a lot of Ford tractors in reasonable condition still out there. Why not make shopping for a tractor an adventurous part of the project? Where you start your search, though, depends a lot on your goals.

If you're buying a tractor strictly as a collector model, which isn't often the case with Ford models, a different set of rules tends to apply. The rules also depend on whether you're collecting the model for its value on the market or its sentimental value to you. Perhaps you just want to own a model like the one you drove on a relative's farm while growing up. If that is the case, it's better to evaluate the tractor as if you were purchasing a model for doing work around the yard or farm. Since many of these models are not rare, it's best to look for a combination of sound mechanics, good cosmetics, and a reasonable price.

On the other hand, if you intend to buy a vintage tractor as an investment, you should plan on doing some research and perhaps check out the credibility of the seller and model being represented. While most enthusiasts are honest people who share the love of Ford tractors as much as you do, there are people who will intentionally or unintentionally misrepresent the products they have for sale. If you're interested in a particular model, study factory literature or tractor books to find out how many of that particular model were built. This will give you an idea how rare that model is and what it might be worth when you are finished. Also find out if there are any distinguishing characteristics of the tractor that might identify it as being the real thing even if the sheet metal or certain components have been changed.

If you're shopping for a collector tractor, you should take a look at the tractor's serial number. As a general rule, the lower the number, the greater the tractor's collector value. Interestingly, Ford started production of the 9N with the serial number 9N1, which would make that particular model fairly valuable if it still exists somewhere.

A high serial number, on the other hand, would indicate that the tractor was one of the last models of its type to come off the assembly line. Of course, it also helps to know some history of the serial numbers assigned to the model you're inspecting.

How To Tell Them Apart

To the inexperienced tractor enthusiast, some of the early N Series tractors look alike or very similar, particularly because the 8N, 2N, and 9N are essentially the same size and the 2N and 9N are the same color. Unless you can look at the serial number, it can be difficult to tell them apart. In most every case, the serial

Even though it's a 9N or 2N painted to look like an 8N, the wheels on this tractor appear to be in good shape, which can make it worth a little more. Original wheels that bolt directly to the top hat–style hubs are extremely difficult to find.

If your goal is to restore a Ford tractor and use it as a work tool, there are a number of models that will work well, including this Model 9N shown at an auction. Ironically, a vast number of 9N and 2N tractors have been repainted over the years to match the color scheme of the 8N. The practice was supposedly started by a number of dealers who found it easier to sell red and white tractors than gray ones.

number is located on the left side of the engine block, just below the head and behind the oil filter.

According to John Smith, a Ford enthusiast from near Peoria, Illinois, the challenge occurs when the number is unreadable or the engine has been swapped from another tractor. "Hybrids, which include 8N models with 9N engines and vice versa, are not uncommon," he says. "A lot of swapping has gone on over the last 50 years and a lot of engines were replaced with rebuilt units on an exchange basis."

Smith has compiled the following checklist of distinguishing features that he uses to identify the different models and model years. Notice that the first-year Ford 9N included several features or differences that were changed the following year; hence, their collectibility among those who restore tractors for their historical significance.

The Model 9N: 1939 to 1942
1939 Serial Number 9N1–9N10275

The first 600 to 700 models were painted dark forest gray like the rest of the model year tractors, but underneath they had a cast aluminum hood and grille in place of the stamped steel components that later followed. The grille also featured horizontal spokes. The rear axle hubs were smooth in the center, and the front radius rods were I-beams. The most notable features are the battery/fuel cover, which is not hinged, and the rear fenders with two crease bars. Front spindle grease fittings were on the forward side, the engine block had no freeze plugs, and the left and right brake pedals were identical and interchangeable. The steering box, battery holder, transmission covers, and instrument panel were cast aluminum. The starter button and key switch were on the dash. The steering wheel was a four-spoke truck type. The hood side panels were smooth and had no mounting holes.

Those who restore Ford tractors for a collection are continuously looking for something unique, like this 9N orchard model. It's especially hard to find a model like this with good sheet metal.

1940 Serial Number 9N10276–9N46017

A safety interlock starter button was introduced at serial number 9N12500, supposedly because someone on the assembly line was injured while starting the tractor in gear. Henry Ford vowed that this would never happen to a customer and ordered it to be changed. The button was moved from the left side of the dash to its new spot just in front of the shift lever. The operator was now required to have the tractor transmission in neutral before the button could be depressed. The aluminum dash panel went through a couple more changes as the starter button was moved, the ignition key ended up on the lower left side, and the red indicator light disappeared somewhere around serial 25000. A hinge was also added to the battery/fuel cover. A wider 10x28-inch rear tire and wheel was offered as an option to replace the standard 8x32-inch rear tires. Around serial number 9N15000, the snap-in battery/fuel cover door was replaced by a new door with a hinge on the front end and a winged latch on the rear to keep it closed. The door could now be flipped forward for access and would stay attached so it wouldn't be lost. The engine now had a visible freeze plug on the center left side of the block. At serial number 9N16953, the small generator was replaced by a

larger version with a spring tensioner. The double ribbed rear fenders went through at least two reductions in the number of rivets that held them together before they were replaced by a single rib model that was used on the N tractors for the next dozen years. The infamous 9N rear smooth axle was replaced by a stronger two-piece riveted axle hub around serial number 9N41500. The last notable change of the year was at serial number 9N45899 when a new steel grille with vertical bars was introduced to replace the fragile aluminum grille.

1941 Serial Number 9N46018–9N88933

By now, the 9N was becoming very established and most changes were minor engineering changes. At serial number 9N47508, the dipstick was moved from the upper left side of the transmission cover in front of the filler cap to the right rear side cover on the differential housing. The grease fittings were moved from the front side of the spindle to the rear side. The brake pedals were redesigned so that the right and left pedals were now different. The tractor's dash was changed from a one-piece cast aluminum to a one-piece cast iron. At serial number 9N80770, it was changed again to a two-piece cast iron column with a steel plate dash panel. The shifter base was also changed to cast iron. The steering wheel changed to a plastic-covered three-spoke design with a chrome nut and washer holding it on. The ignition key moved to the left upper side of the steering column.

1942 Serial Number 9N88934–9N99046
No major changes.

The Model 2N: 1942 to 1947
Introduced amid wartime material shortages in mid-1942, the first 2N tractors were built with steel wheels and magneto ignition. A hand crank served as the starter. According to John Smith, the fact that very few changes were made from the 9N reinforces the belief that the model designation was made, in

According to Ford enthusiast John Smith, there are a number of differences that can help you determine the age of a tractor even if you can't tell from the serial number. As an example, the fenders on the first 9N tractors had two ribs (top). Within a year, the fenders were changed to a single rib.

part, to obtain a price increase during wartime price controls. "Most people," he says, "continue to refer to these tractors as 9Ns, particularly since all 2N serial numbers began with 9N."

1942 Serial Number 9N99047–9N105411
Following Henry Ford's appeal for productive farm equipment, it wasn't long before tractors could again be built with starters, batteries, and rubber tires. Unless steel wheels were used, 10x28 rear tires soon became standard. In the meantime, the toolbox mounting was changed when the battery tray became steel. The Ford emblem on the front of the hood received a small "2N" stamped into it just below the Ford script. A new front axle/radiator support replaced the earlier cast iron support, and the hood side panels now had holes at the lower end for mounting bolts. The grille was changed to have four slots in the center bar. This would be the last change to the grille until the introduction of the 8N. The steering wheel was changed to a hard rubber outside with three uncovered steel spokes in the center. This basic design was used on all Ford tractors through 1964.

1943 Serial Number 9N105412–9N126574
At serial number 109503, the 9N radiator was replaced with a new 2N radiator, which was slightly smaller and was pressurized to 4 psi to increase the boiling point of the coolant. The new radiator cap was stamped steel and was painted black. At serial number 109503, the front steering arms and spindles were changed to a keyed design.

1944 Serial Number 9N126575–9N170017
Partway through the 1944 production year, the front axle radius rods were changed to an oval tube design that was lighter but just as strong as the I-beam radius rods. With small variations in length, this design was used on Ford tractors for the next 20-plus years. At serial number 167488, the front axle/radiator support was updated to a stamped steel design that was used into the 8N production. A longer oil line was added to route the return oil from the oil filter through the governor for added lubrication. Sealed beam Ford headlights became an option and replaced earlier C.M. Hall lights.

The serial number alone can add value to a tractor, especially if it proves that the model was one of the first or last in the series to be produced. Depending upon the model, the serial number may be found in a number of locations.

1945 to 1947

No major changes were made during any of the next three years, but the serial numbers were distinguished as:

    1945: 9N170018–9N198766
    1946: 9N198767–9N258539
    1947: 9N258540–9N306221

The 8N: 1947 to 1952

Due to the fallout between Henry Ford and Harry Ferguson, the 8N, which reflects the 1948 introduction, represented the first redesign of the Ford tractor and the first model to be built without association to the Ferguson name. Production of the 1948 (8N) model actually began in July 1947, so you'll notice some differences between the first models and those built the following year.

Although it still looked very similar to the 9N and 2N, there were a number of improvements that set the 8N apart from its predecessors. Most notable was the bright red paint on the engine and frame with lighter gray sheet metal, hence the "red belly" nickname. The bolt circle of the wheel lug nuts was much smaller than the 9N's and 2N's, running boards were added, the hood had a screened air intake on the right rear side, and the Ford script was embossed into the hood sides.

1947 Serial Number 8N1–8N37907

Early models up to serial number 27940 had a different style clutch pedal linkage that consisted of a bolt that pushed on a lever to release the clutch. At 27941, the linkage was updated to the style that continued through the NAA tractors. Some of the early tractors

If you're aware of the unique changes Ford made over the years, you can often tell the age of a tractor within a year or two, even if the engine—which carried the original serial number—has been replaced. The front axle radius rods, for example, were changed partway through the 1944 production year to an oval tube design (shown here) that was lighter but just as strong as the I-beam radius rods. Based on the evidence, this model is a 2N built sometime after 1944.

still had holes in the grille for the Ferguson system badge that was used on the 2N, but they were covered with brass plugs. The radius rod front clevis resembled the 2N type, and the PTO engagement lever was mounted on a cast-iron cover. The engine block was the same as the 2N block and did not have "8N" cast into it on the left side behind the starter.

1948 Serial Number 8N37908–8N141369

At serial number 42161, the engine block casting was changed for better cooling around the valve guides. At the same time, the old mushroom valves were replaced with straight-stem-style valves, one-piece guides, shorter valve springs, and heavier valve lifters. The engine block now had the 8N casting mark on the left side directly to the rear of the starter. The radius rod clevis was redesigned and the 8N3405-C replaced the 8N3405-A sometime midyear. The camshaft and head were upgraded between serial number 70000 and 85000. At serial 111758, the four-blade fan became standard and the six-blade fan became optional. The generator changed to the larger capacity 8N10000-B generator at serial 137685. Most other changes were minor and not visible.

If it weren't for the wheel hubs, which give it away, it would be hard to tell that this is a 9N. Who knows why it was painted blue, unless it was done in order to look like a Fordson Dextra or a late-model Ford.

Judging from all the rust on this tractor, any potential buyer better figure on using a torch and a lot of penetrating oil during disassembly. If you're lucky, the engine isn't frozen up too.

1949 Serial Number 8N141370–8N245636

There were some notable changes in 1949. At serial number 158162, the cylinder head studs were replaced by bolts. The engine pistons were changed to aluminum with chrome top rings at serial 168356. At serial 179073, the oil filler tube was shortened. A thrust spring was added to the front of the camshaft at serial 187030, and at 197785, the studs in the engine main bearing caps were replaced by bolts. Starting at serial number 215759, the top link rocker was changed from a single-hole to a three-hole design. The steering box was changed to a Spicer type with tapered sector shafts at serial number 216989 for better backlash adjustment.

There are set screw adjusters on both sides of the newer-style steering box. The dash panel was also changed to fit properly with the new steering box. The 8N486A long pin was eliminated as part of the Ferguson lawsuit at serial 237336. Toward the end of 1949 production, an inner grease seal was added to the rear axle housing at serial number 245261 to help stop the common problem of gear lube leaking onto the brakes. New axles were also required to accommodate the new seals.

1950 Serial Number 8N245637–8N343592

This was a big year for changes to the 8N. At serial number 247571, the engine oil pump was redesigned to use longer gears to provide more volume. The one-piece shifter handle with the small forged knob was changed to a threaded handle with a black screw-on plastic knob at serial number 252845. The TSX-33 carburetor that had been used for several years was changed at serial 260596 to the TSX241 model. A new engine block was cast so the distributor could be relocated at serial number 263844. The engine now had a side-mounted distributor with a separate coil on the right side, and the new 8N10001 generator was mounted on the left side of the engine.

The 8N casting mark on the left rear of the block was changed to 8N-B. The Ford script was embossed into the rear fenders at serial number 273178. Also at 273178, the governor was replaced with one that contained a drive for the upcoming Proofmeter (tach and hourmeter), which was eventually added to the instrument panel at serial number 290271. The oil filler cap was changed to a larger model with a replaceable filter element inside at serial 305676. At serial 276115, the carburetor was changed to the TSX-241A, followed by a change to the TSX-241B at serial number 313112, which ultimately solved the problems. At serial number 337916, the engine oil filler/breather tube was modified to keep oil from splashing out.

1951 Serial Number 8N343593–8N442034

At serial number 356950, the engine exhaust valves were changed to the free-rotating type and the valve lifters were changed to the adjustable type. At serial number 403489, a dust shield was added to the inside of the distributor to help extend the life of the contact points. The tractor hydraulic pump base was changed from aluminum to cast iron at serial 429792. The engine block cylinder bores were also enlarged and the sleeves were changed to a cast-iron material with a 0.090-inch wall thickness at serial number 433578 (piston size remained the same). The 8N-B casting mark on the left rear of the block was changed to 8N-C,.and the star on each end of the serial number was changed to a diamond. Because Ford stopped supplying the steel sleeves, many older engines were rebored at overhaul time to use the new cast-iron sleeves. The engine oil pan casting was beefed up to give it extra support to resist cracking from the strain of front-end loaders.

Any high-crop or offset model is highly collectible. In fact, some collectors spend hours searching the country to find a model like this Model 601 Offset Workmaster.

This 8N crawler with a V-8 engine, owned by John Konger from Albion, Indiana, is an unusual item in any collection.

1952 Serial Number 8N442035–8N524076

At serial number 451959, the front tie rod ends were changed to have a longer stud and use a castle nut and cotter pin to keep them from working loose. The spindle arms were also changed to bend upward slightly to make clearance for the castle nut above the axle. At serial 452913, the lube hole for the steering box was put on the front of the upper column between the steering wheel and dashboard. Sometime in late 1952, a change was made to the transmission housing on the left rear side that allowed for a larger reverse idler gear to lower the reverse gear ratio. This change was already in production in the new NAA-Jubilee model. (Note: No documentation has been found to show that the larger NAA type reverse idler gears were ever installed in any of the modified 8N housings.) The upper rear lift arms were beefed up with a more rectangular cross-section shape for increased strength, which was another change that was already in effect on the new Jubilee.

The Jubilee-NAA: 1952–1954

In late 1952, Ford introduced the new NAA Series tractor for 1953, which marked the end of 8N production. In addition to a more powerful overhead-valve engine, the NAA-Jubilee had live hydraulics and redesigned front sheet metal with the Cyclops medallion in the center of the hood.

1952 Serial Number NAA 1–NAA 2379
1953 Serial Number NAA 2380–NAA 77474

The serial number location on the first 22,000 or so NAA models was on the left front of the engine block just below the head. On later NAA models, the serial number location was moved to the left side of the transmission case just below the flat above the starter bulge.

1954 Serial Number NAA 77475–NAA 128965

The Jubilee hood emblem was replaced with a plain emblem; otherwise there were no changes to the tractor.

The Hundred Series: 1954 to 1957 (Model 600-700-800-900)

In addition to the serial number, which is located on the flat area above and behind the starter, the Hundred Series tractors can be identified by a front hood emblem that designates the series.

1954 Serial Number 1–10614
1955 Serial Number 10615–77270
1956 Serial Number 77271–116367
1957 Serial Number 116368–up

In late 1957, Ford introduced the 01 Series. These included the 501 (offset), 601, 701, 801, and 901 Series tractors. The 501, 601, and 701 Series retained the earlier NAA-600–style grille and became known as the Workmaster tractors, while the 801 and 901 were known as the Powermaster tractors. All received a new medallion for the front of the hood and new-styled rear fenders. The 01 series hood emblem was the first one to be made of plastic.

1957 Serial Number 1001–11996
1958 Serial Number 11997–58311
1959 Serial Number 58312–105942
1960 Serial Number 105943–131426
1961 Serial Number 131427–155530
1962 Serial Number 155531–up

The Thousand Series: 1962 to 1964

In 1962 Ford introduced the first Thousand Series tractors: the 2000, 4000, and 6000. The 2000 and 4000 Series tractors were basically the same as the 601 and 801 Series, but with an updated grille that ended 10 years of the cyclops front emblem.

1962 Serial Number 1001–11947
1963 Serial Number 11948–38930

1963 ushered in the first new Ford blue tractors and the familiar red and gray was gone forever.

1964 Serial Number 38931–up

Tap into the Resources

You certainly don't need to go it alone when shopping for a vintage Ford tractor, especially if you're new to the collecting world. There are a number of resources available for help, including bulletin board postings on tractor websites, chat rooms, and collectors who exhibit their machines at antique tractor shows.

It often pays to find someone who knows a little history about the brand. John Smith notes, for example, that the 8Ns didn't change a lot from 1947 to 1952, yet there were some important changes: "In late 1949 the steering box was much improved over the early models. Loose steering was common on the early models and the early steering boxes are more difficult to rebuild satisfactorily. In mid-1950 the distributor was moved to the side of the engine and access to the points at tune-up time got a lot easier. "The later models also had a Proofmeter [tach and hourmeter], which can be handy at times. The early 8Ns are fine tractors, but the later models seem to be more desirable among buyers. This isn't usually reflected in price or value, but people do give it some weight in the decision to buy or not to buy a particular tractor."

Buying the Right Tractor

The time you spend looking for the right model and inspecting each tractor will pay off later in the form of greater efficiency, less time and money spent on restoration, and increased satisfaction with the finished product. If you are looking for a work tractor, the benefits may also include increased safety. Buying a tractor that is not ideal for your needs may be not only inefficient but also dangerous.

Another aspect to consider when looking for a prospective project is the geographic location where the tractor was used. As a general rule, tractors used in the eastern and southern parts of the United States are more apt to have rust problems or a stuck engine, while those from the western part of the country tend to suffer more tire damage due to sun exposure and dry rot. Humidity has a tendency to take its toll, and nothing is worse than salt air.

There are other things that can tip you off to potential problems. If the hose between the carburetor and the air cleaner tube is cracked or missing, the engine may have sucked in a lot of dirt and will need work. Likewise, a missing or cracked shift lever boot can let water into the transmission, and nobody has to tell you what kind of problems water can cause when it repeatedly freezes and thaws.

In contrast, antifreeze in the cooling system and oil in the oil-bath air cleaner tells you right away that

The Ford front bumper was a popular option that is still desired today, especially if you can find an original.

Experienced Ford restorers say it's important to closely inspect the engine block for cracks that might have resulted when the coolant froze over the winter. To make matters worse, the 1939 9N engine didn't have freeze plugs. The block on the right had to be discarded as scrap due to the size and location of the crack.

the tractor was treated well and is likely in good shape. Speaking of coolant leaks, John Smith notes that it is especially important to check for cracks in the engine block before making any kind of offer.

"Look at the left side of the block where the coolant draincock is located," he says. "Check all around the area in front of the draincock and above it for cracks or signs that a crack has been repaired. If someone has let the engine freeze up in the winter, this is where it usually cracks. Be wary of cracked blocks, especially if repairs have been poorly done. A cracked block makes the tractor worth substantially less, and

Regardless of the model, LPG tractors were less common than gasoline versions, which makes them a little more collectible in many cases.

trying to find a good used block for a reasonable price can be a very frustrating task. On the other hand, a crack that has been properly repaired won't affect the performance of a work tractor one bit."

Smith suggests that you do a lot of shaking and wiggling when checking out the tractor. You can start up front by wiggling the fan blade to check the bearings in the water pump.

"Shake the left and right tie rods," he adds. "All four ball and socket ends should be tight. Grab the front tire and push/pull inside and out on it. The wheel bearings and spindles should be tight with no play. Turn the steering wheel left and right to check for excessive backlash in the steering," he continues. "Does one front wheel start to turn before the other starts moving? This indicates a misadjustment or worn sector shafts in the steering box.

"Move to the rear tires," Smith adds. "Grab the top of the tire and push/pull toward and away from the center of the tractor. Does the wheel have side play? Do you hear a clunk when you push/pull? This can indicate a misadjustment in the shims that load the rear axle bearings. There should be very little, if any, play when properly adjusted. If it feels loose, watch the nut on the outside of the rear hub while you push/pull. Can you see movement behind the nut and washer? This indicates a loose hub on the axle. It may be able to be tightened, but if the movement is excessive the hub is most likely shot from running loose."

If the tractor is in running condition, there are several things you should check before and after you start the engine. It would be a good idea to turn to Chapter 5 and run through some of those procedures before you make your final decision.

If the tractor is not in running condition, you'll want to make sure the pistons are not rusted to the cylinder sleeve. One way to do that is to pull one or both of the spark plugs and shine a light inside the cylinder walls to check their condition. If the walls are shiny, the pistons are probably not stuck too badly, if at all. On the other hand, if you can't even

More restorers are looking for implements or attachments to add to their restoration, which makes this combination particularly appealing.

remove the spark plugs due to rust, you might have cause for concern.

For what it's worth, Tom Armstrong includes a humorous tractor buying guide on his N-Complete website that is sometimes all too true. A few sample entries are as follows:

Ad Says:	Really Means:
Rough condition	Too bad to lie about
Engine runs quiet	Using 90W oil
Many new parts	Still not running right
Slight surface rust	No trace of paint anywhere

Negotiating a Price

Before you start dealing on any tractor, you should know your needs, your budget, and what is on the market. Become as knowledgeable about the prospective tractor as you can through research, conversations with other collectors, and physically checking it out. The *Yesterday's Tractors* website, found at www.ytmag.com, can be of value. The site includes a listing of recent tractor sales and lists a variety of models, their condition, and how much they sold for. Another source is www.tractorhouse.com, which provides a listing of tractors for sale throughout North America. With a few clicks of the mouse, you can find numerous Ford tractors, divided by model, for sale by individuals and dealers. If you can find a tractor in the listings that has a similar number of hours that is in a similar state of repair, you have a pretty good idea what the tractor should really be worth or at least where to start your offer.

Ironically, at the time of this writing, there were at least two 2N tractors on the website that had been repainted in the red and gray paint scheme of the 8N. Although they weren't misrepresented, it's another example of why it pays to be able to tell the difference between models.

If you acquire a tractor that's very far from home, you'll need a good trailer that's capable of handling the load. Make sure you have plenty of strong chains along to secure the tractor to the trailer.

If your preview of the tractor turned up any problems, you may find that the seller is willing to come down on the price. You need to decide, however, if you have the time and expertise to correct what problems you have found.

You may find that the tractor won't start or run on the day you look at it. The seller may, in all honesty, tell you that everything worked fine when he or she last drove it, but when a tractor sits for very long, it can develop problems unbeknownst to the owner. In this case, you must start your bidding from nearly scrap level prices, since you have no idea what you're getting into; then go only as far as your conscience and experience will allow. Many collectors also go into a negotiation with the idea that a stuck engine is basically junk. If it can be freed, that's a bonus; hence, your offering price should reflect that possibility.

Finally, know how much you are willing to spend on the whole project before you start negotiations. Many people don't realize how much expense is involved in a restoration. Even if you get the tractor at a decent price, you have to anticipate the cost of engine repairs, bodywork, new wiring, replacement components, and so on. A few things to consider that will add the most cost to your restoration project are tires (figure close to $800 if you have to replace them); the condition of sheet metal, which can be costly if you have to purchase reproduction parts; and fenders.

Many restorers suggest that you assume the worst of any potential restoration. That way you won't be surprised if you can't find parts or if it takes more time and money than you expected to get the job finished.

"Remember that any N Series tractor you're looking at is at least 50 years old and probably has worked hard all its life," relates John Smith. "Add the positives and the negatives and consider the asking price. If there are too many negatives, keep looking. Anything can be fixed with enough time and money, but you may be ahead in the long run to pay more for a tractor

Attachments like this Ford Model 711 loader, commonly referred to as a "one-armed bandit," can make a fairly common tractor much more collectible.

that's in good shape to start with than to buy a rough one and spend a fortune on it to repair everything that's worn out."

Count the Cost

As one final thought, you might keep in mind that N-Complete, based in Wilkinson, Indiana, offers Ford tractors for sale that have been completely remanufactured to better than new standards. That means the engine, transmission, and powertrain have been completely rebuilt; all sheet metal has been repaired and/or replaced; new tires have been installed; and the entire tractor has been stripped and repainted. As owner Tom Armstrong states, they're not restored; they're remanufactured. As a result, each tractor also comes with a full one-year warranty.

The price for an 8N at the time of publication was $8,436 for a standard tractor. That includes the cost of the base tractor. If you have a tractor that you want N-Complete to remanufacture, the cost at the time this book was published was $6,726 for an 8N. You might want to keep these prices in mind when buying a tractor and calculating your cost. It is not meant to discourage you from restoring your own tractor, but if your costs add up to or exceed the price Armstrong is charging for a totally refurbished model, you might be better off sending yours to N-Complete or one of a handful of other companies that restore or rebuild Ford models. If you care to look up other models on the company's website at www.n-complete. com, you'll find that a remanufactured 9N is priced at $8,437 (except the 1939 model), while a Model 600 or 601 is priced at $10,479. Both prices are based on N-Complete furnishing the base tractor. In all cases, acrylic paint is extra, as is a rubbed-out show finish.

CHAPTER 3

Setting Up Shop

Basic Tools

If you're serious about doing a first-class tractor restoration, the first thing you're going to need is a good set of tools. You may already have a lot of the tools you need since Ford tractors, for the most part, are relatively simple. If you don't have a set of tools, look for a set of automotive-quality tools that come with a warranty, such as those offered by Sears (Craftsman), NAPA, or Snap-on.

You'll want to start with a drive socket set that contains sockets ranging from 1/16 inch to over 1 inch. In addition to a ratchet handle, you'll need a breaker bar to loosen stubborn bolts without risking damage to the ratchet.

A set of combination wrenches will also come in handy. There are some places you simply can't squeeze in a socket and ratchet. You can decide which will work best for you and your budget, but choices include open-end, box-end, and wrenches that provide an open-end configuration on one end and a box-end of the same size on the other.

To round out your tool collection, you'll want to add a couple of adjustable wrenches (often referred to as crescent wrenches, even though Crescent is a brand name), a full set of regular and Phillips screwdrivers, a pair of adjustable pliers, needle-nose pliers, and a pair of locking pliers (often referred to by the popular brand name Vise-Grip). Other tools that you'll probably need at some time or another include a good hacksaw, a punch set, and a cold chisel. Don't forget to pick up a couple of putty knives. You'll need those for scraping away grease and grime.

Don't assume you have to go out and buy all new tools. Due to the changes in agriculture and the number of farmers who retire each year, farm auctions are a good place to pick up tools you need at a reduced price.

Specialized Tools

Depending upon how much engine or electrical work you want to get into, there are other tools that you may need. These include feeler gauges, a point dwell meter/tachometer, voltmeter, and compression and vacuum gauges. For tools and gauges that are only used on occasion, consider renting or borrowing from a fellow restorer.

Other tools that can make your life a lot easier include a gasket scraper, bearing and hub pullers, and a seal puller. A pickle fork can be a handy item if you plan to separate the tie rods on the front axle.

If you anticipate doing much engine work, you'll also need tools for making precise measurements. At a minimum, these should include a micrometer for measuring items up to approximately an inch in width; a dial caliper to determine the acceptability of parts, such as the crankshaft and camshaft; a set of feeler gauges; and a dial gauge for measuring certain types of end play.

You'll also need a torque wrench. While most parts of the tractor don't require a specified torque rating, you'll find that many engine components, including the head bolts, must be tightened to a particular setting in order to reduce the chance of head warping and oil and water leaks. While there are several different types of torque wrenches, perhaps the easiest to use is the type that makes an audible click when the correct torque rating has been reached. Since you preset the desired torque with a dial on the wrench, you don't have to worry about having enough light or room to read a scale or being able to see the scale.

Though your work area doesn't have to be anything fancy, it does help to have a place where you can keep the tractor indoors while it is being restored. This is especially nice when it comes time to paint the tractor.

Of course, you can get by with the older style of torque wrench that uses a stationary pointer and a gauge attached to the handle. As the bolt or nut is tightened, the handle bends in response to the applied torque. As a result, the needle, which is fixed to the socket head, moves up or down on the scale to indicate the amount

A number of specialty tools, including feeler gauges and valve lapping tools, can be found at a reasonable price at your local automotive parts store.

of torque being applied. You just have to be able to watch the scale as you're tightening the fastener.

Depending upon how far you get into engine repair, you may also need specialized tools such as a ridge reamer, valve-lapping tool, piston-ring compressor, and cylinder hone. The use of each of these items is discussed in more detail in Chapter 6.

Air Compressor

While an air-powered impact wrench can be a valuable asset when removing stubborn bolts, air-powered tools aren't quite as necessary as the air compressor itself. You'll want a portable air compressor with a tank for a couple of reasons. First of all, an air hose and nozzle are invaluable for blowing dust and dirt out of crevices and away from parts. You'll want to use it to blow out fuel lines, water passages, and the like.

Second, assuming you're going to be painting the tractor yourself, you'll need an air compressor to operate the paint sprayer. Tank capacity is important in this instance. If the tank doesn't have enough capacity and the pump can't keep up, you're going to

You'll need one or more sturdy jacks to support the chassis, since the tractor has to be split in order to work on the engine or transmission.

The staff at N-Complete has designed a set of brackets that bolt to the central housing and hook over the radius rods to support the rear half of the tractor without jacks.

The N-Complete technicians have also developed a stand that bolts to the rear of the tractor to support the rear of the unit during repairs.

be painting a few minutes, stopping to let the pressure build in the tank, painting a few more minutes, and then waiting again. You might want to put things in reverse order and shop for a paint sprayer before you look for a compressor. Most restorers who do their own painting suggest using a compressor with at least 1/2 horsepower that is capable of delivering at least 4 cubic feet of air per minute at 30 psi pressure.

Vise

You don't have to own a vise to do a tractor restoration, but considering the availability, reasonable cost, and the versatility that a vise provides, you'll likely find it worthwhile. Just being able to clamp a part in the vise while you work on it can be helpful at times. You'll be especially glad you have one when you've got a part with a bolt that absolutely won't budge.

For the most versatility, many shop owners recommend at least a 6-inch vise that is bolted securely to a solid bench. You may even want to get a piece of plate steel to attach to the bottom side of the bench for extra strength and support.

Anvil

Another tool that you'll at times find invaluable, especially if you have to straighten sheet metal, is an anvil. You don't have to invest in a commercial shop anvil. For what you'll need most of the time, a 2- or 2 1/2-foot piece of railroad track rail will do. In fact, the rounded edge of the rail will work better than a real anvil for some metal fabrication. If you occasionally need a flat surface or a square end for bending, you can weld a piece of bar stock across one or both ends of the rail so it will stand upright when turned rail side down.

Hoists and Jacks

Last but not least, you're going to need equipment to lift and support the tractor, engine, and other

An oxy-acetylene torch can be equally valuable for cutting metal and heating stubborn parts that refuse to budge.

If you plan to do your own painting, an air compressor with adequate capacity, an inline water filter, and plenty of hose will make the job a lot easier. You'll find compressed air equally helpful when cleaning parts and components.

components. To reduce costs and make the tractor more maneuverable, Ford used the engine on virtually all models as a load-bearing member; in other words, there is no full-length frame. The front of the tractor attaches to the front of the engine, and the rear of the engine attaches to the transmission. To remove the engine for an overhaul, you have to split the tractor in half. That means you'll need a floor jack or bottle jack to support each half of the tractor.

There will come a time when you need to remove the rear wheels, front axle, and front wheels for cleaning, restoration, and painting. You'll need some heavy-duty lifting equipment capable of raising the tractor to the level where you can block it up on stands or wooden blocks. Don't try to get by with concrete blocks! They can crumble or crack too easily and pose a physical danger. Don't try to pile blocks up too high, either. One option is to build cribbing under the frame, which means you place strong wooden blocks log cabin–style under the tractor or axles as structural support until the wheels can be safely reinstalled.

Some restorers like to block up the entire tractor from the start, pull the wheels, strip the tractor down to the frame, and work on restoration from the ground up. Others like to leave the tractor on its wheels as long as possible, work on components as they go, and roll the tractor out of the way when necessary.

Ironically, Ford even offered its own version of a tractor jack called the Dearborn accessory tractor jack. Using hydraulic power from the three-point hitch, the jack stand pivoted beneath the rear axle and raised the rear of the unit as the three-point hitch was raised. The idea was that a farmer could slide the folding unit under the tractor, engage the axle and lift the tractor to remove the tires or adjust the tread width using tractor power alone. If you're lucky enough to own or find one, you can probably use it, as some have done to lift the tractor initially or to work on the tires or brakes. But you'll still need to block up the tractor and remove it before you can work on the hydraulics.

The bottom line is that your lifting and cribbing needs will depend largely on the tractor model you're restoring, how you prefer to work, and what part of the tractor you're working on. Just be sure that you keep safety in mind and that you have the right equipment to do the job; for example, don't try to lift the

You may or may not need a welder during your restoration project. If you do, you can probably find a friend to help you out or take the piece to a commercial welder.

A torque wrench is one of those specialty tools you'll need to purchase or borrow when overhauling a tractor.

Before you start a restoration, one of the first things you'll need to obtain is a good service/repair manual for your tractor model. If for nothing else, you'll need it for tolerance limits and specifications. A parts manual for your model can be equally helpful during reassembly. The largest selections are available from I & T and Jensales.

rear end of the tractor with a single bottle jack, even if it is an 8-ton jack. That's not what you would call adequate stability.

Purchase a Good Shop Manual

Although Ford limited its production to just one model per year until 1954, and there were a number of similarities between models from year to year, this book cannot go into detail on all the differences between each and every model, especially with powertrain restoration. You'll also need a source of specifications, such as tolerance limits, torque settings, and wear limits; therefore, you need to purchase a repair manual for your specific model.

There are a number of good sources for service and repair manuals listed in the appendix. Penton Media (formerly Intertec Publishing) offers a complete line of their I & T (Implement & Tractor) shop

service manuals, which are available for virtually all Ford tractors you're likely to encounter. Jensales Inc. in Manchester, Minnesota, has service and parts manuals for virtually every Ford tractor that was ever built.

You might check with your local New Holland dealer, as well. Depending upon the age of the tractor, an original manual may still be available. Of course, if you want to pay the price, you can still find original service manuals for older tractors for sale by vendors at a number of flea markets, tractor shows, and swap meets.

CHAPTER 4

Getting Started

Take Your Time

The first step in restoring a vintage tractor, once you have it home, is to convince yourself that it's going to take some time. Many of the people who restore antique tractors are retired farmers or mechanics who do it for the enjoyment of seeing an old tractor brought back to life. Others are full-time farmers who spend much of their winter working on a tractor. Once spring arrives, however, their pet project tends to sit until ground preparation and planting are complete.

The point is, unless you're retired or have three or four cold winter months to devote to the project, you need to realize that a quality restoration is going to take up to a year or more. Trying to finish the project too quickly is going to lead to either discouragement or dissatisfaction later on with the shortcuts you have taken.

Establish Your Goals

If you talk to many tractor restorers, you'll soon find that tractor restoration can mean many different things. One of the first things you'll need to do is decide how far you want to take the restoration project. To some enthusiasts, a vintage tractor restoration is nothing short of restoring the tractor to mint condition. That means they go through the engine, transmission, rear end, and every other component that might need attention. They also insist on accuracy in every detail and top it off with a quality coat of paint.

On the other hand, not everyone has the budget to do a first-class restoration. If you're in that category, you need to decide along the way what you can and can't live with. As an example, if you plan to drive your finished product only in a few parades a year and take it to a few antique tractor gatherings, you may

not need to replace that gear in the transmission that is missing a couple of teeth. If you plan on using the tractor to mow the roadsides, plow the garden, and plow snow in the winter, which is perhaps more common with Ford tractors than any other brand, you'll want to restore the transmission to like-new condition or risk further damage. Because of their compact size and maneuverability, Ford N Series tractors, as well as later models like the NAA and 400, have become very popular among hobby farmers and estate owners who use them for small plot cultivation, mowing, and haying operations.

Don't try to cut costs where it doesn't make sense. If there is one common lament among tractor restorers who make their living restoring tractors for paying customers, it's that some clients don't want to spend the money to do it right the first time.

It can take a lot of blood, sweat, and effort to get a tractor to the condition of this beautifully restored Model 501 Offset and cultivator owned by Jim Woehrman of Kansas City, Missouri. Just remember to keep the goal at the top of your mind.

Document the Process

As stated earlier, it may be a year or more before you get to the point where you're ready to reassemble the tractor. It's important that you maintain good records as you disassemble the tractor. Keep a pad and pencil handy for recording measurements and taking notes. You should also consider taking pictures or shooting video as you go. Photos or a video, used in combination with a service manual, can be valuable several months down the road when you are reassembling the tractor.

You'll want some good photos, even if you don't need them for reference later on. One of the first questions people are going to ask you is, "What did it look like when you started?" Pulling out the photos and reliving some of the high points and frustrations is part of the fun.

Another thing to consider is the number of bolts, nuts, and washers you're going to need to keep track of as you start removing the sheet metal, fuel tank, fenders, grille, etc. One way to organize them is to collect a bunch of egg cartons and put the nuts and bolts from different areas into individual egg compartments. You can even use and label separate egg cartons for different parts of the tractor (one for the grille and hood, one for the transmission cover, and so on). For bigger bolts or parts, you can use larger containers, such as coffee cans and plastic butter tubs.

Whatever you do, don't throw anything away unless you are certain you can get a replacement or reproduction part. That's usually not a problem, due to the availability of so many Ford parts and replicas, but you never know when it might be needed as a pattern or for comparison.

The first step in tractor restoration consists of stripping the tractor down and cleaning it up. Start with the layers of grease that have accumulated around the engine and transmission.

While you can still see them, it's a good idea to take measurements of where the decals were located before you strip and clean the panels. It'll make the job a lot easier when it comes time to position new decals.

While you disassemble the tractor and clean the parts, make a list of parts you'll need so you'll have time to search parts sources and swap meets. *Dallas Mercer*

Be careful about using too much force when trying to remove rusted or frozen parts. In your haste to break things loose, it's easy to damage other parts. Quite often, the best bet is to use a combination of penetrating oil, patience, and a properly sized tool.

If the part can withstand the heat, a propane or oxy-acetylene torch and occasional taps with a hammer can be as effective as anything. Alternately using heat and penetrating oil can also be helpful. Just don't apply oil to hot metal or direct an open flame toward a pool of penetrating oil. Be careful about using a torch on a part where the heat can be transferred to a bearing. Unless you know you're going to be replacing any bearings on the shaft, the time you save may not be worth the cost.

Removing Broken or Damaged Bolts

There's a good chance that at some point during the restoration process, you're going to be faced with a bolt that has broken off during removal or the head is stripped to the point you can't get a wrench on it. On the other hand, you may have a bolt or fastener that simply can't be removed by ordinary means. The only option is to drill it out, so let's take a look at the alternatives.

One option is to drill a hole in the bolt, or what remains of it, and use an "easy-out" to back it out of the hole. Unfortunately, many restorers say easy-outs are more trouble than they are worth or cause more damage than if you just drilled the bolt out in the first place. "Easy-outs aren't," states one tractor restorer. "If you break one off, you have just created a bigger problem than you started with. The easy-out is made of some pretty hard steel, so once you've broken one off in place, you can no longer drill it out."

If all else fails, you can always try a technique developed by Paul Cummings, a tractor restorer from Amsterdam, Missouri. When faced with a bolt that has broken off or is rusted in place, Cummings heats the bolt with a torch until it starts to glow red.

You'll be able to find everything from original parts that need work to reproduction parts and decals in the vendor section at many tractor shows.

Holding it by the wick with a pair of pliers, he presses a small birthday candle, like those you'd put on a cake, against the bolt. As it melts, the liquid wax flows down around the bolt and threads and finds its way into any open crevices. In most cases, the combination of heat and the wax coating on the threads allows him to remove the bolt without much additional force. When faced with a broken bolt, he will add the procedure mentioned earlier and weld a nut of the size that would normally fit the bolt to the top of any protruding shaft. In effect, he's created a new bolt head. The wax is already in place around the threads and acts as a lubricant.

One of the last options, and the only one that is really effective for a bolt that can't be removed any other way, is to drill out the old bolt. Start by making a punch mark in the center of the bolt or bolt head. This will allow you to drill a starter hole through the center axis of the bolt. Begin drilling out the bolt using successively larger bits until the hole through the center

is nearly as wide as the bolt. Be careful not to damage the threads in the parent material by using too large a bit or drilling through a hole that is off center. In some respects, this process is like that used by a dentist doing a root canal. Nice thought, huh?

One restorer says he has had good luck using a set of left-handed drill bits to drill out a bolt once a pilot hole has been established. Since the bit is turning in the direction you want the bolt to move, it will often come out as the heat increases and the center is hollowed out by the bit.

Finding Replacement Parts

Before you get too deep into the restoration project, you'll need to consider the challenge of locating and acquiring replacement parts. As you're disassembling the tractor for cleaning, begin making a list of all the parts you'll need to restore the machine to show or working condition. This will give you an idea of how much you may need to spend on parts like bearings,

There are a number of materials on the market that can be used to repair metal parts that aren't subjected to a lot of pressure, including brands like Liquid Steel and J-B Weld.

gaskets, sheet metal components, and so on. It will also give you a head start on locating some of those parts. By knowing what you need ahead of time, you can search the swap meets, salvage yards, and classified ads for the necessary components while you're working on other areas. It will also give you time to place orders with some of the suppliers of replacement parts, especially if you're on a budget and have to spread out the expenses.

Record as much detail as possible, including part dimensions, their shapes, and any serial numbers listed on separate parts. The good news is that parts for antique tractors are much easier to find today than they were just five or ten years ago, thanks in part to the growing interest in tractor restoration. New Holland dealers continue to stock parts for a number of tractor models that date back to the 9N. In addition, there has been a proliferation of companies that

specialize in restoration parts. Through the sources listed in the back of this book and in many of the restoration and tractor club magazines, you can find everything from reproduction hoods, fenders, and grilles to radiator caps, logo emblems, and temperature gauges. There are numerous individuals and companies that can repair your old magneto, carburetor, or distributor.

Keep in mind that the part you need might be available from an unusual source. Some tractor dealerships, including most John Deere dealers, can reference the number on any bearing, regardless of what tractor brand or model it came from, and tell you in a matter of seconds, via the parts computer, whether they have a matching bearing available.

Before you spend a lot of money on new parts, spend some time searching the salvage yards and used parts dealers for original parts that can be refurbished.

The swap meets held in conjunction with a number of tractor shows are a good source of used parts, too. Not only will used parts make your tractor more original, but they may save you money. Just don't rely on used parts in critical areas where a failure could jeopardize safety or cost you more money later on. Breaking a seat spring can be downright hazardous, especially if you're pulling an implement. It's better to go with new or a reproduction.

Shaft Repair

One of the things you'll deal with most often in a tractor restoration is the replacement of seals, bushings, and bearings. Unfortunately, you may also run across the occasional shaft that has been damaged by a defective seal. This is generally evidenced by a groove in the shaft that is deep enough that you can feel it when you run your fingernail across it. Replacing the seal at this point is not going to solve the problem. As long as the shaft is grooved, it's still going to leak.

The good news is that you have a couple of options short of buying a new shaft. One is to sleeve the shaft with a sleeve such as a Speedi-Sleeve that fits over the original shaft to create a bridge over the groove. Speedi-Sleeve is marketed by Chicago Rawhide (CR).

To sleeve a shaft, you'll need to accurately measure the diameter of the shaft at a point where it hasn't been worn. Then, it's simply a matter of taking the measurement and the application information to your bearing or parts supplier. In most cases, the sleeve is thin enough that a different-sized bearing or seal is not required. The trick is getting the sleeve installed on the shaft by using a special tool since the fit is designed to be tight.

Another technique for repairing a groove or nick in a shaft is to fill it with a metal-type epoxy, such as Liquid Steel or J-B Weld. Generally, it's better to apply two or three thinner coats and build it up, rather than one thick coat. After the compound has cured, the shaft can be sanded down until the repaired area is flush with the rest of the shaft. Just be sure to use fine-grain sandpaper or emery cloth to start so you don't scratch the shaft. Finish off the sanding with even finer-grit paper, in the neighborhood of 600 grit, for a smooth surface on the seal or bushing.

In the early stages of tractor cleanup, a putty knife and wire brush can be valuable tools for removing baked-on grease.

CHAPTER 5

Troubleshooting

In many respects, troubleshooting should be a supplement to your tractor-buying procedure. There are several steps that could be considered troubleshooting that you should have already done in the process of evaluating the tractor when you bought it. For the sake of finding out how serious the problems are, let's take a look at a few more things.

Whether you are an experienced tractor mechanic or a novice working on your first tractor, your senses can tell you a lot about what is wrong, if you know what you are looking for. Your sense of smell can tip you off to a problem with the radiator, clutch, or engine. Your sense of hearing can tell a distinct difference between a tick, a knock, and a grinding noise. There can be dramatic differences in the causes of such noises.

Start by looking on and under the tractor for traces of fluid. If what you find is a lighter hue, has the consistency of light maple syrup, and lacks the burned smell of combustion, it is probably from a leaking hydraulic fitting. A darker shade of brown that collects under the oil pan should be obvious. Engine oil is somewhat thicker and has the characteristic smell of having been in an engine; often it will leak out of the engine seals or leaky oil pan gaskets.

Evaluating a Tractor That Runs

Some restorers insist that unless the engine is totally locked up, it's best to start up the tractor and see how it runs in order to best figure out what it needs. If that means overhauling the carburetor or the magneto first, or installing a temporary gas tank, that's what they will do. You can listen to the engine, run it through the gears to see how the transmission and final drive sound, and evaluate the various systems.

Chris Pratt, with *Yesterday's Tractors* online magazine, insists there are a few things you can check to avoid surprises later on. The following inspection points are just part of his troubleshooting and evaluation procedure.

1. Cooling System Inspection

Whether you're checking out a tractor before or after you've made a purchase, it's understandable that you want to fire it up without further delay. It will be to your advantage, however, to check out a few things while the engine is still cold. This includes the cooling system, oil pan, and transmission.

First, carefully remove the radiator cap and check for coolant. There should at least be some type of liquid in the radiator. The best thing you can find is an antifreeze solution. The next best thing is clear water. If you find only clear water, you have to wonder if it was added since last winter or if it has been in there awhile.

If you find rusty water, you can expect to find pitting inside the engine and possibly a radiator that is leaking or is about to leak. Rust in the cooling system is often an indicator that the coolant has become acidic, which means it could also start attacking metal components.

Last, but certainly not least, you'll want to make sure the coolant isn't oily. That can be an indication of seal failures; cracked parts that are allowing oil and coolant to mix; or pitted parts, which can do the same thing.

Oil leaks and certain colors of grease or oil on or around the seal are obvious signs of a leak or seal failure.

If you find that the system is leaking, look for bad hose connections in the cooling circuit, especially where the hose ends meet the radiator or connect to the thermo-siphon components. Also check the radiator core for cracked tubing or leaky ends. If leaks in this area are excessive, the core should be replaced, since the internal integrity of the core itself is probably not worth salvaging.

From the radiator, you'll want to move back to the water pump, if the engine is so equipped. Look for a steady but slow dripping or for antifreeze streaks down the front of the engine housing. Most water pumps have a hole at the base that will leak antifreeze and coolant if the seal on the pump needs to be replaced.

2. Oil, Transmission Fluid, and Hydraulic Fluid Inspection

Next, you should take a look at the oil, but don't just pull the dipstick to see if the level is where it should be. Take a wrench and carefully loosen the drain plug to the point you could pull it out if you weren't holding it in place. Back off just enough pressure to drain out about a cup or less of oil and check it for water and antifreeze. If you get pure oil, you can rest a little more comfortably, knowing that water will settle to the bottom of a cold oil pan or gear case. A small amount of water can simply be condensation and may or may not be cause for concern. If you find antifreeze, it should raise a red flag concerning the mechanical condition of the engine. Repeat this process for the transmission/hydraulic reservoir.

3. Engine Starting Evaluation

Now you're ready to start the engine. Does the engine start easily when cold? Knowing that a tractor starts after just a few revolutions easily eliminates many of your concerns in one check. You may not have a guarantee on the condition of each component, but you immediately know that the battery, compression, ignition wiring, distributor/magneto, fuel flow, and carburetor are in reasonable condition.

If the engine doesn't start easily, you may still be looking at a good tractor, but you know there is a little more work ahead. Unfortunately, if you're looking at the tractor for the first time before buying it, and the unit has already been removed from the shed and warmed up prior to your arrival, you've lost out on a piece of information—namely, the cold start.

4. Engine Running Evaluation

Does the engine run well when it is hot? Taking the time to see how the engine runs after it has been warmed up is particularly important if you are going to be using the tractor to pull a load. Plan to spend at least a half hour running the engine to check for problems that can cause it to run poorly after it warms up. In the meantime, you can look for leaks in both the engine and radiator. After completing your inspection,

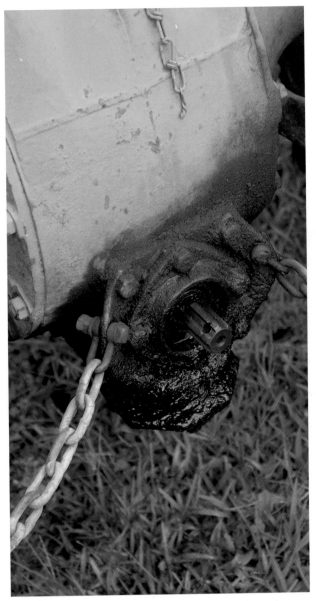

When buying or troubleshooting a tractor, start by checking the obvious areas for problems, such as around the PTO seal.

shut the engine off and see how easily it starts when it is warm.

5. Exhaust Evaluation

Check for smoke from the exhaust. Blue smoke often indicates internal problems, such as problems with rings, pistons, or valve guides, that are difficult and costly to repair. White or black smoke can frequently be corrected with carburetion or ignition changes; however, white smoke can also mean that water is getting into the cylinders, possibly through a bad head gasket or worse, a cracked block.

6. Engine Noise Evaluation

Listen for noises from the engine. A ticking from the top of the engine may indicate the need for a simple valve adjustment, while a clunking or thumping sound deeper in the engine could indicate serious or expensive repairs. If possible, check if the sound becomes more pronounced under load. If a clunk becomes louder when the engine is put under a load, it may be an indication of problems with the crankshaft, bearings, or piston rods.

7. Oil Leakage Inspection

After the engine has been running for a while, shut it off and check the oil for foaming or the presence of water. Either condition is cause for concern. Check for oil seepage from the head and look for structural cracks in the block. These procedures may be difficult to perform if the engine is encrusted in dirt and grease, but they can be time well spent. Check over the cast and steel components and look for hairline cracks.

Checking the engine oil for traces of water, antifreeze, or foaming can tell you a lot about the condition of the engine and cooling system. Whitish oil often indicates water contamination in the engine.

8. Electrical System Inspection

There should be some charge showing on the ammeter when the engine is running. You should also see some change in the charging level when the lights are turned on if the tractor is so equipped. This indicates that the regulator or resistor switch and cutout are operating properly.

9. Governor Inspection

At some point, you'll want to make sure the governor is working correctly. Its job is to adjust the throttle to maintain engine speed as the load changes. One of the easiest ways to check the governor, assuming the steering, brakes, or tires are in good condition, is to go down and up a small hill in second or third gear,

Whether you start the engine or just turn it over, checking for spark at the spark plugs will tell you a lot about the ignition and electrical system.

depending on the number of gears available. As you start downhill from level ground, you should hear the engine quiet down as the throttle backs off. It should automatically throttle back up to maintain the speed as you start back up the hill.

10. Transmission Check

Assuming the tractor is drivable, you should also check the transmission and final drive by driving the tractor around and listening to the gears. If the transmission is worn, you'll probably hear a whine when the transmission is shifted to a questionable gear. As mentioned earlier in the book, this may or may not be a problem, depending upon how you plan to use the tractor.

11. Hydraulic System Inspection

The Ferguson hydraulic system and advanced three-point hitch are the features that set Ford tractors apart from all other tractors of their time. To really check the hydraulic system, Illinois Ford enthusiast John Smith says, "Raise the quadrant control lever to raise the rear lift arms. They should move quickly and smoothly all the way to the top [top position will have the eyes in the outer ends of the lower lift arms around three feet from the ground]. It's best to have a load on the lift arms for testing, such as a heavy rear blade or a mower. If nothing is available, you or someone else should stand on the rear lift arms [hold on to the fenders]. Raise and lower the lift a few times. It should be smooth and not have an excessive amount of knocking coming from the pump area.

"A knocking sound indicates wear in the eccentric bushings that drive the pistons in the pump," he explains. "Most will have some noise, but it should not be excessive. If the lift is jerky coming up, there could be a bad or stuck valve in the pump. Raise the lift to the top position [with load] and disengage the PTO. The lift should hold the load in the up position for 20 minutes or longer without drifting down. Less than 20 minutes can indicate worn rings or a scored lift cylinder. A really tight system will hold the load up overnight with little drift."

Simple Fixes

On occasion, a simple fix is all that is needed to correct what may seem to be a complex or expensive problem.

Always check the simple things first to avoid spending time and money on restoration steps that may not be necessary. Through his experience with tractor restoration, Chris Pratt has come up with the following list of common problems and simple fixes for them.

Runs Poorly When Warmed Up

Before replacing the carburetor, check the fuel line, sediment bowl, and tank outlet. These often become clogged with rust sediment on old tractors and cause the engine to run as if the float and float valve are damaged. Quite often the tractor will run fine when started, but begin to starve out and miss after awhile.

Dies When Warmed Up

If the tractor warms up, suddenly dies with no spark and the spark does not come back until the tractor cools down, the problem is most commonly a bad condenser. Since testing condensers seems to be a lost art, it is easiest to replace them.

Good Battery Won't Actuate Starter

This problem may be most common on tractors with a 6-volt system. Before replacing the starter, check for warmth at the connections of the battery cables. It may be that the cables are of too high a gauge (the wire is too small) or the connections may be less than perfect. As a rule, 6-volt systems draw more amperage than 12-volt systems, and the connections and wiring need to be near perfect for the starter to function as it was intended.

The Engine Is Getting Gas and Spark but Won't Start

If the engine is getting a spark at the right time and gas is getting to the plugs, yet the tractor won't start, it is likely that your gas has gone bad—particularly if the tractor has been sitting for some time. The solution may be as simple as draining and replacing the gas.

Won't Start, Water in Distributor Cap

If you have trouble with your tractor during high-moisture times, such as during a thaw or in damp conditions, check under the distributor cap for moisture. In most cases, all you have to do is dry it out and hit the starter. Since it displaces moisture on electrical connections, WD-40 sprayed on the inside of the

At some point, preferably before buying the tractor, you should check the water in the radiator for traces of rust or oil. The best thing you can hope to find is clean water with antifreeze.

distributor cap can also do the trick. Of course, then you need to find the root of the problem. It's most likely a crack in the distributor cap or a poor seal.

Overheating or Not Charging

Before you replace your water pump, thermostat, and radiator cap, be sure the drive belt is the correct width and profile. Also ensure that it is properly tensioned. These factors can also cause the charging system to appear to be faulty.

Boiling Out Radiator Fluid

If the tractor is boiling out radiator fluid every time it warms up, the first thing you should do before replacing the thermostat is make sure the radiator cap is rated correctly for the system and that its spring and seal are still in good shape. A faulty cap may be letting off steam under what was supposed to be normal pressure.

Burning Oil

What if a compression test indicated good compression on all cylinders and showed that the valves, pistons, and rings are in good shape, but traces of oil smoke are coming out of the exhaust? This can be caused by the oil-bath air filter. Be sure that you are running the correct weight of oil. If the oil is too light,

A compression check measures the pressure built up in each cylinder and helps assess the general cylinder and valve condition. It can also warn you of developing problems inside the engine. When performing a compression check, you'll want to record both the pressure reading and the rate at which the pressure increased. You should also compare the pressure readings between cylinders.

it will be drawn into the engine. Don't go overboard the other way, however. If the oil is too heavy, it won't clean the air. To learn more about oil-bath air filters, refer to Chapter 13.

Compression Testing

If you've had a chance to start or drive the tractor, you probably have an idea how well the engine runs. Before you make the purchase or start tearing it down, you should run a compression test. This measures the pressure built up in each cylinder and helps assess the general cylinder and valve condition. It can also warn you of developing problems inside the engine.

Before you begin, you should start the engine and let it warm up to normal operating temperature. Shut off the engine and open the choke and throttle all the way to provide unrestricted air passage into the intake manifold. Remove all of the spark plugs and connect a compression gauge to the No. 1 cylinder following the gauge manufacturer's instructions.

At this point, you need to either have someone else crank the engine or use a remote starter switch that has been connected to the starter relay. Always follow all manufacturer's safety instructions and make sure the transmission is in neutral and the wheels are blocked or locked prior to engaging the starter.

Crank the engine for at least five compression strokes or until there is no further increase in compression shown on the gauge. Remove the tester and record the reading before moving on to the next cylinder. In addition to the psi rating, you should also note whether the needle goes up all at once, in jerks, or a little at a time.

You'll need to check the service manual for your tractor for the recommended pressure, but generally the lowest pressure reading should be within 10 to 15 psi of the highest. Meanwhile, engine compression specs can vary anywhere from 80 to 150 psi. A greater difference indicates worn or broken rings, leaking or sticking valves, or a combination of problems.

The specific numbers don't matter as much as them all being even. If one or more are significantly lower, you'll probably need rings or worse. If the initial compression test suggests a problem, you might want to confirm your suspicions with a wet compression test. This is done in the same way as your previous test, except that a small amount of heavyweight engine

Squirting a little oil in the cylinder and performing a wet compression check will give you an idea whether a compression problem is caused by faulty valves or worn or broken piston rings.

oil is poured into the cylinder through the spark plug hole before the test. Since this will help seal the rings from the top, it should help pinpoint the problem.

If there is little difference between the wet and dry tests, the trouble is probably due to leaking or sticking valves or a broken piston ring. If, however, the wet compression reading is significantly greater than your first reading, you can assume the problem is worn or broken piston rings.

On the other hand, if two adjacent cylinders have similar low readings during wet and dry tests, the problem is more likely a defective head gasket between the two cylinders or a warped head-to-block surface.

Your notes on how the needle moved up can tell you a lot. If the needle action came up only a small amount on the first stroke, a little more on succeeding strokes, and ends up with a very low reading, it's an indication of burned, warped, or sticky valves. A low pressure buildup on the first stroke, with a gradual buildup on succeeding strokes that leads to a moderate reading can mean worn, stuck, or scored rings.

There can be good news, too. If the readings from all cylinders are within reasonably close proximity, you can assume that the upper end of the engine is in good condition and may not warrant an overhaul. A simple tune-up may suffice.

If you're checking the compression on a diesel engine, the process is basically the same, except you will need to remove the injectors and seal washers. Since the compression is higher on a diesel engine, you'll either need to use a different compression gauge or an adapter for diesel engines.

CHAPTER 6

Engine Repair and Rebuilding

The engine used in all Ford N Series models, which includes all tractors built from 1939 to 1953, is a Ford-built four-cylinder L-head type engine that has all cylinders and the upper half of the crankcase cast on one piece to make it a flat-head engine. Beginning in 1953 with the NAA/Jubilee, Ford switched to a 134-cubic-inch, four-cylinder overhead-valve engine. A 172-cubic-inch engine was used in the 800/801 Series tractors, even though it was essentially the same engine as the 134-cubic-inch engine but with a larger bore. The company didn't use anything larger than a four-cylinder engine until 1962 when Ford introduced the 6000 Series with a six-cylinder engine. That, however, is getting beyond the scope of most vintage tractor restoration.

The first step in engine repair is to find out what you are dealing with and what repairs are necessary. If you're lucky, you are restoring a tractor with an engine that is already in running condition. If that is the case, all that may be needed is a good tune-up. Chapter 5 will have given you some ideas about how much repair to anticipate.

A conversion kit offered by Funk Aircraft Company allowed a six-cylinder engine to be installed in any of the N Series tractors for more horsepower and a three-bottom plow rating. Note the hood extension that raised and lengthened the hood.

On the other side of the coin is an engine that is completely frozen, or a tractor that may have been parked and left to rust after a piston rod broke or the engine block cracked. In either of those situations, figure on a complete engine rebuild.

The more common situation is an engine that will run or start but performs poorly. Perhaps it smokes or has a distinct knock. If you're like some restorers, you may choose to overhaul the engine as part of a restoration. And if you're like others, you may be on a budget that demands just fixing what needs to be fixed. Either way, this chapter will, I hope, guide you through some of the processes.

Funk Conversions

Unless you are totally new to Ford tractors and Ford restoration, you've probably at least heard of a Funk conversion. Nonetheless, there are still a lot of people who don't know much about the concept. It was a kit

for 9N, 2N, and 8N models that modified the tractor to accept a six- or eight-cylinder Ford industrial engine. This conversion was built and offered by a company based in Coffeyville, Kansas, called the Funk Aircraft Company; hence the name *Funk conversion*.

Funk Aircraft started making the kits in 1950 for the six-cylinder conversion, which essentially took the tractor from a two-bottom plow rating to a three-bottom plow rating. From 1949 to 1950 it also had a kit available for a V-8 conversion. This had the potential to push the horsepower from a little 8N to over 100 horsepower. Its very last conversion was for a valve-in-head straight-six conversion in 1952.

Due to the increased length of a six-cylinder engine, a Funk conversion required a number of parts and modifications. Among them were adaptive components for the engine itself, such as a rear engine plate, new flywheel housing ring, new timing gear cover, generator bracket, and a new radiator and

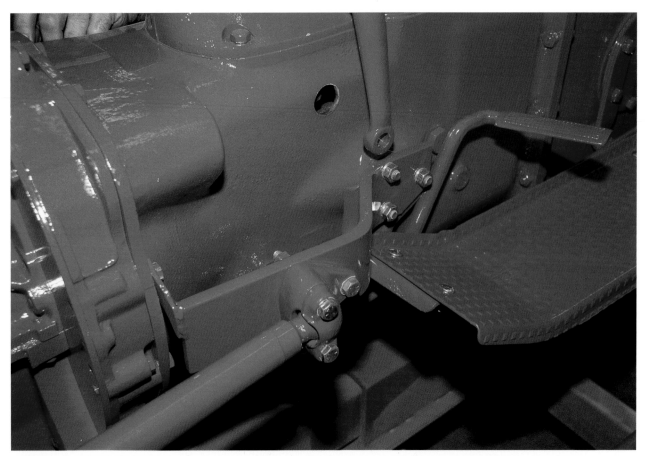

Funk Conversion kits also included the components necessary to stretch the tractor and raise the hood. Examples include a pair of brackets that allowed the radius rods to attach farther forward.

Funk and a few other companies produced kits that allowed a Ford N Series owner to install a flathead V-8 in place of the standard four-cylinder engine.

hoses. The kits also included items needed to lengthen the tractor chassis, including transmission side brackets, steering rod extensions, and hood extensions.

Although the Funk records were lost in a fire in the early 1950s, it's estimated that around 5,000 flathead six-cylinder engine kits alone were sold during the company's tenure. In contrast, only around 100 to 200 V-8 kits were sold. Regardless of which engine was installed, the majority of the Funk conversion kits were sold and installed on new tractors right at the dealer.

Over the years, a number of the Funk Ford tractors have been converted back to the original engine, especially when dealers found they were difficult to sell. Of course, that makes a Funk Ford even more collectible today. Should you find yourself in possession of one, it would be best to find a service and repair manual for the appropriate engine, even if you have to locate an old truck manual. You will want to pay extra attention to detail when inspecting and servicing the transmission, differential, and axle, however,

From the looks of this cylinder block, it wouldn't be surprising to find at least one of the cylinders to be stuck in place. *Dallas Mercer*

because of the extra horsepower to which the tractor was subjected.

Kits to convert N-Series tractors to V-8 power are still available today. Check the appendix for companies like StaufferV8.com and Awesome Henry.

Freeing a Stuck Engine

Ask a dozen tractor restorers how to free a stuck engine and you're likely to get a dozen different answers. Each one seems to have a favorite method. Unfortunately, few of them are quick fixes. They all take time and patience.

Most often, engines get stuck because the pistons and cylinder sleeves have rusted together. This can occur as a result of water directly entering the engine, or by condensation—also called block sweat—inside the engine, which leads to flash rust. With a little time and work, flash rust can often be broken loose fairly easily. Unfortunately, pistons that are practically welded to the cylinder walls are a much bigger challenge.

Before you attempt to break anything loose, there are a few things to keep in mind. First, be careful about towing the tractor in gear in an attempt to free the pistons. Even if you have soaked the pistons for some time, you run the risk of damaging the engine. One possibility is that you will bend the connecting rods or components in the valvetrain, should the pistons—but not the valves—come loose.

You also need to be careful about putting too much pressure on any one piston, such as with a hydraulic press, if all the pistons are still connected to the crankshaft. If the piston on which you're pushing comes loose but three others are still stuck, you risk damaging the piston and the connecting rod or the crankshaft.

One tractor restorer says he likes to soak the piston heads and cylinder walls with the connecting rods attached and the tractor blocked up on one side and in gear. Every few days as he walks by the tractor, he gives the back wheel a push to see if anything has loosened up. If you do attempt to tow the tractor at this point, make sure you use a slow speed and pull it over soft ground or gravel so the wheels will skid. Letting the wheels get a firm traction grip is a sure way to bend something.

Soaking the cylinders and using a press or hydraulic ram to force them loose is an option, too. Another

A few companies, such as StaufferV8.com and Awesome Henry, continue to offer V-8 conversion kits today.

method practiced by some is to put a chain around the engine while it is still in the tractor and pour oil into the cylinders. A round, wooden block is cut to fit the cylinder. Using the chain as a brace, a hydraulic jack is placed against the block and pressure is applied to the piston until it comes loose.

When it comes to the type of lubricant or penetrating oil to pour into the cylinders, everyone seems to have their favorite recipe. Some use diesel fuel, whereas others prefer something as exotic as olive oil. Others prefer a mixture of ingredients that may include brake fluid, penetrating oil, automatic transmission fluid, kerosene, Hoppe's gun solvent, wintergreen oil, Marvel Mystery Oil, and Rislone. One restorer claims to have freed the pistons on 15 different engines with a mixture of one-third automatic transmission fluid, one-third kerosene, and one-third Marvel Mystery Oil. Another prefers to use Seafoam, a solvent available in most automotive stores that is used for everything from cleaning carburetors to lowering the gelling temperature of diesel fuel.

The important thing to remember when trying to free a stuck engine is that it took time for the engine to set up and it will take time to free it. If all else fails, remember that all Ford engines use sleeves in the block, which means you have the option of destroying the piston in an effort to remove it, knowing that you're planning to replace the pistons and sleeves anyway.

Ring Job or Complete Overhaul?

If you have seen traces of blue smoke coming from the exhaust and the engine has been using quite a bit of oil, chances are pretty good that you are in the market for a set of piston rings. Before you can know for sure, you will need to check the piston-to-sleeve tolerances and surfaces, and make sure the valve guides are not sloppy. The valve guides can exhibit the same symptoms as worn pistons and sleeves.

In most situations, it is not advisable to replace only the rings in an engine, because by the time you do the teardown and measurement of the components, you'll find something else that justifies the need for a complete rebuild.

Dallas Mercer, owner of Mercer Tractor Restoration in Excelsior Springs, Missouri, says he seldom ever works on an engine without doing a

In order to perform a complete overhaul, the tractor will need to be split since the engine block and oil pan serve as load-bearing members. The engine can then be mounted on an engine stand.

complete overhaul, which includes new pistons, sleeves, valves, etc. "You can tell the difference in the way it starts, the way it runs, and in the way it sounds," he says. "If everything is tight and like new, the fan will make almost as much noise as the engine," he insists.

If you are planning to replace only the rings, however, you need to first verify all of the following:

- Bore of cylinder is not scored
- Piston is not scored, cracked, or its top surface is not eaten away
- Rings are not stuck to the cylinder wall(s)

- Bottom flanges of sleeve are not cracked
- The engine uses dry sleeves
- Sleeves are not leaking oil into cooling system
- Bore is within tolerance throughout piston travel (up and down and across right angles around the bore)
- Piston ring grooves are within tolerance and not damaged

Engine Disassembly

If you have a service manual for your tractor, it is best to follow the disassembly process outlined by the

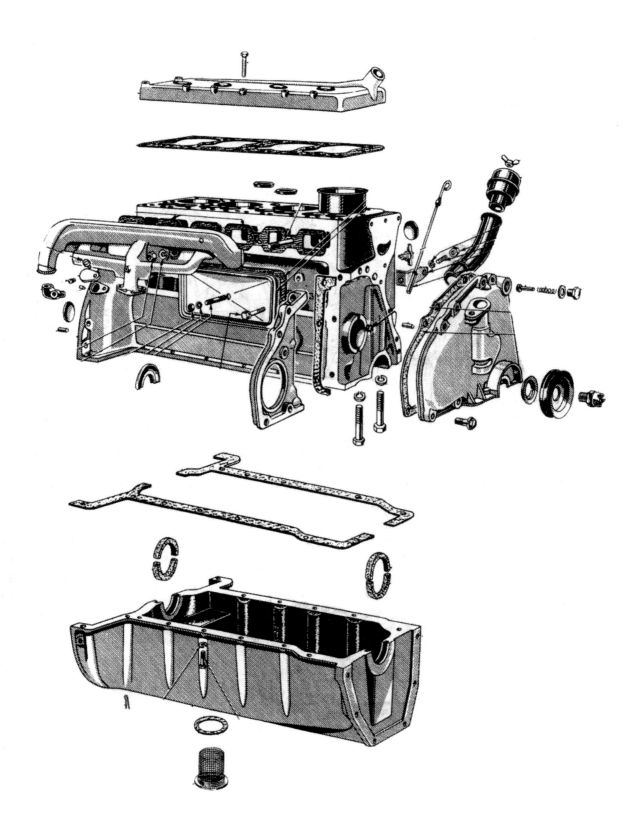

This catalog illustration from *Dennis Carpenter* shows the engine assembly for 1939 to 1950 models.

Remove the manifolds, access plates, and any other components attached to the block in preparation for engine overhaul.

manufacturer. In the absence of that material, the following procedure and tips should apply to most tractor models.

If you haven't done so already, you will need to thoroughly clean the cooling system and drain all the fluids from the engine. This includes water and antifreeze, fuel, and oil. If the cooling system isn't cleaned first, sediment will dry, harden, and affect the cooling efficiency when the engine is reassembled. You'll also need to remove the engine hood, grille, and fuel tank to expose the engine. Place a jack or floor stand under the transmission housing and remove the front axle and radiator assembly.

Since the engine and oil pan are used as a load-bearing unit instead of a separate frame, you'll need to either support the front end or remove the engine altogether and support the rear half of the tractor. At this point it's usually best if you can remove the engine

and mount it on an engine stand that will allow you to turn it over when necessary. First, you'll need to disconnect all other linkages between the engine and the rest of the tractor, including the choke cable, wire from the coil, heat indicator, negative battery cable, and/or Proofmeter cable, depending upon the model. Next, remove any components attached to the engine, such as the coil, starter, generator, spark plug wire brackets, etc. You'll also need to remove the intake and exhaust manifolds at this time. If you're working on an overhead-valve engine, your next step is to remove the valve cover, valve pushrod cover, rocker arm cover, oil inlet and outlet lines, and pushrods.

Begin loosening the head bolts a quarter turn at a time in an alternating pattern. If you have a service manual for the tractor and it shows a tightening pattern, simply loosen them in reverse order. This will slowly relieve the stress on the head and lessen the

When removing the head, especially on a flathead engine, remove the bolts in an alternating pattern.

potential for warping or cracking. If it becomes necessary to pry the head off to get it loose, make sure you are prying against the gasket and not the block. You'll be replacing the gasket anyway.

At this point, you need to take one of two actions. If you're going to replace the sleeves and pistons, you can move on to the oil pan and rod-bearing caps. If you're only replacing the piston rings, however, you'll need to remove the ridge at the top of the cylinder or sleeve. This process can only be done from the top with a tool called a ridge reamer. This ridge is formed naturally as the piston and ring travel up and down thousands of times in the cylinder. In essence, the area of piston travel wears, while the portion above it does not. Since the ridge reamer is one of those tools that is used only occasionally, perhaps you can borrow or rent one.

Removing the oil pan is a fairly straightforward procedure in most cases, but if the oil pan is made of cast material, you should loosen the bolts in an alternating pattern to prevent any warping. As you remove the oil pan, look for any pieces of metal or shavings that might be a clue to engine problems.

You can now remove the rod-bearing caps and pull the pistons out the top of the block. Examine both the pistons and the sleeves for scoring that would suggest the need for more than just ring replacement. Since all

Carefully remove or scrape away the head gasket. If the engine is a flathead model from an N Series, chances are good that the head will still need to be planed.

but a few Ford engines use sleeves in the cylinders, a lot of tractor restorers like to go ahead and install new sleeves if there is any question at all. It's easier to do it now and know you've done a quality job than to go back and have to do it later. In the process, try to keep carbon from getting into the cylinders, particularly the water and oil passages.

Piston Ring Replacement

Once you have removed the pistons and checked them for scoring, you'll need to remove the rings by carefully spreading them from the break or ring gap. This is most easily done with a special tool called a ring spreader. An inexpensive ring spreader looks like a pair of pliers that opens when squeezed. More expensive ring spreaders have the same design but also have a band to wrap completely around the circumference of the ring to ensure that you don't elongate or spread the ring gap too far. This is not that important on your old rings since you are throwing them away, but it is critical with the new ones.

Once the rings are removed from the pistons, examine the grooves that the rings fit into and make sure they are not damaged. You will also need to carefully clean the grooves to remove carbon and dirt that would hamper the correct seating of the new rings. Before installing the rings, you'll also need to check

Remove the rod caps and bearing shells so the pistons can be removed from the top.

The mechanics at N-Complete get ready to overhaul a six-cylinder engine from a Funk Conversion model.

the width of the ring grooves with a new piston ring and thickness gauge.

Before you do that, you'll need to determine the size of the new rings by measuring the bore and determining what size will completely fill the gap when the piston is at the top of its stroke. The manufacturer's required ring gap should also be taken into account. The ring gap is the clearance left at the split in the ring when the ring is compressed in the cylinder. This usually occurs at the top of the piston's stroke.

In most cases, going one size up from the existing rings is sufficient, since ring replacement is done only when there is little wear on the piston and cylinder. If it takes more than one size increase, you might want to consider a more thorough overhaul.

Once you've determined the ring size, you'll need to hone the cylinder to remove the smoothness—

generally referred to as a glaze—from the cylinder bore. If you do not, the new rings will not properly seal. A cylinder hone that fits into a 1/4-inch drill can be found at most any auto parts store.

The intent of cylinder honing is to get a nice crosshatch surface on the cylinder. This requires moving the hone up and down as the drill operates. Never allow the drill to run in one spot, and keep the hone lubricated and cooled with a 50-50 mixture of diesel fuel and kerosene, penetrating oil, or other thin lubricant. Be sure there are no large particles on the bore or hone surfaces that will cause scoring. Cover the crankshaft rod journals while honing to keep them protected from falling debris.

Now it is time to check the ring end gap. As stated earlier, the ring has to have the minimum specified compressed gap when it is in the cylinder bore to allow

Before installing new rings on a piston, squarely position each ring in its respective cylinder, measure the end gap as shown, and compare it to the engine specs.

for expansion that occurs when the engine reaches operating temperature. Without sufficient gap, the ring ends might butt together and cause scoring and ring breakage. Check your repair manual for the exact specification, but it is generally considered to be 0.002 or 0.003 per inch of cylinder bore diameter. For all N Series models, the service manual states that the gap should be between 0.012 and 0.017 inch.

To measure the gap, you'll need to compress the first ring and place it inside the bore. Don't put it on the piston. Push the ring into the cylinder using an inverted piston. This makes it easier to push the ring into the cylinder or sleeve, and it ensures that the ring is square with the cylinder wall. Take your feeler gauge and measure clearance between the ends of the ring. Compare this with the specifications in your manual and determine what changes, if any, are

necessary. Insufficient clearance will require that the ring gap ends be filed down to tolerances.

One of the best ways to do this is to take a file and mount it vertically in a vise. Take the ring, hold it firmly in both hands, and draw it downward over the stationary file. After removing a small amount of metal, check the ring in the bore again and repeat this process as often as needed. Follow this procedure for each ring and make sure you note each gap specification for each particular ring.

After the gap for each ring has been established, take each ring, insert the edge of it into the corresponding ring groove in the piston, and measure the side clearance to determine if the ring grooves are worn. There should be ample room for the proper feeler gauge between the ring and piston lands. This will be another case where you need to check the

Insert the base of the piston into the bore and compress the rings with an appropriately sized ring compressor. As an alternative, Ford restorer Dallas Mercer sometimes places the compressor on the piston ahead of time and leaves enough of the base exposed to slip it into the cylinder or sleeve.

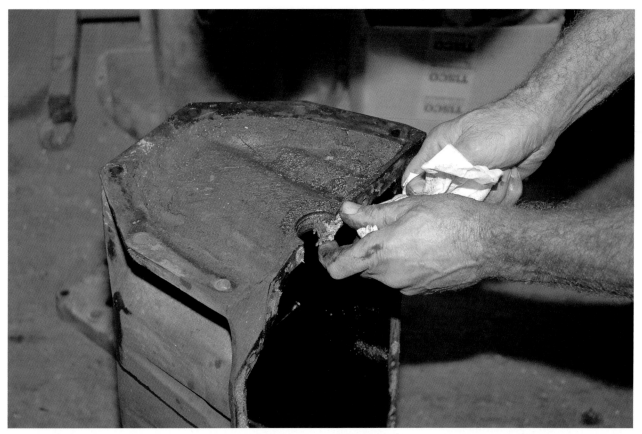

Remove all traces of gasket from the oil pan where it seals to the engine and around the crankshaft.

manual for the specifications. Too tight a fit will keep the rings from proper rotation and movement as the piston moves up and down. On the other hand, excessive side clearance will allow the rings to flutter in the piston grooves when the engine is running. This can result in poor sealing of the combustion chamber or eventual ring breakage. Make sure you place each ring in corresponding order with each piston groove and check the ring for a mark to indicate the correct side up. According to the service manual for all N Series models, the clearance between the ring and the edge of the ring groove should not exceed 0.004 inch. If it is more than that, you should replace the piston.

Once everything has checked out and the ring gap has been established, it's time to install the new rings on the piston using the ring spreader to prevent overexpansion or distortion. If you're not using a ring spreader, carefully spread them by hand and slip them into the ring grooves starting with the lowest ring (the oil ring) and ending with the top ring (the compression ring). Be sure to stagger the piston ring end gaps around the piston for maximum sealing. Note that on

some models, the third compression ring from the top of the piston has a tapered face and must be assembled with the stamped word TOP toward the top of the piston.

It's time to reinstall the pistons back into the cylinder. All components, especially the pistons, should be reinstalled in their original positions if they are being reused. You'll also need to note in your service manual whether the pistons need to be installed in a certain direction. Some have a notch on the crown that has to be oriented toward the front of the tractor. Finally, lubricate the pistons and cylinder walls with clean engine oil.

Using a suitable ring compressor to compress the piston rings, place the piston into the bore. A ring compressor is basically a sleeve that fits around the piston to compress the rings enough to allow the entire piston to be slipped into the bore. Be sure the ring compressor is perfectly clean on the inside and gently tap the piston down into the cylinder. Be careful to ensure the connecting rod studs don't scratch the cylinder walls or the crankshaft journal as

Remove the old piston rings from the pistons and check the ring grooves for integrity.

you're installing the pistons. As extra insurance, you can place pieces of plastic or rubber tubing over the connecting rod studs during piston installation.

At this point, all that is really left is to apply a light coat of engine oil to the connecting rod bearing inserts and install the bearing caps on the connecting rods. Since the rod bearing caps are already off, it's a good idea to also perform measurements to see if the journals need adjustment or replacement. For more specifics on determining serviceability of these components, refer to the following section.

Engine Block Preparation

Before you do anything else with the block you'll need to check it for hairline cracks. It's especially important to inspect all around the area above and in front of the draincock. If someone has let the engine freeze up in the winter, this is where it usually cracks.

John Smith says, "Be wary of cracked blocks, especially if repairs have been poorly done. A cracked block makes the tractor worth substantially less, and trying to find a good used block for a reasonable price

can be a very frustrating task. On the other hand, a crack that has been properly repaired won't affect the performance of a work tractor one bit."

Another potential problem would be a lack of flatness of the mating surface between the head and block. To check both surfaces, you'll need a straight edge, feeler gauges, and your tractor shop manual, which will provide the allowable tolerance. Because nearly all Ford engines are sleeved, this tolerance takes on extra importance: The sleeve stand-up (how far the sleeve sticks out of the block) must be taken into account. If there are radical differences between the cylinders following assembly, you'll need to locate the problems. These can include dirt under the sleeve flange or distortion of the lower mating surface. This can cause leaking at the head gasket and distortion of the sleeve that hampers free movement of the piston.

Main and Rod Bearings

The main and rod bearings can generally be lumped together since the methods used to measure them

Before or during disassembly, check for cracks in the block that can make it unusable. This one had to be scraped and replaced.

are identical. The measurement you are looking for is the existing size of the crankshaft pin or journal. Using this figure, you can calculate which undersized replacements will bring the crank or rod journal tolerance back to factory specification.

The first step in measuring the crankshaft and bearings is to check the surfaces for scoring. Also check for chipped, missing, or worn teeth on the crankshaft gear. If scoring is minimal, it can generally be remedied by having a machine shop turn the crank on a lathe, followed by polishing with No. 320–grit polishing paper. This will cause the journal to be undersized to its original specification, so if the scoring or damage is too bad, you'll have to look for a replacement crankshaft.

Assuming the crankshaft passes the initial inspection, use a caliper to determine if it has equal wear across the surface. If the journal has more wear on one side than the other, you will have to look at having it turned or replaced. Finally, check to see if it has worn unevenly around the diameter of the journal to create

an oblong cross-section. This can be done by taking a measurement, rotating the caliper around a quarter turn, and taking another measurement. Repeat this process at a minimum of four places around the shaft to determine size, out-of-round characteristics, and taper. This will quickly give you an idea whether it is serviceable. The better manufacturers' manuals will explain what are acceptable tolerances in this respect.

If the crankshaft does exceed the manufacturer's wear tolerances, you have two options. The first is to purchase a reground crankshaft. Although this is expensive, it has the benefit of simplifying your measurements, since new bearings that have been pre-measured for the shaft are nearly always provided with the replacement. In this case, you are done with the job.

The less-expensive alternative is to have the crankshaft ground by a local machine shop. While the price is generally reasonable, there is often a wait, especially during certain times of the year, since many of these shops also work on specialty engines, such as those used for racing or tractor pulling.

Kenny Knapp, a mechanic with N-Complete, measures the crankshaft journal to check for out-of-round, taper, and wear.

Before you take a crankshaft in to be ground, be sure you can get the right-sized bearings to cover the amount of material the machinist will remove; otherwise, you may have wasted your money on the machining.

The other journal and bearing measurement process is accomplished by putting the whole assembly back together with Plastigage inserted between the bearing shell and the crank journal. Some manuals will talk about using shim stock to measure the clearance. Since the advent of Plastigage, this technique is seldom, if ever, used anymore.

Plastigage is a plastic-impregnated string that squishes flat as it is squeezed between the journal and bearing shell. You should be able to find Plastigage at any good auto parts store. You'll find that it comes in different colors, like red, green, and blue. The color is a universal code for the range of clearance each particular plastic thread is capable of measuring; for example, red Plastigage is designed to measure a bearing clearance of 0.001 to 0.004 inch. If you take along your service manual or tell the parts person how you want to use it and how much clearance you need,

you shouldn't have to worry about colors. Any knowledgeable parts salesperson should be able to help you find the right size.

To use Plastigage correctly, cut a strip that is wide enough to go across the journal, reassemble the shell and cap with the strip placed between the journal and shell, and torque the bolts to the proper specifications. Never turn the crank during this process. Next, remove the bearing shell and compare the width of the Plastigage against a scale on the package to determine your exact clearance. Once you find this value, you can determine how much oversize will be required to bring the clearance back to that required by your manual. For Ford N Series models, the clearance should not exceed 0.003 inch on the main bearings.

As you've probably noticed, you have now measured the journals twice, once with a caliper and once with Plastigage. This is important with many old tractors. The caliper finds the irregularities and gross undersizes that necessitate crank welding, grinding, or total replacement. The Plastigage process is needed to determine whether shimming is required during reassembly. If Plastigage is the only measurement you use, it may be hard to spot irregularities like conical or oblong journals. On the other hand, you can't measure for the proper clearance without Plastigage.

Camshafts

Although camshafts can bend, it's not likely since the pushrods tend to sacrifice themselves much sooner.

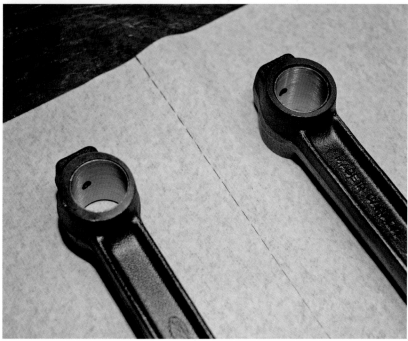

Clean and inspect all connecting rods as part of the overhaul. These connecting rods have already had new bushings installed.

The more common problem with the camshaft is worn or scored bushings and worn or chipped teeth on the timing gear. Both of these parts are readily available and can be easily replaced.

While it is possible to get the shaft turned, the best alternative is generally to purchase a new, used, or reconditioned camshaft. Finally, since Ford engines do not use cam bearings or bushings, you'll need to ensure that the bores in the block haven't become oversized from wear. Should that be the case, which is very rare, the block can be rebored and custom-made bushings can be installed by a competent machine shop.

Rocker Arms

Like the pushrods, you'll need to check the rocker arms for straightness and smooth profile. Rocker arms can be distorted, which can not only make adjustment difficult, but can also cause the pushrod to slip when combined with a slightly bent pushrod. More important, you'll need to check the rocker arm bearing diameter. If clearance exceeds the maximum diameter allowable, the rocker arm, shaft, or both will need to be replaced.

Valves and Valve Seats

Faulty valve action is one of the main reasons for power loss in an engine. Although carbon, corrosion, wear, and misalignment are inevitable products of normal engine operation, the problems can be minimized with high-quality fuel and valve tune-ups.

Carbon is a byproduct of combustion, so it's always going to cause some problems, like fouling spark plugs, which make the engine miss and waste fuel. Valve seats can also become pitted or be held open by carbon particles. These carbon deposits can insulate parts and cause them to retain heat, compared to clean metal, which tends to dissipate engine heat. This increases the combustion chamber's temperature and causes warping and burning.

Unburned carbon residue can gum valve stems and cause them to stick in the guides. Deposits of hard carbon with sharp points can become white hot and cause pre-ignition and pinging.

Valves need to be carefully checked for warping, burning, pitting, and out-of-round wear, especially on the exhaust valve, since it is exposed to the high temperatures of exhaust gases.

Burning and pitting are often caused by the valve failing to seal tightly due to carbon deposits on the valve seat. This in turn permits exhaust blow-by, although it may also be due to weak valve springs, insufficient tappet clearance, warping, and misalignment. Warping occurs chiefly in the upper valve stem due to its exposure to intense heat.

Out-of-round wear follows when the seat is pounded by a valve whose head is not in line with the stem and guide. Oil and air are sucked past worn intake valve stems and guides into the combustion chamber, which causes excessive oil consumption, forms carbon, and dilutes carburized fuel.

Misalignment is a product of wear, warping, and distortion. Such wear, which is often hastened by insufficient or improper lubrication, will eventually create sloppy clearances and misalignment. On the other hand, distortion is generally caused by unequal tightening of cylinder head bolts.

Valve Guides

Valve guides tend to warp because of the variation in temperatures over their length. Consider, for example, that the lower part of the guide on an overhead valve engine is near combustion heat, while the upper is cooled by water jackets. Any wear, warping, or distortion that affects the valve guide destroys its function of keeping the valve head concentric with its seat, which obviously prevents sealing. On overhead-valve models, it's also important that you check the clearance between the valve stem and guide with a small hole gauge and micrometer. On NAA models, this clearance should be 0.002 to 0.003 inch.

Remove the piston pin from the piston and check the tolerance as outlined in your service manual. Usually the manual calls for a tight press fit.

New sleeves should be carefully unwrapped and examined prior to installation in the block.

Valve Springs

Valve springs must be of a uniform length to be serviceable. To check the springs, place them on a flat, level surface and use a straight edged ruler to determine whether there is any irregularity in height. Unequal or cocked valve springs should be replaced.

Spring tension that is too weak will allow the valves to flutter. This aggravates wear on the valve and seat and can result in valve breakage. If the springs are less than 1/16 inch shorter when compared with a new one, they should be replaced.

Pistons and Sleeves

Just as you did with the crankshaft, you'll want to examine the piston and sleeves for any visual damage, such as scoring, out-of-roundness, and greater width on the sleeve at the highest point of piston travel, not including the ridge that forms above the high point of

travel. Scoring will indicate the need for replacement regardless of the measurements. The other conditions can be determined through precise measurement.

To check for out-of-roundness, use an inside micrometer to take a measurement at the top and bottom of the cylinder. Repeat the process at right angles to the original measurements. With these numbers, you can see how conical the cylinder is and how oblong it has become. Repeat the process using your caliper on the piston. There will usually be a factory specification for what is acceptable.

If the differences at the top and bottom are acceptable, you may still need to determine if there is too much distance between the piston and the sleeve. This will be most noticeable at the top of the stroke. Most shop manuals suggest using a long feeler gauge of a certain size placed between the piston and sleeve with the piston inserted in the sleeve. A scale is then used

If you are going for a total rebuild, it's often best to send out the engine block, head, and any other major grease-carrying components for professional cleaning in a hot chemical bath.

to pull the feeler gauge out of the bore. The amount of drag required to pull it free, as measured on the spring scale in pounds of pull, determines its serviceability. This process needs to be done without the rings in place, and the measurement is usually taken 90 degrees from the piston pinhole.

If you have any doubts about the condition of your pistons, one of the best options is to just purchase a kit that includes new pistons, rings, and sleeves. This will save a tremendous amount of measuring and practically guarantee a matched fit. Replacement pistons and rings are also available.

Piston Pins

The piston pin is difficult to measure without using calipers to measure the pin, and the results of this may be meaningless to the home mechanic. The main objective is to ensure that there is no detectable

looseness. The pin should generally require a "light-press" fit when the piston assembly is at room temperature (70° F). After the piston reaches operating temperature, the pin will float in the piston pin bore.

Rebuilding the Engine

If you're planning to completely overhaul the engine, you may want to consider purchasing an engine rebuild kit. Most have all the replacement parts you'll need for overhauling an engine without going to the store to separately purchase gaskets, special measuring tools, or miscellaneous parts. Don't let the matching sleeves, pistons, rings, and bearings lead you into a false sense of security. They should still be measured and installed in a workshop environment.

If you are going for a total rebuild, your best bet at this point is to also have the engine block, head, and any other major grease-carrying components

Each new sleeve in a rebuild kit comes with a matching piston and rings.

Carefully check the camshaft for straightness, as well as any damage to the lobes or gear teeth.

professionally cleaned in a hot chemical bath. This process will not only strip those components of grease and paint, but it will also remove carbon, varnish, and oil sludge from the inside and outside of each part.

While the engine components are out for cleaning, it's also a good idea to have a professional Magnaflux the engine block and head to search for cracks that are not visible to the naked eye and would have been overlooked in your original inspection. This investment alone could save you a lot of time and money.

Meanwhile, smaller parts can be cleaned in the shop using a solvent tank, then dried, inspected for integrity, and placed on a clean rag. When the engine comes back from the machine shop, it should, ideally, be mounted on a rotating engine stand and prepared for reassembly.

Use an air hose from your air compressor to blow out the engine block. Be sure to hit all the openings and bolt holes to remove any residue that may be left

Most connecting rod bearings are of the slip-in precision type and are available in both standard and various undersized sets. Note how both the piston rod and bearing cap are notched to accept and hold the new bearings.

in the engine. A clean solvent rag can be used to wipe off the internal surfaces to remove any film left over from the tanking process. Let's hope that the machine shop has reinstalled the casting plugs (sometimes called freeze plugs) and oil galley plugs.

It is generally recommended that the head be reworked in its entirety by the machine shop. Pressing in valve guides, getting the correct angles on the valve seats, setting the proper valve-to-head recession, and measuring and milling warped surfaces, among other things, are really beyond the scope of the average home shop.

Unfortunately, 9N-2N-8N flatheads will almost always show some warping in the head, according to John Smith. Be very careful when milling or resurfacing the N flathead to not remove too much stock. A number of N-Series heads have already been milled during previous rebuilds.

"Valve clearance is rarely a problem," he says, "but very little material can be removed before the pistons start hitting the head. Always check the piston-to-head clearance on the N-Series engines when assembling, especially if the head has been resurfaced. A simple method is to place the head on the block with no gasket and just start a couple of bolts to line it up. Then rotate the engine and watch for the pistons to hit the head and lift it up. If the piston lifts the head, you can use a feeler gauge to measure the interference. If the pistons are hitting the head, some machining will need to be done on the combustion chambers in the head to remove just enough metal so the piston does not hit. Then, when the gasket is installed, you will have approximately 0.050 inch clearance between the piston and head. That is about the minimum needed to allow for thermal expansion. If the head has been milled too much, it will need to be replaced with a new or good used one."

By the same token, crankshaft and camshaft measuring, grinding, and polishing are also out of the

Before reinstalling the cylinder head, slip a new head gasket over the mounting bolts and make sure it is correctly oriented. You'll also need to install new gaskets on the manifolds, as shown.

realm of the average home shop. It is wise to always double-check the machine shop's work with a feeler gauge, dial indicator, and Plastigage. It is important to check the crank end play with a feeler gauge and to check each bearing journal with Plastigage before starting the reassembly procedure.

If your rebuild includes cylinder sleeves, you may also want to look at having the machine shop install these. Just remember that the pistons and sleeves come as matched sets so you'll need to identify what piston goes in which sleeve before turning loose of half the kit.

Smith notes, "If your engine is serial number 8N433578 or later, you have the 0.090-inch-wall-thickness cast-iron sleeves. All earlier engines could have either the 0.090- or 0.040-inch sleeve since many were rebored at overhaul time. The only way to know for sure is to disassemble the engine and take a look. I've heard that some suppliers of sleeve kits only sell the heavy-wall sleeve and tell you that the older block must be rebored for the newer sleeve," he adds. "This is not true. The 0.040-inch-wall-thickness sleeves are available and will still work fine in the older engines."

If you plan to replace the sleeves, there are numerous methods for removing and replacing the old ones. The easiest and safest way is to use a commercial sleeve puller set. Reverse the puller setup process to

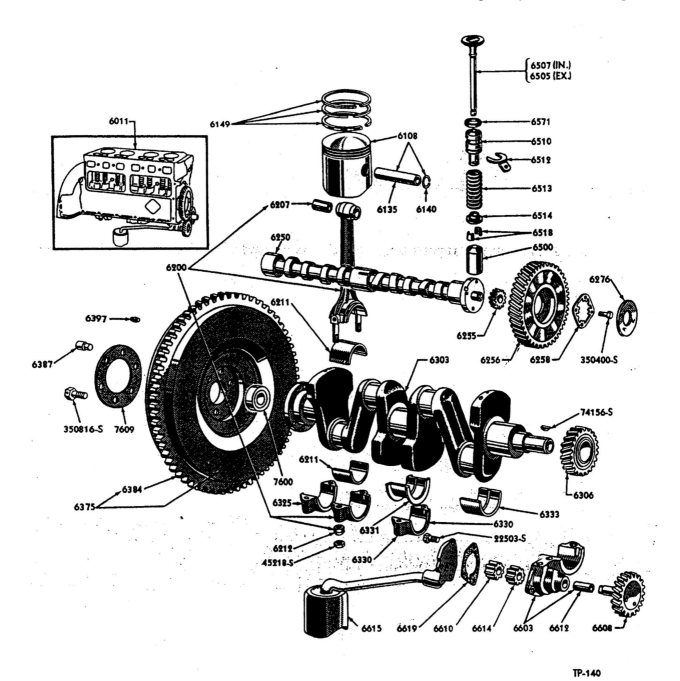

6507 (IN.)
6505 (EX.)
6571
6510
6512
6513
6514
6518
6500
6276
350400-S
6011
6149
6108
6135   6140
6207
6250
6200
6211
6255
6256   6258
6303
74156-S
6397
6387
6306
350816-S   7609
6384
6375
6211
7600
6325
6333
6331
6330
6212
22503-S
45218-S
6330
6615   6619   6610   6614   6603   6612   6608

TP-140

The internal engine assembly didn't change much from 1939 to 1952, as illustrated in this exploded view that covers all 13 years.

install the new sleeves. Most machine shops that do engine rebuilds will have one, and it's usually a pretty reasonable price for them to remove and replace the sleeves for you. You may be able to rent a sleeve puller set or you could make your own that will do the job.

According to Smith, "The 0.040-inch thin-wall steel sleeves—commonly referred to as tin can sleeves—can be removed by using a tool to crush the sleeve inward away from the cylinder wall. This is a risky proposition, however, as many cylinder walls have been damaged and even broken by people trying to wedge a screwdriver or other tool between the sleeve and cylinder."

"That's about the only way I remove the thin-wall sleeve," says Dallas Mercer, admitting that an inexperienced hand can scratch the cylinder wall. "Otherwise,

I use a homemade sleeve driver for both taking out the old ones and putting in the new ones."

Smith notes that another method that seems to work well on both types of sleeve is to run a bead of weld (make sure it isn't too hot) from top to bottom of the sleeve. As the weld cools it contracts the sleeve and you can usually slide it out by hand.

Clean the bores of carbon and scratches but do not remove any stock or you may find that the new sleeves are loose. For this process, Mercer says he lightly runs the hone through the bore just long enough to remove the rust.

When it comes time to put the new sleeves back in, some restoration enthusiasts recommend putting the sleeves in the freezer for a couple of hours. This will cause the metal to shrink just enough to slip into the cylinder bores a little easier. Don't stop midway for any reason because the natural heat from the block will quickly cause the sleeve to expand and increase the risk of breakage. Only stop when the sleeve is flush with the top of the block.

"Unfortunately, I've never had a lot of luck with freezing at home, since the sleeves warm up by the time I get them from the freezer to the engine block," Smith relates. "Usually, the sleeve will press in the bore by pushing it down by hand. Place a short length of 2x4 across the top of the sleeve and lean on it. Make sure the sleeves are starting into the bore straight! You can tap on the 2x4 lightly with a soft mallet, but never hammer on the sleeve itself," he insists. "If the sleeves are tight in the bores and won't push in, make a puller to pull them in. Get a piece of heavy flat stock that will span the top of the sleeve and another that will span the bottom of the engine block. Drill a 5/8-inch hole in the center of both pieces of stock. Use a length of 5/8-inch threaded rod and two nuts between the two pieces of stock to pull the sleeves in. The top of the sleeves should be flush with the top deck of the block or have a slight standout [0.002 to 0.003 inch]."

The sleeves are also intended to be a light-press fit into the bores. If you find that one of the new sleeves is loose in the bore, try another sleeve. Don't assemble the engine with loose sleeves. Call a machine shop and see what other options they can offer.

If you're simply honing the old sleeves or the cylinder walls, you can refer back to the piston ring replacement section for this process. Cylinder sleeves that come in a kit with the pistons do not require honing after installation, but should be checked for distortion or high spots.

Now that the sleeves are in place or the cylinders have been honed, the next step is to match the pistons to each cylinder. Refer to your shop manual and locate the piston-to-cylinder wall measurement or amount of pull required to remove the feeler gauge. To obtain this measurement, you'll need to locate a long feeler gauge, commonly called a ribbon gauge. Install the piston in the bore and see if the specified feeler gauge will slip in next to the piston. The proper fit is when the ribbon gauges can be pulled from between the piston and sleeve with a specified inch-pound pull as verified by an inch-pound scale. If you don't have the recommended scales, you should at least make sure the feeler can be pulled out freely with moderate pressure and without binding. You should also check the piston at the top and at the bottom of the cylinder for proper clearance in case the sleeve is tapered. Don't assume that if the piston freely falls through the bore that the clearance is adequate. If the clearance is inadequate, the cylinder bore (or sleeve) will have to be honed and rechecked. Take the time to do it right.

Each piston will come with a certain number of piston rings. Unwrap the rings and lay them next to each piston in the order of installation. The instructions for measuring and installing the piston rings are basically the same as for piston ring replacement, so refer to the previous section in this chapter about piston ring replacement.

Once the piston rings have been installed, the next step in assembly is to check the piston pin-to-bushing tolerances. Once again, this is a close tolerance and is best done at a competent machine shop. An insertion pressure of pin to bushing will be slightly looser than that of the pin to piston. When dealing with clearances of 0.0002 inch or less, it is important to have the proper measuring tools. A pin too tight or too loose will cause a piston and rod to break apart under the stresses of engine operation.

Valvetrain Overhaul

Depending upon the condition of the engine when you started, you may or may not have to do major work on the valvetrain. If the engine was running

A valve spring compressor is used to compress the valve springs for access to the keeper when removing and replacing the valves and springs.

Once they've been removed, carefully check each valve for warping, burning, pitting, rust damage, and out-of-round wear. It's also important to check the valve springs for irregularity in height or spring tension. Here, the valve springs have already been inspected, measured, and matched to the valves.

The valve seats will need to be ground and/or lapped. When properly finished, both the valve and the valve seat will have the type of smooth surface that ensures a tight seal.

when you acquired the tractor, a good visual inspection and adjustment of the tappets may be sufficient.

When water gets into an old engine, though, it seems that the valves are among the first components to suffer. As a restorer who likes to focus on orphan tractors, Bill Anderson of Superior, Nebraska, has seen his share of valvetrains that not only required one or more new valves, but valve-seat restoration, as well. This can generally be accomplished by using a valve-seat tool to regrind the seats. If damage to one or more valve seats is severe, though, it may be necessary to have a machinist cut recesses into the block or head that will accept special hardened valve seats.

To inspect, grind, or lap the valves and seats, you'll first need to remove them from the head or block, depending on whether it is an overhead-valve engine or a valve-in-block engine. To do this, you'll need a valve-spring compressor so that you can compress each of the valve springs. Once the spring is compressed, you can remove the clip or keeper from the base of the valve spring. At this point, the valve can be lifted out. Be sure to keep the valves separate so each one can be replaced in its original seat.

Depending upon the condition of the valves, you'll have one or more options. If the valves have notches or burned sections, you'll need to replace them. If the valve faces and seats are simply a little rough and dirty,

Make sure all valve tappets are suitable for reuse. If they aren't in good enough condition, it's easier to replace them now instead of down the road.

they can be cleaned and renewed with valve lapping. To do this, make sure the valves are returned to their original position after inspection so you're lapping each valve into its original seat.

Before you install the valve, place a small bead of medium-grit valve-lapping compound around the face of the valve where it mates to the valve seat. Using a valve-lapping tool, rotate the valve back and forth in the seat, alternating between clockwise and counterclockwise rotation. In the simplest form, a valve-lapping tool is little more than a suction cup on a stick that you spin in your hands. Other, more sophisticated versions have a suction cup on a shaft driven by a device that looks a little like an eggbeater. Some older lapping tools engaged a slot or recesses in the valve head. At any rate, you can move on when you have a smooth, clean surface all the way around the valve face with a matching surface on the valve seat. If necessary, add more compound during the process.

Valve lapping should not be a substitute for having the valves professionally reground. If they're in rough enough condition that a few minutes of lapping doesn't polish up the mating surfaces, you're probably better off having a machinist grind the valves and seats. This basically consists of clamping the valve stem into what looks like a large drill chuck and turning it against a grinding wheel that renews the face to the correct angle.

All that is left is to thoroughly clean all the parts, including the keepers. Check the valve springs to make sure they meet service manual specifications, and reassemble the valvetrain and coat all parts with clean engine oil as you go.

Once the valves and springs have been assembled back into the head or block, you'll need to finish up by adjusting tappet clearance according to specifications. Correct clearance contributes to quiet engine operation and long valve-seat life. Insufficient clearance causes the valve to ride open and results in lost compression and burning. Too much clearance retards timing and shortens valve life.

Oil Pump Restoration

Any thorough engine overhaul should include an inspection of the oil pump. Although oil pumps can be of the vane or gear type, almost all vintage Ford tractors use the latter. Like the gear pumps used in some hydraulic systems, the pump uses two gears that mesh together to create an area of high pressure on one side of the gears and low pressure on the other

Every thorough engine overhaul should include an inspection of the oil pump, since it provides the lifeblood to engine parts.

side. As one gear drives the other and the teeth mesh, oil is carried around the outside between the gear teeth and housing.

Inspection involves cleaning or replacing the pickup screen and checking the gear surfaces and housing for wear and cracking. Be sure to check for worn bushings or bearings and ensure that all oil passages are clear. Check your repair manual if you have any doubt about wear criteria. Several sources offer a complete oil pump repair kit that includes a new drive gear, internal pump gears, bushing, and gasket. You'll also need to check the oil pump relief components, including the plunger and spring. These items are available for most tractors.

The oil pump used on the 9N, 2N, and 8N tractor engines is unfortunately made integral with the front crankshaft main bearing cap. If one of these pumps cannot be rebuilt and requires replacement, the block and new pump will need to be line bored at a machine shop to get the proper fit on the front main bearing.

Finally, the pump should be primed before replacing the oil pan. One way to do this is to pack it with a lithium-based grease, commonly called white lube, before replacing the oil pan.

If you intend to test run the engine before complete tractor assembly, which isn't a bad idea, you'll need to rig up some kind of temporary fuel tank. You must be very careful how you handle gasoline in a semi-open container.

The head for an 8N engine has already been cleaned and planed as part of the engine overhaul.

The engine on this 8N is finally finished and has been remounted in the tractor so that the remaining components can be reinstalled. *Dallas Mercer*

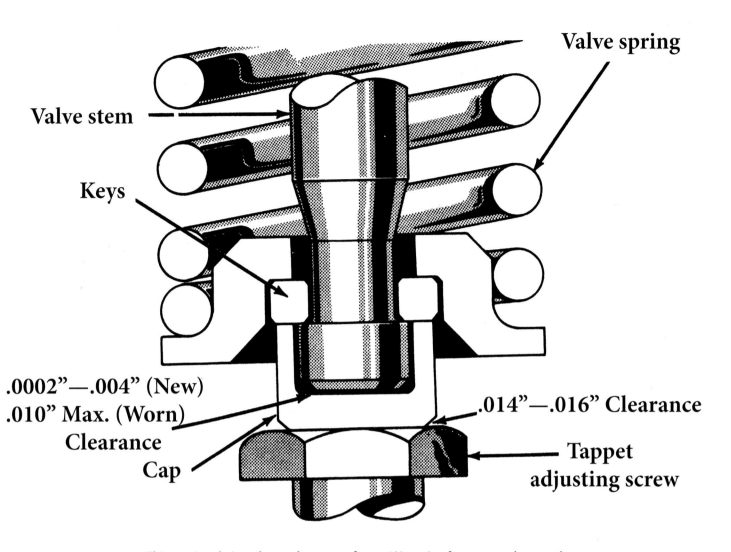

Valve spring

Valve stem

Keys

.0002"—.004" (New)
.010" Max. (Worn)
Clearance
Cap

.014"—.016" Clearance

Tappet
adjusting screw

This sectional view shows clearances for an 8N engine free-type exhaust valve.

CHAPTER 7

Clutch, Transmission, and PTO

I f the tractor is in running condition, you should have had the opportunity to drive it and run it through the gears before you made the purchase. This would have given you an idea where the trouble lies. Often it will be with one of the gears that saw a lot of fieldwork, particularly if there were only three or four gears in the transmission, as was the case with most vintage Ford models.

Other things to watch out for are the effects of dirt and water. Just as with a modern transmission, dirt is the gearbox's biggest enemy. There's still a good chance that you will get lucky and find that all it takes to get the transmission in working order is to drain it, clean it up, and refill it with fresh transmission fluid. In fact, most tractor enthusiasts say that's all that has been needed on the majority of the tractors they have restored.

That's probably not the case with the clutch, though. During your test drive, assuming the tractor is in running condition, if you found the clutch slipping or chattering, you'll need to take a closer look. The problem is most likely a worn clutch plate. At any rate, the clutch is probably going to need more attention than the transmission.

Although they look a little dry from lack of use, the gears in this transmission appear to be in pretty good shape and should be serviceable after a good cleaning.

Transmission Inspection and Repair

As was stated earlier, transmissions used in tractors built in the 1930s and beyond were generally heavy-duty enough that they don't present any major problems, even after sitting for several years. It is still a good idea to at least open up the transmission to check out the gears and clean them up. To do this on a 9N or 2N, you'll need to first remove the steering assembly. On the 8N and later models, the transmission has a separate cover that can be removed without disturbing the steering assembly.

Several restorers say they like to drain any fluid they find in the transmission case and replace it with diesel fuel. Keep in mind that after sitting for several years, the fluid can be pretty thick. While you're draining the transmission, keep an eye out for pieces of metal or fine shavings that can tip you off to problems.

To access the clutch in any Ford tractor model, you'll need to split the tractor since the engine and transmission are used as structural supports.

Drive the tractor around the yard for several minutes to circulate the diesel around the transmission case in order to coat and rinse all the gears. If the tractor can't be driven but can be towed, that would be your next-best option. A word of caution though: Since the N Series shares the transmission oil with the hydraulic system, it would not be a good idea to use any of the hydraulic system until the fluid has been replaced.

It's easy to spot the damage on these gears. Chipped teeth and rounded corners were quite often caused by speed shifting a transmission before the tractor came to a stop.

Here's another set of gears that needed to be replaced. These came from an 8N being overhauled by Dallas and Chris Mercer. *Dallas Mercer*

If you can't use gear action to do the work, you'll need to clean every part you can reach with cleaner and a stiff brush. Next, inspect all the bearings, shafts, and seals for damage. Rotate the gears with your fingers as you go through the cleaning and inspection process. At the same time, check for looseness and rough action. If it wobbles or shakes, it's probably going to need repair.

Keep in mind that transmissions built in the early part of the twentieth century were not synchronized like they are today. If farmers, or more likely their teenage sons, didn't wait until the tractor stopped before shifting, they had a tendency to round off the gears. This was particularly the case with the road gear. Consequently, you may find a gear or two that needs replacement due to ground teeth.

According to the service manual for all N Series models, noisy transmissions are sometimes due to incorrect adjustment of the transmission shaft bearings. A great deal of care should be taken when overhauling the transmission to make sure the correct number of shims are placed behind the bearing caps to make a good snug fit, yet allow the shafts to turn easily by hand.

The main cause of noisy transmissions is damaged teeth on one or more of the gears. Sometimes even the slightest indentation of a gear will cause a distinct noise. Quite often, the damaged teeth can be smoothed up with a grinding stone passed back and forth over the damaged area. If this doesn't work, you'll need to find a replacement gear. Keep in mind that due to the similarity between Ford models, you will often be able to find the appropriate gear from another model. If you're faced with a transmission that needs extensive repair, another option is to buy a rebuilt transmission or a used transmission that's in better shape from a salvage yard.

While inspecting or rebuilding the transmission, it's also important to pay

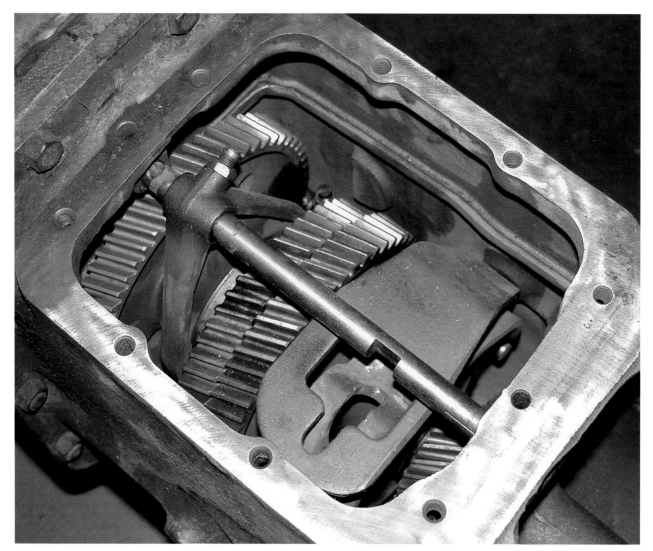

Everything in this transmission appears to be in good shape after the gears have been cleaned and the gasket surface sanded to accept a new seal.

particular attention to all transmission bearings. It should go without saying that any bearings and seals that look bad should be replaced. Unfortunately, any repairs to the transmission, including shafts, gears, or bearings will require the transmission to be completely removed from the tractor on all models.

Select-O-Speed Transmission

The Select-O-Speed transmission, which was introduced in 1959 on the 01 Series, is a solid-drive transmission that was developed by the Ford Tractor and Implement Division exclusively for Ford tractors. While it seemed to be a great idea that put Ford ahead of its time, the concept was unfortunately rushed into production before the design was proven. As a result,

If it does become necessary to replace a gear, the transmission must be completely disassembled.

The Select-O-Speed control, which is attached to the dash, consists of a valve body connected to the transmission by a single line.

Select-O-Speed transmissions continue to plague Ford tractor owners to this day. The Select-O-Speed transmission was available on three vintage Ford tractor models: the model x11 Ford tractor, the model x71, and the model x81. The different model designations refer to the PTO option available as outlined in Chapter 2.

In simple terms, the Select-O-Speed transmission consists of a mechanical system of gears, which are always in mesh. The transmission is also a manually selected, hydraulically controlled unit that transmits engine torque through a system of four serial planetary gear sets, three servo-operated brake bands, and three multiple-disc, hydraulically-operated clutch packs. This provides a total of ten forward speeds and

Quite often, you'll run across a Ford N Series model that has been fitted with an aftermarket auxiliary transmission, such as those produced by Sherman. Since they were generally installed inside the center housing, the only thing showing is the shift handle or a shift cable, which protrudes through the housing.

two reverse speeds to the operator. In addition, there are two stationary positions: park and neutral.

Due to the complexity of Select-O-Speed and the complications that Ford itself experienced, it is generally beyond the capability of most restorers to make repairs. Consequently, you may want to have the transmission serviced by the local equipment dealer or a qualified mechanic. If you choose to attempt the repair yourself, make sure you're equipped with a detailed service manual.

Sherman Transmission

The popularity of the Ford N Series tractors and their high sales numbers created a huge market for additional accessories for the tractors. Many companies started making products to improve the Ford's usefulness or make their operators more comfortable. But, according to Ford enthusiast John Smith, Sherman products stood out by the sheer number of goodies it sold.

"The Sherman brothers were insiders with Henry Ford and Ford's dealers would sell and service many of the Sherman's products," Smith explains. "Front loaders and backhoe attachments were popular, while other items, such as the aluminum head and the live PTO, didn't go over as well.

"Far and away Sherman's most popular add-on was the auxiliary transmission," he adds. "By the introduction of the 8N, tractor buyers could order a Sherman transmission when they ordered their new tractor and Ford would ship the tractor with the Sherman attached to it. The dealer mechanics then installed the transmission before delivery," he adds, and noted that the Sherman option was installed inside the bell housing between the engine and standard transmission. "The first offering was the step-up transmission, which gave the owner twice the gear selection he had before. Step-up first and step-up second gear were between the regular second and third gears. It was basically an overdrive unit for the transmission input."

The company later introduced the Sherman step-down transmission. It used the same gear case as the step-up model and essentially worked the same way, except it lowered the gear ratios rather than raised them to give the tractor a slower ground speed. The most popular model, however, was the Sherman

Install new gaskets on the transmission case and center housing cover when replacing the covers and/ or steering assembly (on 9N and 2N).

Be sure the starter lock plate and starter switch assembly are correctly installed when reassembling the transmission on most N Series models. The engine can't be started if it is incorrectly installed.

In addition to checking the splines and shaft condition, be sure to inspect the condition of the clutch fork, clutch release shaft, release springs, and associated bushings and seals.

step-up/step-down combination transmission. Once installed, it offered customers 12 forward speeds, 3 PTO speeds, and 3 reverse speeds.

One of the last Sherman models was the creeper single step-down transmission, which offered a 9:1 reduction ratio. The Sherman Company wasn't without its competition, though. After seeing the success of the Sherman transmission, other companies joined the market and offered their own versions of an auxiliary transmission.

"One such company was the Hupp Corporation," Smith explains. "Their Dual-Drive over/under transmission was similar to the Sherman unit but the shift lever was on the right-hand side of the tractor. Hupp offered two models of the Dual-Drive—one with different gear ratios and one in a straight-overdrive (step-up) model."

Others included the F & T overdrive transmission, the Howard gear reduction unit, and the Everett trencher transmission. The Everett and Howard units

were designed for applications, such as trenching or running a rototiller, where a lower ground speed was needed while still maintaining the higher PTO speed. To accomplish this, the unit had to be installed behind the tractor transmission, rather than in front like the Sherman and Hupp units.

Obviously, since they were auxiliary add-on units, none of these transmissions are covered in the Ford repair or service manuals. In addition, a number of them were rather rare, according to Smith and his sources. "The Howard transmission, for example, was originally designed to be used with the Howard Rotovator, which was a rear-mounted rototiller," Smith explains. "Unfortunately, the transmission itself was somewhat fragile if abused and broke gears easily. As a result, replacement gears for these units are nearly impossible to find.

"If someone is thinking of adding an auxiliary transmission to their N Series Ford, the best bet today for availability is still the Sherman transmission,"

Smith adds. "Used Sherman models and parts for the transmissions can still be found in salvage yards, at swap meets, etc."

Smith has Sherman transmission installation instructions, as well as Sherman overhaul procedures on his website at www.oldfordtractors.com. In general, the process isn't too much different from overhauling the standard transmission, which calls for cleaning and inspecting the gears and replacing the appropriate bearings, seals, and gaskets.

Clutch Inspection and Rebuilding

Once you've finished with the transmission—either having cleaned it and verified its condition, or replaced the appropriate gears and bearings—it's time to move on to the clutch. These two components essentially work together anyway.

Overhauling a clutch is never an easy job, but it's one of the most important, partly due to the safety issues. Obviously, you want the tractor to stop when you push in on the clutch and apply the brake. But if you have a tractor on which the clutch has rusted to the shaft, it's also possible for the tractor to move when the engine is started, even if the transmission is in neutral.

Although the clutch disc appears to have some wear left on it, this clutch plate has a bigger problem, as evidenced by the stripped splines.

The stripped splines on this driveshaft will unfortunately be a bigger problem to remedy than the mating splines on the clutch plate.

While some of the early tractors, including steam tractors, had positive engagement clutches, the move toward internal combustion engines necessitated the use of a friction clutch that could be slipped as the drive was engaged. All Ford models therefore use a plate clutch that is attached to the engine flywheel. This means the tractor needs to be split at the bell housing for clutch replacement or inspection.

If you drove the tractor before you purchased it or started restoration, you should already have an idea whether the clutch needs attention. Usually the trouble is obvious and falls into one of three categories:

- The clutch slips, chatters, or grabs when engaged
- The clutch spins or drags when disengaged
- You experience clutch noises or clutch pedal pulsations

If the clutch slips, chatters, or grabs when engaged, or drags when disengaged, the first thing you should do before tearing into the clutch itself is see if the clutch linkage is improperly adjusted. In some cases, free travel of the clutch pedal is the only adjustment necessary for proper operation of the clutch. Free travel is the distance the clutch pedal can be pushed before resistance is met. Refer to the repair manual for your tractor for this dimension. On most N Series models and the NAA Series, it should be adjusted to allow 3/4 inch of free travel. To adjust the clutch, remove the clevis pins on the clutch linkage, and turn the adjustment eye bolt counterclockwise to decrease pedal travel and clockwise to increase travel.

Beyond clutch linkage adjustment, the causes of most problems are generally found in the clutch housing where clutch components may be worn, damaged, or soaked with oil, which will cause the clutch facing to slip. Most often, the culprit is weak or broken pressure springs, or worn friction disc facings. As a result, clutch restoration generally consists of cleaning and checking all parts for wear, replacing bushings in the sleeve (if necessary), and replacing the clutch lining.

Although the clutch lining is attached with rivets on the majority of vintage tractors, some tractors use a drive plate to which the friction disc is bonded. Your best

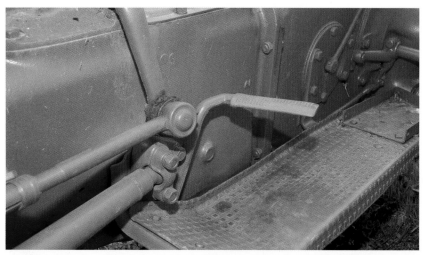

Although the transmission case may look similar among the N Series models, there were slight differences over the years; for example, the bulge behind the clutch on this 8N model was added to accommodate a larger reverse gear.

The final step in transmission/clutch restoration is adjusting the amount of free travel on the clutch pedal. On later models, this is done by adjusting the clevis on the end of the clutch pedal rod.

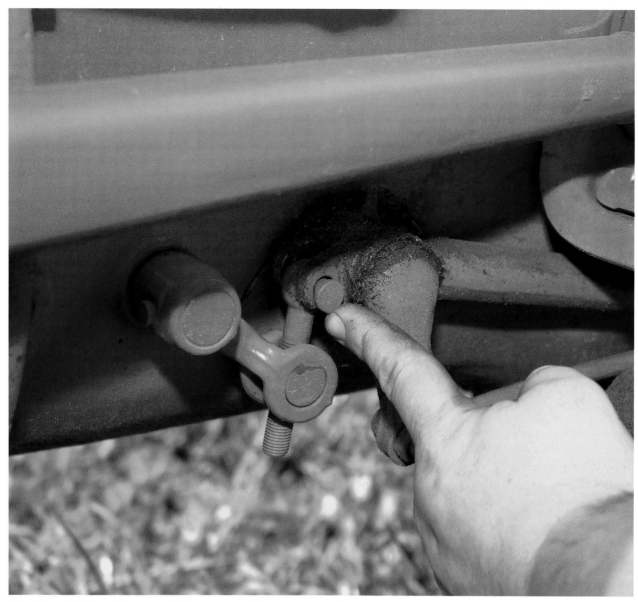

The 9N and 2N models use a different type of arrangement for clutch-pedal free travel.

bet is to replace the entire clutch plate with a reman-ufactured part if one is available. If you're working with an older tractor, you may have to have a machine shop reline the existing plates by riveting new linings in place.

Clutch Release Bearing

Another potential problem spot is the throw-out or release bearing, which compresses the springs to release pressure on the plates when the clutch is pushed in. Characteristics associated with a defective throw-out bearing include squealing when the clutch is released and rough actuation. Replace the release

bearing if there is any hint of roughness, looseness, or discoloration.

Power Take-Off Repair

Although a power take-off (PTO) was standard on all Ford tractors, beginning with the 9N in 1939, that doesn't mean the PTO was any less frustrating in the days before live PTO became a factor. It means the tractor has to be moving or in neutral with the clutch engaged for the PTO to operate. Many farmers can still remember mowing hay fields with a transmission-driven PTO. If the sicklebar started to plug or you had to stop in the middle of the field, you could almost count on getting it plugged even worse because the minute you stopped, so did the sickle. That factor hasn't changed, so be prepared to improvise if you plan to use an N Series model as a work tractor.

Things changed in 1954 when Ford introduced the Hundred Series with the option of a live PTO. The live, or independent, PTO utilizes its own clutch within the transmission, which means that the PTO can continue to operate in relation to the engine speed, rather than slow or stop its function as the tractor is slowed or stopped. By the end of the 1950s, nearly all tractors had a live PTO, although Ford continued to offer it as an option for a couple more years.

Whether your tractor is equipped with a transmission-drive PTO or an independent-drive system, you should check its condition as part of transmission inspection and repair. The most common problem tends to be seal leakage. Other ailments can include clutch problems with live PTO systems and worn gears and bearings. Due to the different variations used, overhaul procedures are best explained in your tractor repair manual.

Belt Pulley

Unlike many tractors used prior to the 1950s, which had belt pulleys mounted on the right side of the tractors as standard equipment, the unique configuration

The most prevalent problem with the PTO on Ford tractors, or any tractor for that matter, is worn and leaking seals around the shaft.

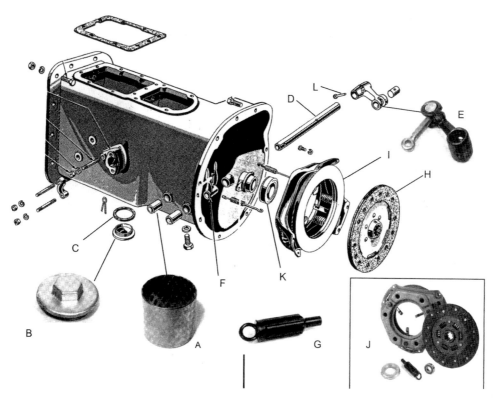

An exploded view in the parts manual can be as helpful as the repair manual when reassembling the clutch.

of the Ford N Series required an alternative arrangement. Through much of the twentieth century, a belt pulley was a necessary component on a tractor used for driving feed grinders, corn shellers, and threshing machines. Although the Ford tractor was a little light for driving heavy equipment, there were still jobs that required a belt pulley on a Ford tractor; accordingly, Ford introduced a separate belt pulley assembly that was bolted to the back of the tractor where it engaged with the PTO shaft.

Ironically, the belt pulley unit can be installed in any one of three different positions, although the most common is horizontal to the right or left. Since the belt pulley assembly requires power from the PTO shaft to be turned 90 degrees to the belt pulley drive, restoration primarily consists of inspecting the drive gears and shafts and replacing the appropriate bearings, gaskets, and seals, just as you would with the transmission or differential.

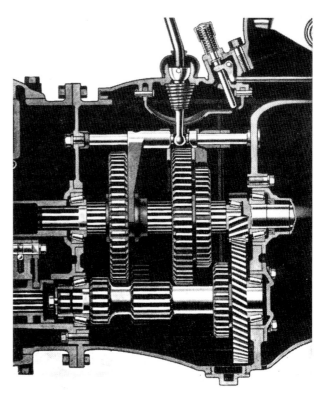

This side-section view of a Ford transmission shows the simplicity of the early three-speed gearbox.

CHAPTER 8

Final Drive and Brakes

Your first thought may be that the final drive and brakes have little in common and really don't go together in one chapter. But when you consider that the role of the brakes on a tractor is to stop one or both rear wheels, you can begin to see how the two fit together.

In general, there are two points of application with the brakes used on most vintage farm tractors, depending on the type of final drive you find on the tractor. Most models that used bull gears to drive the axles have brake housings located on the sides of the transmission/final drive case. These are generally expanding-drum brakes on a splined shaft that engage the bull gears or bull gear pinions. In effect, the brakes aren't stopping the axles or the wheels, but rather the pinions or bull gears that drive the axles.

In contrast, tractors that utilize a pinion shaft and ring gear in combination with a spider gear set don't have a braking point on the gear sets themselves. This is the case with virtually every Ford tractor ever built, starting with the 9N in 1939. For this reason, the brakes are located on the drive axles or in the wheel hubs.

Differentials and Final Drives

The differential and final drives on most vintage tractors were tough enough to take all the torque the engine and transmission could generate and then some. It wasn't until engines got bigger that manufacturers began to have trouble. The bottom line is that the final drive on most vintage tractors needs little attention other than replacing bearings and seals and changing the fluid.

Due in part to their automotive heritage, vintage Ford tractors were all built with a hypoid- or bevel-gear-type differential to transfer engine torque from the transmission to the axles. Composed of a bevel pinion and shaft, bevel ring gear, and a set of pinion and side gears, the differential provides a means of turning the power flow 90 degrees and dividing the power between the two rear wheels. The differential also provides further gear reduction beyond the choices provided by the transmission for additional torque to the rear wheels.

Although many manuals state that the drive gear assembly (including the differential gear case) and the drive pinion are only sold in matched sets, which means that if either is damaged, both must be replaced, that statement was dispelled in a Ford service bulletin dated August 19, 1948. The revised directions state that the ring gear and drive pinion are furnished separately as service parts; hence, it is not necessary to replace both if only one is damaged. Just make sure they mesh properly when installed. Of course, it should go without saying at this point that the axle housing and the center housing should be replaced if either is cracked or bent.

In most cases, the final drive doesn't require anything more than a good cleaning and inspection of the gears. Unfortunately, this model had a problem with the axle shafts.

The drive axles on most tractors have at least two seals on each shaft: one inner seal and one outer seal.

You may need to pull the driveshafts just to check the bearings and replace the seals.

The splines on the outer end of this axle and wheel hub have been stripped to the point they are unusable.

Differential and Final Drive Inspection and Repair

Inspecting and rebuilding the differential and final drive is not too much different from working on the transmission. It basically means draining the old fluid if it is different from that in the transmission, cleaning the gears, and checking for worn bearings and seals and missing gear teeth. The different models and series built over the years used a number of different configurations, so you'll need to refer to your tractor service manual for inspection or replacement procedures.

Unlike most tractor brands, Ford does not permit ring gear and pinion mesh or backlash to be adjusted. The manual simply instructs you to "Be sure to install a standard thickness gasket between the axle center housing and rear axle housing to maintain correct adjustment of the differential carrier bearings." With the exception of the NAA models, the rear end on most Ford models was pretty durable and reliable, which means you stand a good chance of being lucky.

Axle Shafts

Rear axle seals leaking gear lube onto the rear brake shoes and wheel rim is very common on some models, especially the early 8Ns, before the company added an inner seal. The major causes of seal leakage are improper (loose) axle bearing preload and worn (loose) hubs on the axle shafts. Installing the correct number of shims to obtain proper bearing preload when replacing seals is critical, as is having good hubs. If the hubs were loose on the axles before, they will probably need to be replaced. Once the hubs are worn, they will no longer tighten against the taper splines on the axles and you'll never stop the leaks.

As John Smith relates, "I have personally never had to replace an axle shaft. Severe wear from loose hubs has always been in the hub itself and the harder axle shaft was still good. You may not be so lucky," he adds. "Inspect the hubs and axle shafts closely for wear. If the hubs were tight on the axle and required some force to remove them, they are most likely okay. Replacing the seals is not too hard of a job if you're used to working on old rusty mechanical things, have a copy of the service manual, and some basic tools."

Should it become necessary to tear into the rear end this far, be sure to check the integrity of all bearings, bearing cones, and seals. Also, make sure there are no chipped or missing teeth, just as you would with the transmission.

Smith notes that if your tractor is a 1948 or 1949 model, there is only one outer seal. If you have a 1950 to 1952, it will have both an outer and an inner seal.

According to Smith, removing the backing plate and axle after you've removed the hub on older models is somewhat unnecessary, but you should go this far anyway in order to reseal the area where grease can leak between the backing plate and axle housing flange. Also make sure you have the right amount of shims to properly load the axle bearings.

"This is the time to inspect the axle bearing and cup for wear and to reset the axle bearing load," he says. "Make sure the bearing looks good; no pits in the cup or on the rollers. Make sure the backing plate, bearing retainer, and all shims and/or gaskets are clean. I select the shims needed to load the axle bearings to zero load. Zero is hard to describe. It's no bearing load and no end play. If you're not sure how many shims to use, follow the procedure in the shop manual to set the load."

It's important to realize that if you're working on a Ford row-crop tractor, these models feature a final drive assembly located at the end of the axle housing. The differential assembly is also removed from the right side of the center housing instead of the left as in general-purpose tractors. In essence, the drop housing used on row-crop models incorporates another set of

If you're lucky, you may be able to bring the brake band linings back to life by roughing up the surface with sandpaper or using a torch to carefully dry out oil-soaked pads. If not, you'll need to replace the brake band lining and perform a thorough cleanup.

It can sometimes be a challenge to install the new brake shoes while holding the adjustment screw assembly in place and attaching the spring. Brakes for 1939–1947 models have a different arrangement.

gears that raise the rear axle and provide additional torque via the different gear ratio.

The housing also contains its own oil reservoir that needs to be maintained at the proper level via the filler plug and drain plug for adequate gear lubrication. Like the rest of the drivetrain, inspection and repair involve checking the gears for wear and replacing components as necessary, including bearings, oil seals, and O-rings. Despite the different configuration, the brakes are still on the end of the lower driveshaft where it attaches to the wheel.

Brake Restoration

Let's be honest. The brake system is not the place to cut corners. You might be able to get by without overhauling the transmission or opening up the

The brakes are finished and now the axle hub and drum may be installed.

rear end, but you'll want to give the brakes the attention they deserve. This isn't just for your safety, but for the safety of those around you. If you take your tractor to any shows at all, you're going to need to unload it off a truck or trailer, and this is not the place to have your brakes fail to hold. Also consider how you would feel if you lost control of your tractor in a parade, with people along both sides of the street. Fortunately, brake restoration is not a difficult job.

Brake Inspection

Before you begin any brake repair project, remember that brake springs can fly off unexpectedly and in who-knows-what direction if they are not handled properly. Always wear safety glasses when attempting any work on the brakes. Since you will no doubt be lifting the rear of the tractor off the ground, you should also double-check to make sure the tractor is secure from rolling or tipping.

While it's important that you start brake troubleshooting by checking all brake adjustment points, it's also important to examine the brake linings. If brake linings are glazed but aren't badly worn or oil soaked, you may be able to bring them back to life by roughing them up with sandpaper. Other restorers have used a torch to dry out oil-soaked brake shoes that have sufficient wear left on them. Keep in mind that the brake pedal pressure required to obtain sufficient braking action will increase as the linings wear thinner.

If you find that the brake linings have become oil soaked or worn too far, it's fairly easy to find a replacement set through the nearest Ford/New Holland dealer or one of the suppliers listed in the parts appendix. In the meantime, any local machine shop should be able to turn any problem brake drums on a lathe to remove grooves or out-of-round spots. It's worth noting that the left and right disc brake assemblies are identical, which means that all parts are interchangeable in the event you need to find a replacement drum.

Once you've checked or replaced the brake shoes, you need to make sure the brake drum contact surfaces are clean and free of rust. A piece of emery cloth or sandpaper will do the trick.

Make sure the brake shaft engages the brake shoes correctly.

The axle hub and brake drum have been installed and this job is finished.

To adjust the brake on each side, insert a flat-blade screwdriver in the adjustment hole and engage the cogs in the adjustment screw assembly.

Brake Adjustment

Whether the brake pads have been renewed, touched up, or approved in the current condition, it is important that the brakes be adjusted. On 8N models and later, which use foot brakes that are adjacent to each other, it's particularly important that brakes are adjusted to a comparable setting with an equal amount of free travel; otherwise, one brake may be applied while the other drags. Unequal braking action is generally indicated by the tractor pulling to one side when the brakes are applied simultaneously. This isn't a problem on 9N and 2N models where the left and right brake are operated by pedals that correspond with the driver's feet.

The easiest way to adjust the brakes is to raise the rear wheels off the ground and remove the appropriate brake adjustment cover. Turn the adjustment to tighten the brake until you can no longer rotate the wheel by hand or until it at least drags with the pedal in the released position. Back off the adjustment until the rear wheel turns with only a slight drag. If you're working on a model that has both brake pedals on the right side, shorten or lengthen the left-brake tie rod by using the clevis until both brake pedals are in line with both brakes engaged.

Foot brakes that are adjacent to each other or can be locked together need to be adjusted to a comparable setting with an equal amount of free travel. This will prevent the tractor from pulling to one side when both brakes are applied in an emergency.

After the first hour of operation after the brakes have been adjusted, occasionally feel the brake drums to make sure they are staying cool. If the drums are hot from excess friction, readjust the brakes as previously outlined. At the very least, you should end up with around 1 to 1 3/8 inches of pedal free play before the brakes make contact.

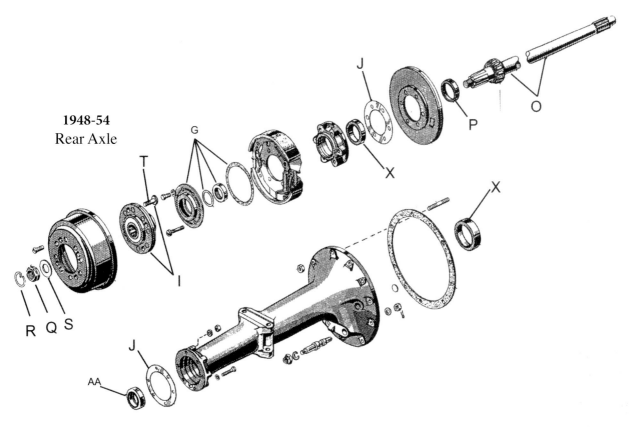

1948-54
Rear Axle

G

T

I

R Q S

J

AA

J

X

X

P

O

High-clearance models and tractors with a tricycle front end use an extra set of gears on the end of each axle to attain the added ground clearance.

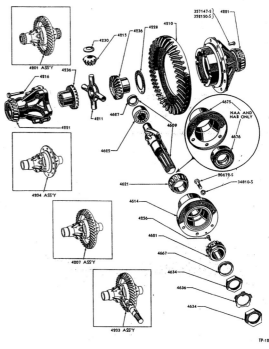

The exploded-view drawings of the rear housing and axle on 1939 to 1954 models give you an idea of what to expect when replacing the various seals and retainers. *Courtesy of* Jensales *and* Dennis Carpenter

CHAPTER 9

Front Axle and Steering

Steering in a New Direction

As we all know, Ford did a lot of things differently when the company introduced the Ford 9N in 1939. Most notable was the innovative three-point hitch known as the Ferguson system. Ford also took a different direction on configuration and steering. In the early part of the twentieth century, the tractors being developed were for draft operations, such as pulling a plow. Cultivation, planting, and row-crop operations were still being handled by horses.

By the 1930s, however, nearly every manufacturer had also introduced a tricycle configuration for use in cultivation and row-crop applications. To accommodate the needs of tractor owners, most companies offered a choice of single- or dual-wheel tricycle front ends. By the time World War II had ended and many veterans were going back to the farm, some dealers had a hard time selling a tractor with a wide front end.

Not only did the tricycle front end fit between corn and vegetable rows of the time and make shorter turns at the ends of the field, but most farmers also liked the visibility the narrow front axle offered when using a front-mounted cultivator. Unfortunately, tractors with a narrow front axle also proved to be more dangerous than those with wide axles, especially if they were top heavy or turned too fast on sloping terrain.

Henry Ford had a different idea. With the development of the three-point hitch by Harry Ferguson, Ford was able to mount a cultivator, planter, plow, and a host of other implements on the back of the tractor. In his mind, mounting the implements on the rear of the tractor instead of on a high-clearance competitive design would permit a lower operator station on the tractor and eliminate the need to round up all the attachments for front and rear cultivation. It would also lower the center of gravity and help prevent tractor rollovers.

Ford wanted a tractor that could replace a team of horses for all jobs at a price any farmer could afford. The best design was a low-profile tractor with a wide front axle that could be used for every job, whether it was pulling a plow or cultivating row crops.

In an attempt to accommodate the desires of farmers who wanted a tractor with a narrow front end, Ford finally made concessions to build two models in a tricycle-style row-crop model in 1954. The 700 Series was a tricycle version of the 600 Series, while the 900 Series was a tricycle version of the 800 Series. By the time the 01 Series came out in 1957, Ford offered a tricycle version with a single front wheel.

As equipment got bigger and the turning radius improved on standard tractors, farmers found they didn't have to turn such tight corners. They also discovered that they could guide the tires on a wide front axle between the rows as easily as they could keep dual tricycle wheels in a single-row width. Besides, the rows were getting narrower. Consequently, tractors went back to wide front axles on all models, including the Ford Model 6000 introduced in 1962.

Steering Configurations

The steering systems on early Ford tractors were pretty simple in comparison to today's power steering systems. In fact, the steering system used on the 9N and 2N tractors built from 1939 to 1947 was designed to "make the Ford tractor steer as easily as a passenger car." It consists of a spiral beveled pinion and twin sectors with a high gear ratio and tapered roller bearings on the steering column to reduce friction. On Ford 8N and later models, Ford switched to a recirculating-ball-bearing, worm-and-nut type system. Anti-friction

Unlike most tractor companies, Ford didn't introduce a tricycle-style row-crop model until late into its production series. With the exception of a Fordson model that appeared much earlier, Ford's first tricycle model appeared in 1954 when the 700 Series was released as a narrow-front tricycle version of the 600 Series.

The biggest problem with most wide-front tractors is worn bushings that allow too much free play.

The steering gear assembly on 9N and 2N tractors built from 1939 to 1947 consists of a spiral beveled pinion and twin sectors with a high gear ratio and tapered roller bearings on the steering column to reduce friction.

steering is achieved by steel balls that serve as rolling contacts between the work and nut.

Rotation of the steering tube shaft moves the ball nut along the worm. The right-hand steering sector engages the rack on the ball nut, and is thereby rotated through an arc by the movement of the ball nut. The left sector engages the right sector and rotates the same number of degrees in the opposite direction. The pitman arms transfer the motion of the sector to the spindle arms through the drag links to the front wheels.

Front Wheel Tread Adjustment

The front wheels on Ford tractors equipped with a wide front axle are adjustable from 48 to 76 inches in 4-inch increments. To adjust the axle, jack up the front end of the tractor and remove the bolts holding the three sections of the axle together. Move the front wheels together or apart until the desired tread width is obtained. It's important to always leave one or more

On Ford 8N and later models, Ford switched to a recirculating ball bearing worm-and-nut type system. Anti-friction steering is achieved by steel balls that serve as rolling contacts between the work and nut.

open holes between the bolts. It is possible to obtain front wheel spacing wider than 76 inches by reversing the wheels.

Steering Gear Adjustment/Repair

When the wheels are in the straight-ahead position on wide-front-axle models, all backlash should be removed, but if the wheels are turned to the extreme right or left, a slight backlash will be present due to the gear tooth design. This characteristic allows for a backlash adjustment for wear between the worm nut teeth and the sector gears.

Steering gear adjustments should be checked before removing the unit from the tractor or disassembling the unit. Adjusting the steering gear on the tractor in many cases will eliminate excessive backlash caused by improper adjustment between the sectors and the ball nut. To determine the cause of excessive backlash, first check the adjustment of the steering tube bearing. To do this, you'll need to disconnect the drag links from the pitman arms. Follow the instructions in your repair manual to measure the

force required to rotate the wheel. This will require the use of a spring scale to pull the wheel.

If it becomes necessary to remove and repair the steering assembly, your service manual will provide the proper technique for overhaul, as well as the specifications for adjustment. You'll need to use caution in a few places, though. The steering gear is one such place. When it is partially or completely disassembled, the ball nut assembly must not be allowed to turn so that it reaches the end of the worm on the steering shaft, since this can damage the ball retainer. Extreme care must also be exercised during reassembly to make sure that no balls are outside the regular ball circuits. Finally, you'll need to remove or install the appropriate number and thickness of shims to adjust the steering shaft tube bearings.

Steering Assembly Lubrication

Whether the steering gear assembly needs repair or not, it needs to be well lubricated to work properly. Ford enthusiast John Smith notes that the steering box typically uses 90-weight gear lube. A number of owners have tired of leaking seals, however, and now fill the box with thick, heavy gear oil or grease.

"If you're using grease, I'd recommend a soft black moly grease that will stay fluid and not pack away from the moving parts or dry out," Smith advises. "The biggest problem with the lube is the upper thrust bearing, which is above the full level in the box and seems to fail from lack of lube. Overfilling with a free-flowing grease seems to solve this problem. The early (1947, 1948) 8N steering box had a 1/4-inch pipe plug on

the upper right side of the box. It could also be filled by removing the nut that holds the steering wheel on and pouring the oil down the hollow steering shaft where it flowed out a cross-drilled hole and over the upper bearing.

"The improved steering box (after 1949 serial number 216989) had a 1/8-inch pipe plug on the upper left side of the box hidden under the dash support bracket and was nearly impossible to access," Smith continues. "The 1950 to 1952 models could be filled through the

Quite often, there will be a need to replace the front axle center support pin bushing due to years of axle pivoting.

Carefully inspect the right and left spindles for wear and scoring. Replace the bushings and thrust bearings for a tighter tolerance. The spindle on this tractor has been scored beyond use near the top and had to be replaced.

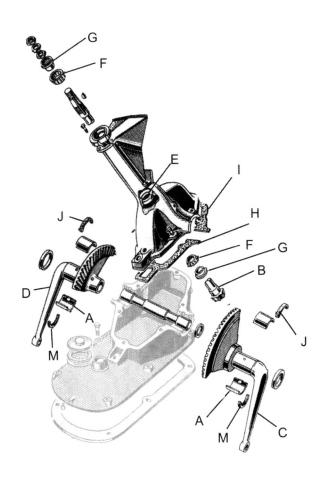

The steering gear on 1939–1947 models used a simple shaft and pinion that engaged two steering sectors.

upper right-hand side bolt hole where the dash panel attaches to the steering box.

"After serial number 452913, a screw was added to the front side of the steering column between the dash and steering wheel to allow adding lube from there. This let the oil again flow over the upper thrust bearing on the way down the same way the early models did."

Front Axle Repair

The life a vintage tractor led before you acquired it has a lot to do with its condition and the repairs that it is going to need. The condition of the steering gear and front axle is a textbook example. A tractor that spent most of its days mowing or raking hay fields isn't going to have near the wear on the knuckle bushings and axle pivot pin as a model that spent every working hour crossing corn furrows and turning around on end rows. This is just one more reason to find out

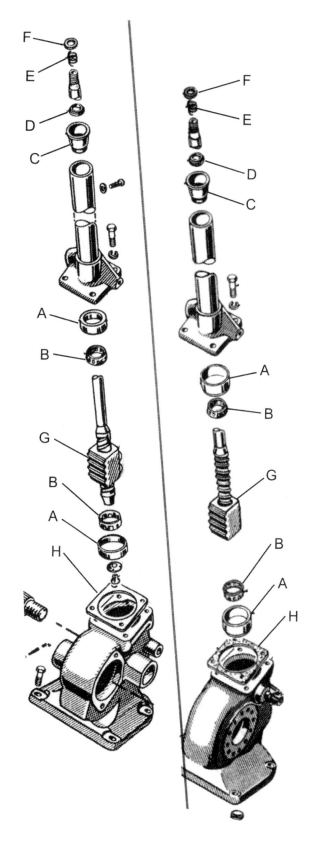

Later models incorporated ball bearings into the system to reduce friction.

all you can about the tractor before you make a purchase or calculate repair costs.

That said, the only satisfactory way to overhaul the front-axle assembly on a wide-front tractor is to remove it from the tractor and make a complete check of all bearings and bushings. That includes the center pivot pin, steering arms, radius rod sockets, spindles, steering drag link ends, spindle bushings, spindle thrust bearings, and radius rod to front axle pins. Wear in any and all of these areas can affect steering and front axle performance.

If there's too much free play, it may be necessary to replace the radius rod pivot brackets and/or the radius rod to front axle pins.

Check the condition of the drag links, especially the ends where they connect to the steering arms and front axle.

When reassembling the front axle assembly, make sure the chisel marks on the spindle and spindle arm are aligned to ensure proper front-end toe-in. The marks were applied at the factory after the toe-in was set during manufacturing. In the event the spindle is replaced, it will be necessary to adjust the toe-in because the replacement part will not carry this mark. Correct toe-in is 1/8 to 1/2 inch.

On models with a tricycle-type front end, inspection primarily consists of checking and replacing wheel bearings and seals. Depending upon the amount of free play in the bolster, it may also be necessary to replace bushings, bearings, and seals in the upper or lower sections of the bolster.

One of the steps in steering system restoration on narrow-front models is checking for free play in the bolster.

Power Steering

As with the hydraulic system, the maintenance and repair of the power steering system requires absolute cleanliness of all parts. It's also important that all parts be free of nicks, burrs, or scoring that can affect performance. Basically, the control valve is the heart of the hydraulic steering system. In fact, it is mounted on the steering shaft itself with the shaft passing through the center of it. The control valve's role is to direct the flow of fluid to the proper side of a hydraulic cylinder that essentially assists the manually operated system. Hydraulic fluid is supplied to the cylinder from an engine-driven pump and is returned to the tractor hydraulic system reservoir from the cylinder. To inspect and service the system, it's best to follow the procedure outlined in the tractor service manual, since service involves checking pressures; adjusting flows; and inspecting various valves, washers, springs, and end play clearances.

Steering Wheel Repair

Unless your tractor has been protected from the elements for most of its life, there's a pretty good chance the steering wheel is going to be severely cracked. Fortunately, there are several solutions available to you. Should you prefer to have the steering wheel professionally repaired, there are several companies that specialize in refurbishing steering wheels. Minn-Kota Repair is one of the most notable. It can take your old wheel and mold new plastic around the steel rim, complete with the original grooves, ribs, or finger ridges.

Should you choose to repair a cracked steering wheel yourself, there are a couple of options practiced by restorers. One professional restorer says he uses Fiberstrand body filler to fill all the cracks and crevices. Another uses a body filler, such as Evercoat polyester glazing material, and follows with a coat of fast-fill primer. With either product, the steering wheel must be sanded smooth after the material hardens, and then painted.

You can always buy a reproduction or refurbished steering wheel. Just be sure you get the right style for your particular model, assuming authenticity is important to you. The first 9N models, for example, used a four-spoke Ford truck steering wheel in an attempt to save money and speed production. It had been replaced with a three-spoke wheel by 1941.

The power steering unit on Ford tractors consists of a separate pump and reservoir mounted on the engine that supplies fluid to an inline valve and cylinder on the steering arm.

For a professional look on a hard rubber-rimmed steering wheel, you might consider sending it to one of several companies that specialize in refurbishing plastic-rimmed steering wheels.

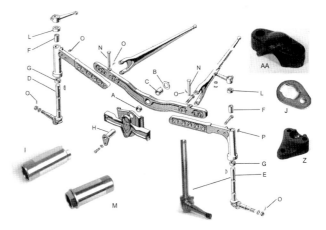

This exploded view of the front axle on most N Series models illustrates the various bearings and seals that should be checked during front axle restoration. *Courtesy of* Dennis Carpenter

CHAPTER 10

Tires, Rims, and Wheels

Just so you've been forewarned, tires and wheels can be a costly and frustrating part of a restoration project. By the time you pay for new tubes and mounting, you can easily sink $350 to $600 into a pair of rear tires, depending upon the size and the desire to replicate the original look.

Of course, Ford tractors are unique in that they were equipped with rubber tires from the start of production, beginning with the first 9N models released in 1939. Low-pressure pneumatic tires hadn't even made an appearance on a farm tractor until six years earlier, in 1932. Allis-Chalmers actually initiated the concept when the company mounted a pair of 48x12 Firestone airplane tires on a Model U. By 1934, all of the leading manufacturers offered rubber tires, even though the country was in a depression.

Consequently, by the time Ford and Ferguson were ready to introduce their first model, rubber tires were standard equipment and well accepted. The irony is that Ford actually took a step backward when the 2N was introduced in 1942. In order to continue tractor production when rubber was vital to the war effort during World War II, the 2N was equipped with steel wheels for at least a year and a half.

Ford is somewhat unique in that virtually every model built from 1939 through the 1960s uses a two-piece wheel that consists of a wheel and a rim center. The rim and center could be mounted in different configurations to adjust tread width. This configuration also makes it easier and more economical to replace a wheel. Even if the rim portion of the wheel is rusted out or damaged, the center portion is usually fine, which means simply replacing the wheel itself at a cost of around $100 to $150.

Rear Wheel Removal

Rear wheel removal on a vintage Ford tractor is pretty simple, compared to the procedure for removing a wheel from a competitive model that employed a sliding hub on the driveshaft. To remove a Ford wheel, you only need to jack up the axle, remove the wheel bolts, and remove the wheel. You may have to fight a little rust, but it's not like trying to get a hub to slide off a rusted shaft.

The bad news is that if you want to adjust the tread width of the rear wheels, you have to interchange the rear wheel components in the proper combination, which is a lot more time consuming than sliding the wheel in or out on the driveshaft. In most cases, the rear wheels are adjustable from 48 to 76 inches in 4-inch spacings. The tread width is widened by installing the wheel disks in convex or concave position and/or installing the rims in any of four positions illustrated in this chapter. Of course, this may also mean removing and remounting the tires so that the tires are always rotating in the proper direction for traction and cleaning the tread.

Considering that wide tires with all-season tread were never used as stock equipment, this tractor will need new front tires to return it to original condition.

Before you remove the rear wheels, it's important that you check the tires for calcium chloride. The Ferguson system was unique in that it transferred weight to the rear axle for pulling three-point-hitch-mounted equipment. The light weight of the tractor itself, however, meant that weight had to be added

Neglect and years of exposure to calcium chloride as a rear wheel weight have obviously taken a toll on these wheels. The worst damage is almost always around the valve stem.

if the tractor was to pull loads that weren't attached to the three-point hitch. This was also important for counter balance when using a front-end loader. That usually meant adding calcium chloride to the rear tires, since it isn't often convenient to add rear wheel weights and cover the wheel bolts. Unfortunately, calcium chloride is extremely corrosive and can destroy the rim if it leaks inside the tire. One of the first places you'll notice this corrosion is around the valve stem.

To see if the tires are filled with a calcium chloride mixture, position the valve stem near the bottom and carefully let a little air out of the valve stem. If the tires are filled, you will see liquid come out. It's important that you handle the tires carefully until you know for sure. Tires filled with the mixture are very heavy and could easily cause injury if you were to remove the bolts and have one fall over on you.

If you intend to use the tractor as a work tractor once you've finished with restoration, and plan to put fluid back in the tire, keep in mind that tires should never be filled more than two-thirds full. Any more than that can contribute to instability on slopes and hillsides.

Tire Repair and Restoration

Unless your Ford tractor has been carefully cared for or it has been a working tractor on which the tires have been replaced, there's a good chance that the tires are in pretty poor shape. If you're only looking for a working tractor, any tires that fit the rim will generally be acceptable. The newer-style tires, with their 23-degree bar or long-bar/short-bar design, may even offer better traction than the 45-degree lug tires originally found on the tractor.

If, however, your goal is to restore a vintage model to show condition and you're after accuracy, the challenge is a little greater. Not only did the tire companies change their size standards, but they also changed tire styles as more effective patterns were developed. Fortunately, there are several independent sources for the most sought-after sizes and types of tractor tires.

They include M. E. Miller, Wallace W. Wade, and Dennis Carpenter (see appendix). If you want to be authentic, replicas of the original tires are available. Dennis Carpenter offers 4x10 single-rib front tires with the Firestone logo molded into the sidewall for $85 each (at the time of this printing) and 10x28 rear tires with the 1940s-style tread design and the Ford script molded into the sidewall for $295 each. M. E. Miller also lists a closed tread Ford rear tire for $295 each.

One option for repairing tires that are worn or slightly damaged but still usable is to install a set of tire reliners. These are made from old tires that have had the lugs ground down to make the reliner about 1/4-inch thick. Reliners generally come in half-moon shapes so they can be easily inserted into the old tire, where they partially overlap. Some companies also offer spot reliners. The inner tube is inserted into the tire where, once inflated, it holds the reliners in place.

Other tire repair products include rubber putty that can be used to repair cracks, gouges, weather checking, and other minor problems. Unfortunately, it can't be used to repair a hole. Various companies carry a concentrated black tire paint that can be used to revive the color of old, gray-looking tires. Mix it with paint thinner according to the directions on the label and apply it as you would paint. Gempler's stocks a variety of reliners, tire sealant products, and tire repair components. It also carries calcium chloride and kits to put it into the tires, although that is often better handled by your local farm tire dealer.

The original-style wheels that bolt directly to the top hat–wheels used on early N Series tractors are becoming hard to find.

Any replacement wheels are generally equipped with loops on the wheel for attaching the rim to the wheel.

Wheel and Rim Restoration

As mentioned earlier, calcium chloride has been the enemy of many an old Ford tractor, especially if the tube has let go or was damaged at some time and released the corrosive material inside the tire. There's also the chance that the tires have rotted away after years of sitting outdoors and the wheels came into contact with the ground, allowing rust to take its toll.

If you've been fortunate enough to find rims and wheels that are in relatively good shape, the restoration process may be as simple as sandblasting the appropriate parts and applying one or more coats of primer prior to painting.

If one or more of the wheels are too far gone or if a rim is in very bad shape, you basically have two options, depending on the planned use of the restoration. If you're planning to use your machine as a work tractor, your best bet may be to purchase a replacement rim from one of the many replacement parts suppliers listed in the appendix. Most are available for as little as $100, which makes wheel replacement as simple as picking up the phone.

If you're restoring a work tractor, newer-style tires with a 23-degree bar generally offer better traction than the 45-degree lug tires originally found on the tractor.

Unfortunately, the replacement wheels bear little resemblance to the original. Instead of having a solid flange around the inside of the rim, the replacements use a series of loops through which the mounting bolts are installed.

As Ford enthusiast John Smith explains, "The N Series models built from 1939 to 1955 used a unique rear rim that has been nicknamed the hat or top-hat style. The top hat refers to the cross-section of the rim, which has a raised center resembling a top hat that bolts to the wheel center.

"Any Ford restorer looking for originality must have the correct style top-hat rims, which makes good used ones very valuable today," Smith continues. "Because so many were eaten up by calcium chloride, good originals are hard to find, and nobody makes a replica."

That leaves the restorer bent on authenticity with only a couple of choices. Frequent auctions, swap meets, salvage yards, and classified ads in search of an original replacement or try to repair the old one.

If you're only dealing with a few rust holes on a rim or some calcium chloride corrosion around the valve stem, you should be able to take care of those by thoroughly cleaning the holes and filling them in with

Steel wheels were only used on the 1942 and some early 1943 Model 2N tractors built at the beginning of World War II. They were available on 9N tractors as a special order option. Note the steel front and rear wheels attach to the standard hubs and rear wheel discs.

Interchanging Rear Wheel Assemblies Give These Combinations

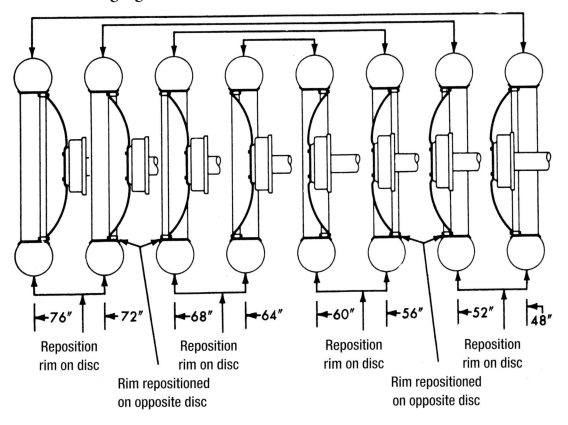

|←—76"| |←—72"| |←—68"| |←—64"| |←—60"| |←—56"| |←—52"| |←48"|

Reposition rim on disc   Reposition rim on disc   Reposition rim on disc   Reposition rim on disc

Rim repositioned on opposite disc   Rim repositioned on opposite disc

Rear tread width on early Ford tractors is adjusted by interchanging the rear wheel assemblies in different combinations.

small beads of weld or some type of filler, such as J-B Weld. You'll want to use a filler primer before painting to further smooth imperfections.

If you're good with a welder or know someone who is, you may be able to repair larger rust areas by totally replacing the damaged area. The first step will be cutting out the corroded or rusted portion of the wheel. Quite often, this will be the outer edge of the rim, where it has rested on the ground, or the area around the valve stem. Next, you'll have to find a scrap wheel or rim that is identical in size and style from which you can cut a replacement piece. Make sure all edges have been ground smooth, clamp the splice into position, tack weld around the whole piece to keep it from warping, and carefully weld it into place. Once you've finished welding, grind all splices down until they are flush with the surrounding metal and prepare the wheel for painting.

Ford eventually came out with a rear wheel design that allowed farmers to change the tread width without removing the wheel or sliding it on the axle. The operator simply loosens a set of locking bolts and rotates the wheel disc within a set of tracks on the rim until the desired width is abtained.

CHAPTER 11

Hydraulic System

While hydraulics weren't much of an issue on most vintage tractors, the hydraulic system is really the foundation of the Ford tractor brand. In fact, the Ford line might not have come into existence had it not been for the Ferguson hydraulic-lift system. As explained in Chapter 1, the history of Ford and tractors to this point involved the Fordson models, which had been moved to factories in Ireland by the 1930s. It wasn't until Henry Ford saw Ferguson's unique three-point hitch that used hydraulic force to raise and lower implements and attachments that Ford took another serious look at tractors. He realized that the Fordson couldn't be adapted to the new three-point hitch and that it would take a whole new tractor, from the ground up, to incorporate such a system, so Ford tractors and hydraulics have gone hand-in-hand since day one.

Basic Principles

Before we look at troubleshooting and repairing the hydraulic system, let's look at some of the basics associated with hydraulic systems. First of all, hydraulic fluid is just like any other liquid. It has no shape of its own and acquires the shape of the container. Because of this, oil in the hydraulic system will flow in any direction and into any pump or cylinder, regardless of the size or shape.

Like any fluid, it is also practically incompressible. As a result, when force is applied to hydraulic fluid, it transfers force to the work site. Hydraulic fluid has one other characteristic. It has the ability to provide substantial increases in work force, which means that one pound of pressure on the piston in a small pump is converted to several pounds on a larger cylinder or piston. If you use a hydraulic bottle jack to lift your tractor, you already know how this works.

Let's look at the application of this principle on your tractor. Instead of pressure being supplied by a jack handle and piston, it comes from a hydraulic pump. From there it flows through a valve, which directs its path to the appropriate point, and finally to a hydraulic cylinder on the three-point hitch, power steering, or remote.

Most hydraulic pumps used on farm tractors today are one of three types: a gear, vane, or piston pump. Although Ford used a vane pump on the NAA and a few other models from 1952 to 1955, a piston pump was used on all other models, including the 9N, 2N, and 8N, which incorporate a unit that is simple in design, yet well advanced for its time. Positioned in the bottom of the reservoir sump, it runs directly off the PTO shaft and incorporates internal control valves and a lift cylinder that is connected to the rear lift arms.

Hydraulic System Contamination

The two biggest enemies of a hydraulic system are dirt and water. If these two contaminants were kept out of the system by the previous owner, you may not have any problems with the hydraulic system. But if they managed to work their way into the system, you may have some repairs ahead of you.

Just as in the engine, dirt can score the insides of cylinders, spool valves, and pumps. Water will break down the inhibitors in the hydraulic oil and cause it

Although the power steering unit assembly uses hydraulic pressure for the power steering system only, it should be inspected and repaired in the same manner as the main hydraulic valve and pump system.

The hydraulic pump used on all N Series models from 1939 to 1952 is mounted in the bottom of the transmission/ rear housing where it is driven off the transmission. It also shares the oil reservoir with the transmission.

The pump unit drops out of the bottom of the rear case for easy repair. Most valves are also internal, should service be required.

to emulsify and lose its lubricating ability, leading to scoring of cylinder walls and breakdown of internal seals. Unfortunately, the tolerances in many hydraulic pumps and spools are even tighter than those in an engine.

One way dirt can get into the system is through the careless handling of the hoses, particularly if a broken or damaged hose is replaced. This should be a hint to practice cleanliness when making hydraulic repairs or inspections.

Dirt isn't the only enemy to hydraulic fluid. Sludge, which is formed by the chemical reaction of hydraulic fluid to excessive temperature changes and/ or condensation, can also cause problems. That's why it is especially important to keep the hydraulic oil clean and changed at regular intervals in the N Series models. Since the pump is located in the bottom of the sump where it shares five gallons of oil with the transmission and the rear end of the tractor, it has a tendency to accumulate moisture from condensation

Refer to the service manual for overhaul procedures. You can also remove the entire unit and take it to a New Holland service center if in doubt.

inside the gear cases. Water can also collect in the bottom of the sump where it is drawn directly into the hydraulic pump. If this water freezes hard enough in cold weather, it can break the chambers in the pump and cause real problems. If the oil looks milky, it very likely has water in it and needs to be changed. If enough sludge builds up on the pump's internal parts, it will eventually plug the pump. To add insult to injury, a restriction on the inlet side of the pump can starve it of fluid, and heat and friction will cause the pump parts to seize.

Troubleshooting

Like many other systems on the tractor, you should have an idea whether the hydraulic system actually works and how well it works from your initial test drive, assuming that the tractor was in running condition when you acquired it. If the tractor has power steering, did it work? Did the lift system raise and lower properly?

Unlike today's three-point hitch units, the Ford N Series models use an internal hydraulic cylinder to pivot the lift arms.

If your tests indicate a weakness in the system, the first thing you should do is check the fluid level in the reservoir and make sure it is filled to the proper level with the recommended grade and type of fluid. Improper fluid can cause low or erratic pressure and eventually deteriorate seals and packing, particularly if it contains incompatible ingredients. Since the pump on the N Series models runs off the PTO shaft, it's important to make sure the PTO is engaged and the shaft is rotating.

Ford enthusiast John Smith came up with his own list of troubleshooting steps, which proceeds as follows:

Just like the pistons in the engine, the hydraulic piston uses piston rings that occasionally need replacement.

Q. The lift isn't working at all.

A. If you've already checked the oil level and made sure the PTO is engaged, turn off the engine and remove the right-side access cover (the one with the dipstick). Slide your hand down along the control rod into the oil and feel the end of the rod where it goes into the control valve pivot. Make sure the rod is connected and that it is moving the control valve spools in and out as you move the lift control lever up and down. Other possibilities are a defective relief valve or a ruptured oil tube that goes from the pump base to the top cover. To check these items, leave the side cover off and start the tractor. Have a fairly heavy weight or load on the lift arms. Raise the lift control lever and watch inside the cavity for oil spraying out in the area of the relief valve or from the side of the cavity where the tube is located. If no oil is spraying out anywhere, you could have a bad pump. Check the pump pressure as outlined in the appropriate repair manual.

Q. The lift only comes up half way then stops.

A. This is a very common complaint and can almost always be attributed to a worn cam follower pin in the lift control linkage. Loosen the four bolts holding the quadrant control lever bracket to the top cover. Slide the quadrant bracket toward the rear of the tractor (bolt holes are elongated). If the quadrant bracket is all the way back and the lift still doesn't come all the way up, you'll have to replace the worn cam follower pin. Remove the top cover and place it bottom side up on the workbench.

To find the worn pin, disassemble the control linkage until you can get the part with the worn pin out of the assembly. Press or drive the

Be sure to check all tolerances and adjust them to the manual specifications before reinstalling the unit.

worn pin out and replace it with the correct hardened dowel pin, part number 374072S from Ford/New Holland. This is listed as a 5/16x7/8-inch dowel pin, but it is actually 0.309-inch diameter, not 5/16 inch (0.3125). Pressing or driving a common 0.3125-inch pin into the 0.309-inch hole can cause major problems and I strongly advise against it. Some thrifty folks rotate the old pin 180 degrees and reinstall it to get another few years of wear out of it. That usually works okay if you can't spare the two bucks for a new one. Reassemble the linkage and adjust as per the shop manual instructions.

Many times you will find that replacing the worn pin will take care of the problem without any further adjustments, but you have to completely reassemble the tractor to find out if you are lucky or not. Before replacing the top cover, take the time to inspect everything else in there for wear or other problems. This is an excellent time to rebuild the lift cylinder as well.

Q. The lift drifts down when the PTO stops.

A. Leakdown is probably the most common complaint with the N Series tractors, but it's usually easy to fix.

If you have an implement on the lift and it drifts down over a few minutes time after the tractor is shut off, you have some leakage. If the implement drops as soon as you push the clutch pedal in, you have major leakage. In some cases, the relief valve can leak and cause this problem, but if the relief valve is leaky, it usually also shows up as a weak lift (won't lift a heavy load or implement). The control valve spools in the pump base can leak due to scoring in the bores, but this is rare and generally not repairable except by a major pump rebuild.

The most common cause of leakdown is worn lift cylinder piston rings. You can determine if the leakage is coming from the lift cylinder by removing the right side cover (the one with the dipstick) and starting the tractor. Have a fairly heavy weight or load on the lift arms. Raise the lift control lever and watch inside the cavity for oil leaking out from above in the area of the lift cylinder. If the cylinder is leaking, you will see it. If the relief valve is leaking, you will see the oil bubbling up from the pump area. The N tractors originally had a piston with three cast-iron rings to seal it. These rings are still available, inexpensive, and will work just fine, but a small amount of leakdown is normal and is to be expected with them.

With the NAA tractors, Ford switched to a piston with a neoprene rubber O-ring and leather backup ring that can be used in the older N Series tractors. This provides a much more positive seal to eliminate the small leakage from the cast-iron rings. The NAA piston and seal will cost more to replace than just buying new cast-iron rings.

The determining factor in most cases is the condition of the cylinder bore. Remove the lift cover and remove the four bolts holding the cylinder to the cover. You can remove the piston from the cylinder by applying a little compressed air to the oil inlet hole in the cylinder. Don't use a high pressure or else you'll blow out the piston.

To settle terms of a lawsuit with Harry Ferguson, Ford switched to a vane pump on NAA models as well as a few other models from 1952 to 1955 that was driven off the engine. An engine-driven piston pump was used on other models from the 1950s on.

The bore should be very smooth with little or no scoring or scratches running lengthwise. It can (and probably should) be lightly honed to a cleanup. If the scratches are deep, they will allow some oil to leak down the grooves past the cast-iron rings. In this case the NAA seal will work better, but only for a short time. The scratches or grooves will chew into the new neoprene seal and it will leak worse than ever. If there are deep scratches and you do not want to spend the money to replace the entire cylinder assembly, you should use the cast-iron rings and live with the small leakage. If the cylinder bore is in good shape or has only very faint scratches or grooves, use the NAA piston and seal.

Q. The lift went up, but now it won't go down.

A. This is nearly always caused by the control valve spools in the pump base getting stuck in the bore, which is most likely due to water or dirt in the oil. Turn off the engine and remove the right-side access cover and slide your hand down along the control rod into the oil and feel the end of the rod where it goes into the control valve pivot. Make sure the rod is connected and that it is moving the control valve spools in and out as you move the lift control lever up and down. Chances are you will find that the valve pivot is stuck and not moving. You may be able to break it free by prying lightly on it with a screwdriver between the pivot head (ball socket) and the pump base. When it breaks free and starts working again, change the oil. If it's really stuck tight, you'll have to pull the pump and rebuild it.

Q. The lift works by itself but not with a heavy load on it.

A. This could be severe leakage at the cylinder, a bad relief valve, or a badly worn pump. Check for lift cylinder leakage and relief valve leakage as described in the questions above. If no major leakage is noted, check the pump pressure as outlined in your service/repair manual. A rebuild is probably in order.

Q. The hydraulic pump makes knocking noises under load.

A. What you're hearing is the sound of worn cams/pistons in the pump. When the pump is new, it runs quietly, but as the cams wear, they begin to knock as they actuate the pistons from side to side in the pump. The louder the knock, the more wear there is on your pump. It's generally not an immediate, pressing problem. If the knock is faint, you can probably put off repairs for quite a while. If it's knocking loudly, you should buy a pump repair kit and do a rebuild before it quits all together.

Q. The lift is very jerky and erratic when raising.

A. This is usually a sign of a defective or sticking valve in the pump. The pump piston pushes the oil out and pulls it back in as it returns. It is time for a pump rebuild. Although most of the plumbing on the N Series tractors is internal, there may be a need to check hoses on later models for kinking or leaks. In this case, keep in mind that hydraulic

Always check the integrity and condition of hydraulic hoses before reassembly.

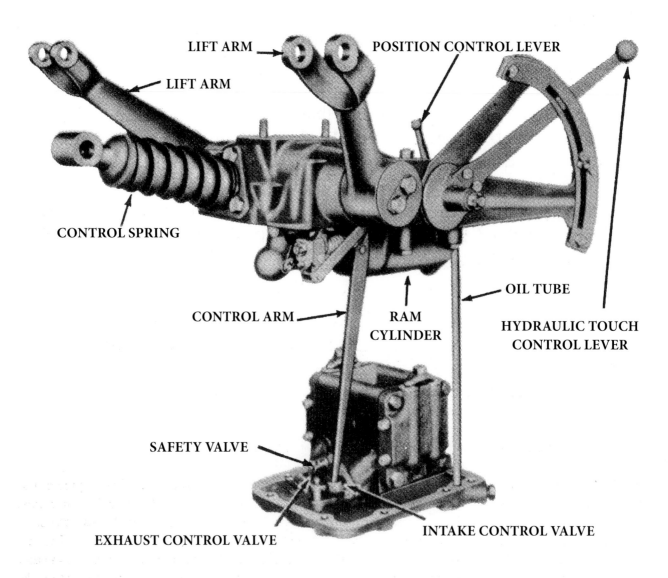

LIFT ARM

LIFT ARM

POSITION CONTROL LEVER

CONTROL SPRING

CONTROL ARM

RAM
CYLINDER

OIL TUBE

HYDRAULIC TOUCH
CONTROL LEVER

SAFETY VALVE

EXHAUST CONTROL VALVE

INTAKE CONTROL VALVE

This illustration from the Ford 9N-2N-8N manual shows the relationship between the hydraulic pump and the three-point hitch lift assembly.

pressure escaping under high pressure through a pinhole leak can actually penetrate the skin and lead to gangrene poisoning if not treated quickly. You should never check for leaks with your bare hands or even with leather gloves. Instead, pass a piece of cardboard or wood over any suspected areas to check for escaping fluid.

Hydraulic Seals

It almost goes without saying that due to the high pressure within the system, no hydraulic circuit can operate without the proper seals to hold the fluid

under pressure, as mentioned in the troubleshooting section. Seals also serve the purpose of keeping dirt and water out of the system.

Hydraulic seals generally fall into one of two categories: static seals that seal fixed parts and dynamic seals that seal moving parts. Static seals include gaskets, O-rings, and packings used around valves, between fittings, and between pump sections. Dynamic seals, in contrast, include shaft and rod seals on hydraulic cylinder pistons and piston rods.

As for seal types, they can include O-rings, U- and V-packings, spring-loaded lip seals, cup and flange

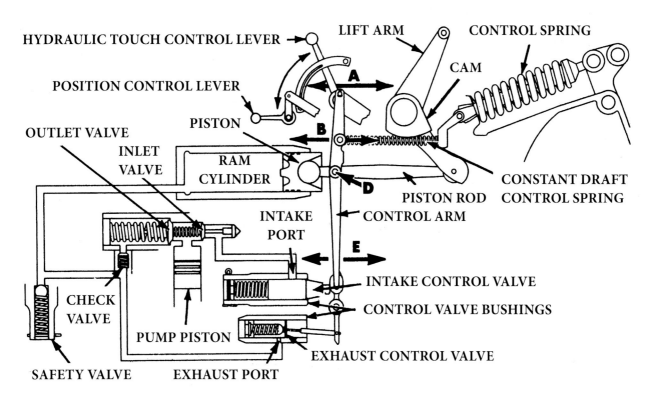

A flow schematic explains how fluid moves through the valves to the ram cylinder.

packings, mechanical seals, metallic seals, and compression packings and gaskets. Troubleshooting naturally consists of looking for leaks; however, even though the perfect seal should prevent all leakage, this is not always practical or desirable. In dynamic uses, a slight amount of leakage is needed to provide lubrication to moving parts.

On the other hand, internal leakage, either from static seals or excessive leakage from dynamic seals, is hard to detect. Often, excessive leakage from an internal seal must be indicated by other means, such as pressure testing.

As a general rule, it's usually best to replace all seals that are disturbed during repair of the hydraulic system. As is the case with the engine, transmission, and most other major components, it's a lot cheaper to replace a few seals or gaskets during restoration than to come back later and repair leaks.

It may sound a little extreme, but you should also give seals the same care during handling and replacement as precision bearings. This means keeping them protected in their containers and storing them in a cool, dry place free of dirt until you're ready to use them.

Following installation, static O-rings used as gaskets should be tightened a second time after the unit has been warmed up and cycled a few times to make sure they seal properly.

Dynamic O-rings should be cycled or moved back and forth (as on a hydraulic cylinder) several times to allow the ring to rotate and assume a neutral position. In the process of rotating, the O-ring should allow a very small amount of fluid to pass. This is normal since it permits a lubricating film of oil to pass between the O-ring and the shaft.

Unless directed otherwise in your service manual, you should always dip all cylinder and valve parts in hydraulic fluid when reassembling a cylinder and/or valve unit. It's also wise to lubricate all O-rings with petroleum jelly or an equivalent before installing them.

CHAPTER 12

Electrical System

When the Ford 9N was introduced in 1949, it was already ahead of most tractors in that it incorporated a full electrical system, including a battery, generator, and starter. Electric lights were optional until 1955, when headlights became standard equipment on the 640, 650, 660, 840, 850, and 860.

Ironically, Ford actually took a step backwards in 1942, when it introduced the 2N. Due to the shortages of rubber and copper, the War Board allowed some tractors to be built in order to support food production, as long as they didn't use either vital material. The 2N did not, therefore, include a starter, distributor, or generator; and steel wheels were standard. These "war model" Ford 2N tractors were equipped with a magneto to allow hand-crank starting. As material became available, which was the case by late 1943, rubber tires and a complete electrical system came back as standard equipment.

According to Ford enthusiast John Smith, the number of "war model" 2Ns built with steel wheels, magnetos, and no electrics was actually very limited. There are no numbers available, he relates, but fewer than half of the 1942 production units were war models and almost none of the 1943 models were built that way. Restrictions on materials were lifted after a short time when Ford successfully argued that the tractor was an essential part of the war effort. Within a matter of months, starters, generators, lights, and rubber tires could again be used, which means that all other Ford tractors produced from that time through the end of Ford tractor production were equipped with a distributor.

Consequently, 1942 and 1943 model year Ford 2N tractors are equipped with a magneto to allow hand-crank starting, while all other Ford tractors produced from mid-1943 through the end of Ford tractor production were equipped with a distributor.

Magneto Systems

Since Ford used a magneto for only two years, there was only one unit that was ever used: a Fairbanks-Morse. A magneto works much like a miniature spring-driven generator. As the drive cog is rotated, the magneto drive wraps up a spring that is positioned between the drive link and the magneto rotor. At the appropriate moment, the spring is released and the rotor is quickly rotated within a magnetic field to generate a charge of electricity; hence, the clicking sound associated with magneto operation. The distributor portion of the magneto determines which of the four cylinders receives the spark.

Due to the complexity of the spring-drive system, the need for special tools and testing equipment, and the internal workings of a magneto, it's best to have any adjustment or rebuilding done by a professional shop. There are several listed in the appendix in the back of this book. Some of the things you can check and replace yourself include the points, condenser, rotor cap, and rotor tower cap.

You'll also need to make sure the magneto is reinstalled properly. This is especially important because the magneto must initiate the spark before the piston reaches the top of the compression stroke. On the other hand, the impulse coupling is designed to retard the timing during slow engine

Ford was unique in that the electrical system on its very first model used a starter, battery, generator, and distributor, which is actually a combination unit that incorporates the coil.

revolution, such as when it is being started. The result is a stronger spark for starting the engine and a reduced chance of kickback, which can occur when the spark reaches the cylinder before the piston has reached the top of the cylinder. If you do not hear the click, your

Since magnetos don't require a battery or electrical circuit for power, they were used on a number of early-model 2N tractors built during World War II to provide spark to the cylinders.

magneto may have a broken impulse coupler. Options for fixing this are to buy a new magneto or send the magneto to one of the businesses that specialize in restoration.

Magneto Inspection and Service

While there are a couple of ways to check for electrical output, one of the easiest for a novice is to attach a spark plug via a piece of electrical wiring to the coil output terminal. Ground the spark plug to the base of the magneto and test for a spark while rotating the drive lug. A word of warning: Keep your hand clear of the coil and coil output terminal. If it's working properly, the coil can put out nearly 30,000 volts.

Most auto parts stores carry a spark tester that makes testing even easier. A spark tester looks like a

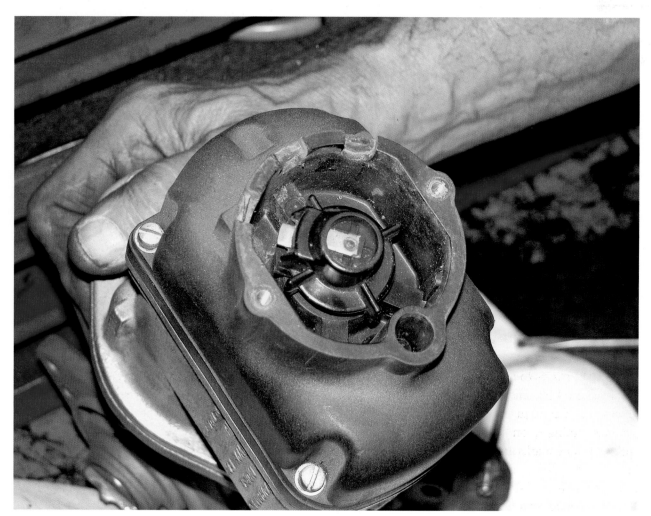

Unlike modern electrical systems, the magneto operates like a generator, coil, and distributor wrapped into one unit. The Ford magneto also incorporates a 90-degree drive so it can run off the front of the engine in the same manner as the distributor that it replaced.

spark plug with a large alligator clip. Hook the device to a plug wire and connect the clip to ground. When the tractor is cranked, the tester will flash if you have sufficient spark.

The presence of a spark won't be a guarantee that the magneto is putting out enough current, but it can give you an idea of how well the unit is working and if the spark is hot enough for ignition. If there isn't any spark, you at least know you're wasting your energy. The testing alternative is to connect a special multimeter that records and stores readings in excess of 30,000 volts.

If you choose to disassemble the magneto and try to service it on your own, the first thing you should do is inspect all the gaskets and insulators that isolate the generating components from the body of the unit. This especially applies to any bolts that protrude through the magneto body. Any voltage leakage can ground out the unit and make it ineffective.

You'll also want to clean all dirt and grime out of the unit by using a combination of compressed air and electrical parts cleaner. Finally, inspect and replace any seals or bearings that appear to be faulty. While you have the unit apart, it's also a good idea to have someone recharge the large horseshoe-shaped magnet that generates the magnetic field around the armature.

Before putting everything back together, apply a light coat of oil to all drive parts and bushings. Be careful not to over-apply the oil. Lastly, replace any tune-up components for which you can find parts. This includes the condenser, points, rotor tower, and rotor cap. It's easier and cheaper to replace them now than struggle with problems later on.

Timing the Magneto

There are two phases to magneto timing. The first step is to get the magneto roughly timed. The second is to get it adjusted for final timing. To begin the timing process, you'll need to crank the engine until the No. 1 piston is coming up on the compression stroke and the ignition timing marks are in register. The marks will be in different locations, depending upon the model, but your service manual should explain this in detail.

As soon as you have tightened the mounting bolts by hand, rotate the body of the magneto as far as possible in the direction of normal rotation. Slowly turn the engine through one complete revolution until

The Ford 9N, 2N, and early 8N models built through serial number 263844 in 1950 use a combination distributor/coil unit that is mounted on the front of the engine.

you have the No. 1 piston at the top of its compression stroke again and the timing marks are aligned as before. Slowly rotate the magneto in the direction opposite of its normal rotation until you hear the pronounced click of the impulse coupler. This indicates that the magneto is right at the point where it will fire

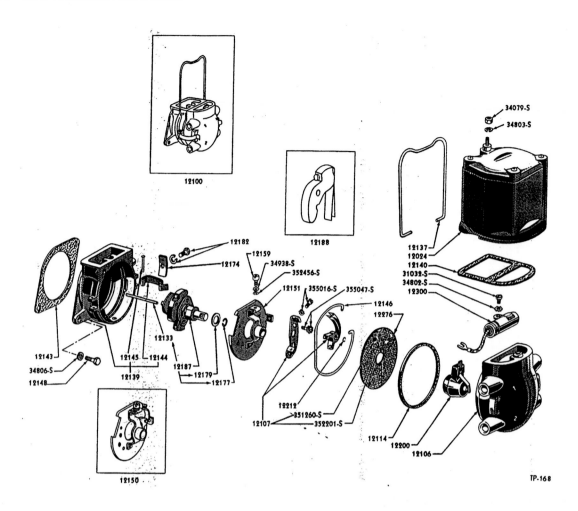

While there are some similarities, there are also a number of differences between the front-mounted distributor and the side-mount version.

the No. 1 piston. Tighten up the bolts, attach the spark plug wires to the cap, and try starting the engine.

If you are hand cranking the engine, be sure you follow the hand-cranking safety precautions in your manual, since you are trying to start an untested engine. There are several factors beyond magneto timing that go into backfires, or you may have made a mistake. This isn't a time to be careless.

Distributor

Unlike a magneto, the distributor doesn't actually produce electricity, but only serves to distribute the spark to the appropriate cylinder. Moreover, the typical distributor provides automatic spark advance, which is controlled by centrifugal weights mounted in the distributor base. As engine speed increases, the spark must occur earlier at the spark plugs to give the fuel/air mixture sufficient

time to ignite. Consequently, centrifugal weights incorporated in the distributor design advance the breaker cam to provide a predetermined variation in spark timing at any given engine rpm. That's why an accurate measurement of spark timing at any given engine rpm can only be accurately determined with the aid of a timing light. Service and rebuilding are much easier.

Except for those 2N models equipped with a magneto, all Ford tractors built from 1939 to 1950 use a front-mounted unit that incorporated both the distributor and the coil assembly. In contrast, the distributor used on Ford tractors from 1950 to 1964 is mounted on the side of the engine, as is the case on most other tractors, and uses a separate coil. The change took place at serial number 263844. At serial number 403489, a dust shield was added to the inside of the distributor to help extend the life of the contact points.

This battery appears to be a little oversized.

Inspection and Repair

Unless you plan to replace the spark plug wires, start distributor restoration on either type by grasping the spark plug and coil wires and gently twisting the boot as you remove them from the cap. It's also a good idea to label the wires with tape and a marker so they can be reinstalled in the correct position.

If you plan to do much work on the distributor or engine, you may want to go ahead and remove the whole distributor at this time and move it to a workbench where it will be easier to work on. Getting it reinstalled and timed correctly isn't that much different from reinstalling a magneto. To save some time, though, make a note of which plug wire tower serves the No. 1 cylinder and make a mark on the side of the distributor housing that corresponds with this tower.

The first step in inspection and restoration is to check the inside and outside of the distributor cap and individual cap towers for cracks, burned spots, and corrosion. To do this with the front-mounted

The front-mounted Ford distributor is pretty basic compared to most distributor units. During the overhaul, inspect the bushings, make sure the weights swing freely, and check inside and outside of the distributor cap and individual cap towers for cracks, burned spots, and corrosion.

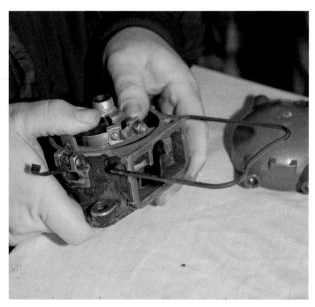

A quality distributor rebuild should include new points, condenser, and rotor. Replace the distributor cap if there is any doubt about its condition.

distributor, you'll need to first remove the plug wires from the distributor cap and high-tension wire from the top of the coil. Next, unsnap the coil bail and distributor cap clips and remove the coil and cap. If there is any doubt about the condition of the cap on either type of distributor, it's best to replace the cap.

Before you throw the cap in the trash, check for carbon tracking around the plug towers and the cap base. Defective spark plugs or spark plug wires can cause sparks to travel from the tower to the nearest ground, which is usually the mounting clip. The evidence is a small carbon trail that resembles a tiny tree root. You should also take a look at the inside of the cap for carbon tracking that can indicate past problems with cross-firing, backfiring, or missing. In this case, the lines will usually connect from one post to the next.

Once you have inspected and cleaned all parts at the top end of the distributor, it's time to take a look at the bottom end. Start by checking for any free play or

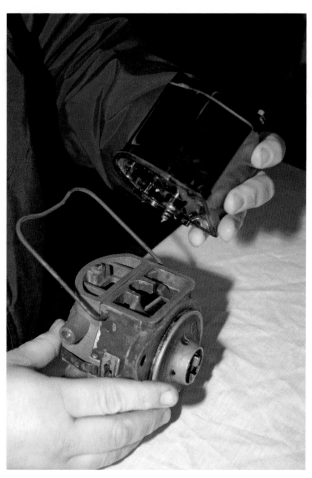

The coil portion of the front-mounted distributor/coil assembly can easily be replaced as a unit and snapped into place.

wobble in the driveshaft on side-mount models. There are generally two bushings or thrust washers on the shaft: one at the top and one at the bottom. If either one is badly worn, it should be replaced as part of the rebuild. To access the bushings, remove the drive gear, which is usually held on by a pin through the shaft and gear. This will allow the entire shaft to slide out of the housing.

Next, remove the points and condenser. Beneath the mounting plate you'll find a spark advance system of springs and counterweights. Replace any springs that are broken or weak, and make sure the weights aren't rusted and that they move freely. The springs must be replaced in pairs and by springs of identical size. In the meantime, clean all pieces in solvent before reassembling. Although some restorers like to reuse the points and touch them up with a file before they're reinstalled, a quality rebuild should include new points, condenser, rotor, cap, and spark plugs.

Setting the Point Gap and Distributor Timing

You will need to adjust the gap between the points. To do this, rotate the shaft to a point where the cam lobe separates the points to create a gap. Using a wire-type feeler gauge, adjust the points to match the specifications in your service manual and tighten the mounting screws.

Be sure you remove any oil film from the feeler gauge before inserting it between the points. Oil on the contact points can cause the points to burn or become pitted. Finish off point adjustment by lubricating the rubbing block with a small amount of high-temperature grease. At this point, you can install a new rotor, line up the casing marks, and reinstall the distributor in the housing.

Reinstalling the Distributor
Front-Mount Distributor

The front-mount distributor on Ford models built between 1939 and 1950 is unique in that the timing needs to be done before the distributor is reinstalled,

In 1950, Ford redesigned the block to accept a side-mounted distributor with a separate coil.

Note the cylinder firing order molded into the engine block. This can help if there are any problems reinstalling the magneto or distributor, timing the engine, or reconnecting spark plug wires.

rather than after. To set the timing, place a straight edged ruler on the wide side of the shaft. Rotate the shaft until the straight edge is 1/4 inch away from the outside edge of the smallest distributor mounting hole. This will also be the mounting hole nearest the timing plate. At this distance, the distributor points should start to open. If they don't, loosen the timing plate lock screw and turn to advance or retard the timing. Keep making adjustments until you obtain the proper 1/4-inch setting. As you adjust, eliminate backlash by turning the shaft backwards and bring the shaft forward to measure your setting. This 1/4-inch setting will get you static timing at top dead center.

When reinstalling the front-mounted distributor, keep in mind that the slot in the end of the camshaft (front of motor) is offset. Consequently, the tang on the distributor can only mate easily to the slot on the engine camshaft one way. Mounted correctly, it will slide on easily without force and fit flush to the motor. If the tang is 180 degrees off, the distributor will have to be forced on. This should be a warning, because if you tighten down the mounting bolts at this point, you will break the casting on the distributor.

Once the distributor has been fine-tuned for timing, tighten the mounting bolt to secure it in place.

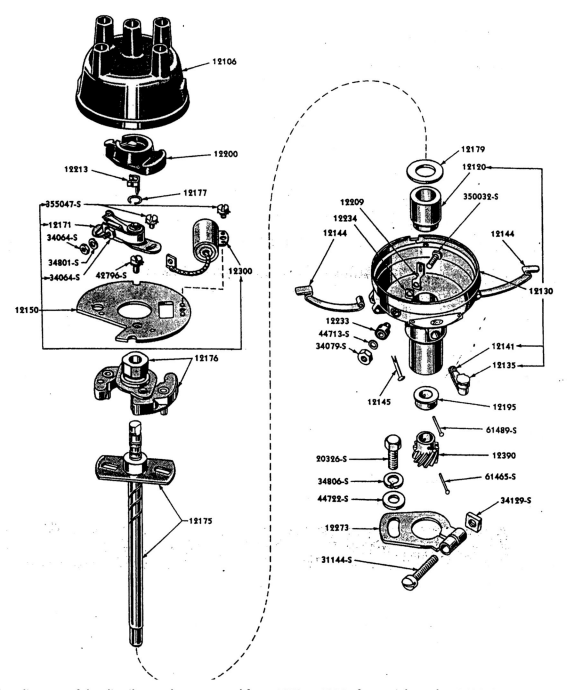

Here is a diagram of the distributor that was used from 1950 to 1952 after serial number 263843.

Side-Mount Distributor

If you've compensated for any gear taper during installation, the mark on the distributor casing should line
up with the rotor tang. If not, it shouldn't be off by
more than one tooth. If the distributor is completely
off, there's no need to panic. Most service manuals
include a detailed procedure for timing the engine.

Start by slowly turning the engine until the No. 1
piston is coming up on the compression stroke. You
can tell this by placing your thumb or finger over
the spark plug hole with the plug removed and feel for
the compression. Continue turning the engine until the
ignition timing marks are in register. Although the location of these marks will vary depending upon the model
you're restoring, they can generally be found by removing the timing hole cover on the flywheel housing.

Check the procedure outlined in your service
manual. For the 8N, the manual says to crank the

The function of the generator is to replace any electricity in the battery that has been used elsewhere in the electrical circuit. An electric starter was standard on Ford tractors with the first 9N model; hence the need for a generator and battery.

engine until the timing mark 0 (dead center) exactly aligns with the pointer in the timing window. For NAA models, the instructions call for 8 degrees before top dead center. Either way, the distributor assembly should be inserted, and with the gears fully meshed, the rotor should point to the No. 1 spark plug wire. The 8N instructions say the rotor should point to the right front cylinder head bolt.

Install a new distributor cap and spark plug wires, and finish the timing process with the ignition on. To do so, slowly turn the distributor in the direction of normal rotation and watch for the exact moment that a spark occurs at the plug. If you missed it, back the distributor up and try it again. The engine should now be timed properly. Tighten the distributor mounting bolt(s). If you have a timing light available, you may still want to check everything with one.

The brushes on generators and starters alike should be replaced if they are worn more than halfway.

Side-Mount Coil

Perhaps the easiest way to check the coil used with the side-mount distributor is to gently pull the wire that runs from the coil to the distributor and hold it about 1/8 inch from the engine block or a good ground. A strong spark should jump the gap when the engine is turned over. The coil should also be clean and dry. If you're not confident that the coil is in good condition, consider replacing it.

Electronic Ignition

Although it was never standard equipment or even an option on vintage Ford tractors, modern technology and the interest in tractor restoration have led to the development of electronic ignition systems for a number of older vehicles, including some Ford N Series models. Dennis Carpenter lists both 6- and 12-volt kits for tractors built from 1950 to 1964. Genesee Products lists conversion kits for 8N side-mount, NAA, and 600-4000 Series four-cylinder engines. Conversion kits are also available for the front-mount distributor used on early 2N, 8N, and 9N tractors; however, the kit includes a remote-mount canister-type coil to do away with the existing square coil. It may be something to consider if you want to eliminate the problems inherent with a coil and distributor.

Generators and Voltage Regulators

If you ever did any experiments with electricity or with a generator in a high school science or physics class, you may already have an idea how the generator on your tractor works. But if not, don't despair. It's not that complicated.

By the simplest explanation, one way electricity can be created is by moving a conductor through a magnetic field. If you look at this principle in terms of a generator, the armature, which serves as the conductor, is moved, or in this case spun, inside of two or more magnets. But think back again to science class. Remember the time you wrapped electrical wire around a nail and attached it to a battery? You created an electromagnet. The generator on your tractor just uses a larger version.

Now you can envision the field coils as electromagnets attached to the generator case. As the armature spins within this magnetic field, electricity moves through the armature to where it is allowed to flow though the brushes.

If you intend to use your restored tractor strictly as a work tractor, you might want to install an alternator and convert the electrical system to 12 volts. On the other hand, if that has already been done by a previous owner and you want to restore your tractor to its original condition, you'll need to find a generator.

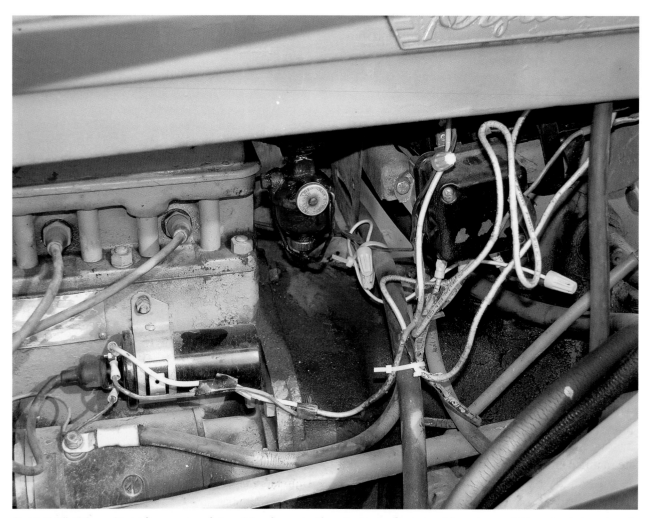

Sometimes it's easier to buy a complete wiring harness than to try to figure out how to rewire or repair worn and patched wiring.

The wire that makes up the coils actually begins at the F terminal of the generator, winds its way around the case, and terminates either at a third brush on a three-brush generator or connects to the wire going to the output brush or A terminal on a two-brush generator. Unless the generator has been replaced, it most likely uses two coils.

The magnets are actually a two-piece arrangement consisting of a coil of wire that fits around a pole shoe made of a special kind of metal. As the armature spins within the magnetic field, it begins to generate electricity—some of which is used to charge the battery or run electric lights, while the rest goes back into the field coils to make the magnetic field even stronger. The role of the regulator is to control the generator by manipulating the ground connection of the field coils.

Among the most important components are the brushes, which serve to gather the electricity that is being produced. The brushes ride on the commutator and allow the generated electricity to travel to the voltage regulator, and ultimately the battery or other load, then back into the field coils.

As a result, the primary problem areas on a generator are the brushes, commutator, and bushings. Generally, brushes should be replaced if they are worn more than halfway. Quite often the bushings and bearings that support the main shaft will also be worn and require replacement.

To perform any of these repairs, it will be necessary to disassemble, clean, and inspect the generator. Don't try to remove the field coils unless it is absolutely necessary. If you take them out, it will be difficult to get them back in without the proper tools. There are only two things that can go wrong with the field coils—either the wires have lost their insulation somewhere and are touching ground (such as the generator casing) or they have broken and have created an open circuit.

Considering the cost and availability of rebuilt generators, most restorers will tell you it's seldom worth your time to try to repair a generator yourself. Moreover, most communities have a machine shop or automotive shop that can test and rebuild your generator to factory specifications.

The same could be said about the voltage regulator. If there is doubt about whether it is working properly, your best bet is to take it to a shop that specializes in starter and generator rebuilds and let them test it. If it can be repaired, they'll be able to take care of it; and if not, they should be able to suggest the correct replacement.

Starters

As mentioned earlier, the only Ford tractors not equipped with a starter were the 1942 2N models and part of the 1943 models that were produced during the early years of World War II. In essence, the starter is much like the generator, only it operates in the opposite manner. Instead of generating electricity, it takes electricity and uses it to turn a drive sprocket. Like the generator, it contains an armature, coils, brushes, and commutator that can wear or short out in much the same manner. Overhaul consists of inspecting the brushes for good contact with the commutator and making sure the latter is reasonably clean and smooth. If it is not, it will need to be turned down on a lathe.

Just as you did with the generator, you'll also need to check for worn, dirty, or damaged bearings. Again, it may be easier and less costly in the long run to have these things done by a shop that specializes in starter and generator repairs or trade it for a rebuilt unit.

Before you pull the starter off the tractor, you need to remember that every Ford tractor produced after 1939 was equipped with a neutral start interlock switch that prevents the tractor from being started if the tractor is in gear. If the interlock switch is faulty, you may be wasting your time on the starter itself.

You may also have problems related to the battery or loose or corroded connections. To check for these, connect a fully charged battery to the starter using a

Light kits were a dealer-installed option for several years on Ford tractors. Ford used two types of mounts over the years. The wing-style mounts, shown here, were used up until mid-1950 when they were replaced in the kits with the stamped-steel round mounts.

The optional taillight never looked anything like this one. The previous owner apparently thought a boat trailer light was a lot cheaper and just as effective.

set of jumper cables. If there is a significant difference in the way the starter turns over, check the battery; then inspect, clean, and tighten all starter relay connections, as well as the battery ground on the frame and engine. If the starter still does not crank with the jumper cables, plan on removing and replacing or repairing the starter.

Wiring

Unless your tractor has been treated with tender loving care for the past 50 years, it's doubtful that you will get by without replacing at least part of the wiring. At the very least, you will want to replace the spark plug wires as part of the engine rebuild.

Replacing crimped, spliced, and inferior wiring on the rest of the tractor not only improves the looks of your restored tractor, but it also can be a safety measure. The first step in wiring restoration is locating a

wiring diagram. With luck, this will be included in your service and repair manual. If you're working on a Ford N Series model, you can also find one on the Internet. If worse comes to worst, you can always trace the wiring from the power source, or the battery, to each switch and component. But don't put too much stock in what you find. Previous owners may have replaced the original wiring with a different gauge of wire, the incorrect type of wire, or they may have even taken shortcuts with the routing.

If there is any doubt, talk to other tractor owners or try to find a well-restored model like your own and take notes. As a general rule, you should use at least 10-gauge wiring for circuits that carry a heavy load, such as from the generator. Switches and other components can be wired with 14-gauge wire. Remember, the larger the gauge number, the smaller the wire diameter.

This is much more representative of what the rear taillight should look like. This model has also been equipped with a rear work light.

New gauges, including the Proofmeter, which was introduced in 1950, really set off the dash on this 8N restoration.

Make sure the starter switch on the transmission cover is in good operating condition to avoid later problems.

If you have a lot of wiring to replace, it might be easier to just purchase a complete wiring harness for your tractor. Available through various sources, such as those listed in the appendix, an appropriate wiring harness is made up with the correct gauge and color of wiring for each switch, gauge, and component and is prewrapped to match the routing.

Spark Plug Wires

Contrary to their rugged appearance, spark plug wires are quite sensitive. That's because most secondary wires consist of a soft copper-core wire surrounded by stainless steel or carbon-impregnated thread mixed with an elastomer-type conductor. The outside covering of a heavy layer of insulation prevents the 12,000 to 25,000 volts from bleeding out when the wire is carrying current.

Consequently, the resistance-type wires do not handle sharp bending or jerking and can break internally and ruin the wire. Excessive exposure to oil and antifreeze can chemically break down the coating. Perhaps the most damaging effect is caused when someone pulls on the wires to remove them from the spark plugs. This can separate the conducting material and cause internal arcing.

It's important that you keep spark plug wires clean and separated from each other with any wire clips that are integral to the routing. To remove wires from the plugs during service or restoration, grasp the rubber boot and not the wires. Keep in mind that secondary wires, including the coil wire and spark plug wires, can appear in good condition yet be faulty.

One way to check their condition is to measure the wire resistance using an ohmmeter. In general, the wires should register around 8,000 to 12,000 ohms per foot. This will also test the wire for continuity to ensure that there are no breaks in the copper wire core.

Lights

As has been mentioned earlier, lighting kits were only available as an option on all Ford N Series tractors. That trend continued until 1955, when head- and taillights became standard equipment on many, but not all, models.

Besides broken lenses and deteriorated wiring, the most common problem you're likely to encounter is a rusty, faded, or worn housing. Most restorers start the renewal process by disassembling the light and cleaning it inside and out. One restorer likes to bead blast the light housing to a smooth finish—although he admits paint stripper can have the same effect. Then, it's simply a matter of painting the shell at the same time you're painting other tractor components. As a point of accuracy for those looking for authenticity, C. M. Hall lights were used from 1939 to 1944, when they were replaced with sealed-beam Ford headlights. Sometime in the mid-1950s, the

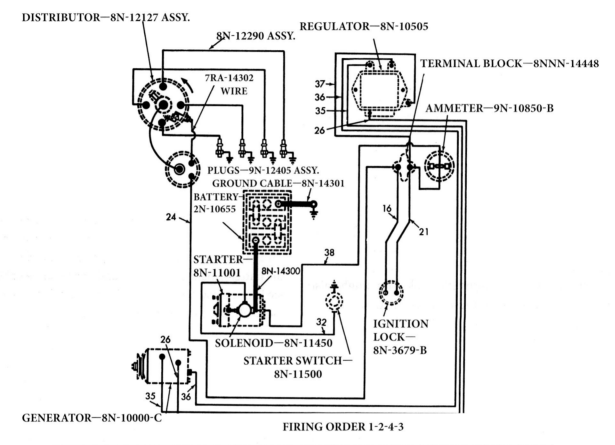

KEY		
CIRCUITS	WIRE NO.	COLOR
Wiring junction block to ignition lock	16	Red–Green Tr.
Wiring junction block to ignition lock	21	Yellow
Coil to writing junction block	24	Red
Generator ground to regulator	26	Black–Red Tr.
Starter solenoid to starting switch	32	Red–Blue Tr.
Generator field to regulator	35	Black–White Tr.
Generator armature to regulator	36	Yellow–Black Tr.
Regulator to wiring junction block	37	Yellow
Starter solenoid to wiring junction block	38	Yellow

A wiring diagram can be a tremendous help when rewiring a tractor or tracing electrical problems.

dealer-installed accessory lighting kits also eliminated the headlight wing mounts used on earlier models and replaced them with round stamped-steel mounts.

Should you need to find a replacement light, swap meets, salvage yards, and dealer parts counters are all good sources. There are also a number of vendors, including Dennis Carpenter, that offer exact reproduction headlight assemblies, as well as replacement sealed-beam bulbs, wiring, headlight mounts, and headlight rings.

Gauges

Gauges used to be a real problem for the restorer trying to obtain an authentic look. Often the gauges worked fine but looked a little worse for wear and detracted from the whole appearance of a nicely restored model. Fortunately, today's Ford tractor restorer has several different options. Stewart-Warner (S-W), for example, makes gauges that work fine for many older tractors. Many of them even look a lot like the original except they have the S-W logo at the bottom of the gauge face. In fact, if you're not terribly concerned about authenticity, you can replace any gauge that is no longer working with an off-the-shelf model.

If you want an authentic look, you might also want to contact one of the vendors listed in the back of this book and find a specially built reproduction. Available units include the Proofmeter assembly used in 8N and later models. Don't overlook the local Ford dealer. Due to the popularity of older Ford models, Ford/New Holland dealers continue to carry a number of parts for older units.

Depending on how you plan to use the tractor and the condition of the existing gauge, you may just want to refurbish the one you have, particularly if the face plate is in relatively good shape. First, you'll need to carefully remove the bezel ring that holds the glass in place. On some gauges, you may have to bend up the lip around the edge of the gauge to do so. It's just a matter of cleaning it up, making sure the mechanisms work properly, and repainting it.

Since a starter was standard on most N Series models, a battery and generator were also included, beginning with the first Model 9N. For best performance from the battery, make sure the ground and positive cables are in good condition and are large enough to carry the load, especially on 6-volt systems.

This wouldn't qualify as the proper way to hold the battery in place.

CHAPTER 13

Fuel System

There can be a wide variation in the amount of work a fuel system is going to need, depending upon the age of the tractor and whether it was running at the time you bought it. If you had a chance to drive it before the purchase or before you started tearing it down, you should have a good idea about how smoothly it was running. On the other hand, if you're restoring a treasure that has been sitting in the weeds or an old barn for the past 20 years, chances are there's a lot of rust, varnish, water, and who knows what else in the system.

Unlike most vintage tractors, which were designed to start on gasoline and run on kerosene, Ford models were built to run on gasoline unless someone specifically ordered an all-fuel model. This was an option from 1939 to 1954, which allowed the engine to run on cheaper kerosene through the aid of a special kerosene vaporizer or carburetor.

Fuel Tank

You can rebuild the carburetor, clean or replace the fuel lines, and change the fuel filter, but all that does little good if the fuel tank was the source of contamination. The first step in fuel system overhaul should be to clean the tank and reseal the interior if necessary.

Everyone seems to have his or her own story about how to clean a fuel tank. Some have been known to stick the sandblast nozzle in the fill opening and move it around to hit all sides with silica sand or glass beads. The risk is that you might blow a hole through any weak spot in the tank. Plus, you'll need to get all the sand out of the tank.

Judging from the twisted fuel line and the oil leak around the air cleaner, the fuel system on this tractor will need a little extra attention.

A more common option is to fill the tank about one-third full of water and add a few handfuls of 1/2-inch nuts, shingle nails, or pebbles. The key is to provide a slight abrasive action to clean up the inside. A word of caution is in order, particularly if you want to avoid frustrations later on. Check to see if the filler neck extends into the tank to act as a baffle that keeps fuel from splashing back out. If it does and you add a non-metallic abrasive like pebbles or even brass nuts, you may have a hard time getting all the material out of the tank. It will be a little like trying to shake pennies out of the slot in a piggy bank. Most professional restorers prefer nuts and bolts because the stragglers can be fished out with a magnet.

The next step is to agitate the tank rather vigorously with this mixture sealed inside. One restorer claims the best way to agitate the mixture, assuming you do some farming, is to strap the tank to a tractor wheel with bungee cords and let it rotate while you do a day's field work. Another restorer says he secures the tank in the back of his pickup and hauls it around for about a month while he's working on other parts of the tractor. If you're going to use that method, it helps if you live on country roads. You get the picture. You need to agitate the tank vigorously enough and long enough to scour all the rust and residue out of the tank.

If the tank is in really bad shape, you might want to start by adding a lye-based cleaner to the initial mixture for the first 15 or 20 minutes and then switching to a clean water-and-abrasive mixture. Once the tank has agitated for a sufficient period of time, remove the abrasive material and rinse the tank with clean water. You may have to repeat the rinsing process several times until clean water comes out of the tank.

If you find that the fuel tank leaks, do not try to solder it yourself. Regardless of what kind of instructions your friends have given you—like filling the tank with exhaust gas from your car's exhaust pipe, which supposedly makes it safer—it is impossible to get the fuel tank clean enough to safely solder in a home shop. Shops that repair automobile gasoline tanks usually steam clean the insides for an hour or more to ensure that no residual gasoline is emitted from the pores in the metal during heating. Even then, soldering a gas tank can be a dangerous proposition. That's why many professionals also fill the tank with an inert gas or liquid before heating the tank.

In order to remove the carburetor, it's necessary to first remove the fuel line and all throttle and choke linkages. Then, unbolt the carburetor from the intake manifold.

Soaking the disassembled carburetor in a bucket of cleaner should be the first step in the overhaul process.

One thing you can try on your own is patching the hole with an epoxy, assuming the patch will be hidden beneath the tractor sheet metal. Several restorers have reported success with materials marketed as Magic Metal, J-B Weld, and other gas tank menders sold in automotive stores. The key is getting the surface clean with a good parts cleaner prior to mixing and applying the epoxy.

Most sealer formulas recommend that you first etch the tank with phosphoric acid or an acid metal-prep solution to stabilize any remaining rust prior to adding the sealer. Be sure to leave the fuel tank lid off when rinsing the tank with acid, since the reaction with the metal creates a gas. Rinse the tank several times with clean water and air dry the tank with a warm air source to prevent any further rust.

As soon as the tank interior has adequately dried, pour in enough sealer to cover all sides of the tank interior. In most cases, the sealer instructions will tell you to allow several days for the material to cure before adding fuel. While you're waiting, you can finish up the fuel delivery system by cleaning the sediment bowl assembly and replacing all gaskets and screens.

If all else fails, the good news is that due to the popularity of Ford tractors, replacement gas tanks are readily available. At around $250 by the time you pay shipping, however, you might want to try every avenue listed above before you place the order.

Fuel Line Inspection

The fuel lines and fuel filter may look fine right now, but taking a few extra minutes to thoroughly examine them could still save you a lot of headaches later. Start by inspecting the fuel hoses for kinking, damage, or loose connections at joints and elbows. Make sure fuel lines are not running near an exhaust manifold or pipe, which could lead to a vaporizing problem on hot days. If the fuel turns into a gas in the line, it can cause the fuel circuit to vapor lock and stop delivering fuel to the carburetor.

Finally, make sure fuel is flowing freely to and from the fuel filter. A partially plugged fuel filter can lead to a leaner fuel mixture and cause backfiring, spitting, and misfiring. Unfortunately, when the engine dies, back pressure from expanding vapor can push debris from the filter back into the fuel tank, thereby hiding the problem. The engine will start and run like normal until debris finds its way back into the filter element.

Carburetor Repair

To your benefit as a tractor restorer, the carburetor on most vintage Ford tractors is not as complex as it would appear. To begin, there was no such thing as a fuel pump on early tractors. The fuel tank was mounted above the engine and the fuel was fed to the plain tube, updraft-type carburetor by gravity. The carburetor itself is equally simple. Moreover, the carburetors used on Ford tractor engines from 1939 to 1962 are Marvel-Schebler models of basically the same type, with the same operating principles. The models used through 1954 are detailed in the chart below.

According to a Ford service bulletin, a modified 8N carburetor became standard in production starting with serial number 8N-313112. The Marvel-Schebler part number can be found on the boss located on the right-hand side of the carburetor body. Due to problems and complaints, Ford went back and forth on carburetor models several times, as indicated in the chart above. According to the service bulletin, "The operation of tractors equipped with the TSX-241 carburetor, in which the engine tends to 'stumble' either while idling or when placed under load, can be improved by installing the economizer jet, Part No. 8N-9914. The installation of this jet along with proper carburetor adjustment, will in most cases correct this 'stumbling' condition."

The bulletin also notes that the 8N and the 9N carburetor are both adjusted in much the same manner. "In some cases," it states, "it may be necessary to open the idle adjustment needle of the 8N carburetor as much as one and one-quarter turns and the main adjustment needle one and one-half turns to obtain

Ford Model	Marvel-Schebler Part No.	Carburetor Description
9N-9510	TSX 33	9N carburetor used on tractors prior to serial no. 260596
8N-9510	TSX 241	8N carburetor used on tractors between serial nos. 260596 and 276115 (without economizer jet)
8N-9510	TSX 241A	8N carburetor used on tractors between serial nos. 276115 and 313112 (with economizer jet)
8N-9510	TSX 241B	8N carburetor used starting with serial no. 313112 (modified)
8N-9510	TSX 241C	The 241C deleted the economizer jet again. The 241C was later 8N original production and was cheaper to build than the 241B it followed. Because of this, the 241C was eventually superceded by the earlier 241B.
Golden Jubilee/ NAA	TSX-428	

Farm equipment dealerships and automotive parts stores are a good source of carburetor kits. Notice that this one even includes full instructions for carburetor overhaul.

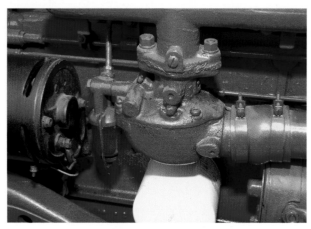

Be sure to clean all fuel passages, including the inlet and outlet from the sediment bowl. On some models, the sediment bowl is right below the fuel tank, and on others it is mounted inline with the carburetor.

proper engine performance. In adjusting the 9N carburetor, turn the idle adjustment needle approximately three-quarters of a turn open and the main adjustment needle one full turn open."

As a final suggestion, the bulletin states, "In cases where a tractor with an 8N carburetor does not operate satisfactorily, even after the carburetor jets have been installed and the carburetor properly adjusted, it is recommended that the entire carburetor assembly be replaced."

With the exception of the 8N problems, the main difference in the carburetors was the sizes of the main jets, which varied depending upon the size of the engine. That means that interchange of carburetors on the manifold is possible within the early N Series Ford tractors, but not between the later Ford tractors (600, 700, 501, 601, 701, and 2000 Series) equipped with 134-cid Red Tiger gasoline engines or the 800, 900, 801, 901, and 4000 Series equipped with a 172-cid Red Tiger gasoline engine. The carburetors are of different sizes and the manifold stud spacing is different for each size carburetor.

Carburetor Rebuilding

The first step in rebuilding a carburetor is to remove it from the tractor and get it cleaned up. Start by closing the valve on the fuel tank, if this hasn't already been done or if the fuel tank hasn't already been removed, and disconnect the fuel line from the carburetor. You'll also need to disconnect any choke cables and governor linkage on most carburetors.

Remove the carburetor from the intake manifold and the air cleaner and move it to a clean workbench or other area where you can disassemble it without losing pieces. Remember that until you empty the bowl, the carburetor still contains a small amount of gasoline. Treat it as flammable until you've cleaned it out. If the carburetor is equipped with a drain plug or a drain valve, and if it's not rusted in place, it's best to drain the fuel before you go any further.

Begin by removing the top half of the carburetor and dumping any gasoline that is still in the bowl into a safe place. Next, carefully disassemble the carburetor and inspect all parts for wear as you go. Before you remove the idle-mixture and main jet-adjusting needles, carefully tighten each against the bottom of the seat, noting how many turns it takes to do so. When reassembling the carburetor, you can tighten the needles to the seat and back off the recorded number of turns. That will at least give you a starting point to dialing in the carburetor. If you have a good service manual, it will also tell you how many turns are needed for initial settings. Of course, final adjustment must be made when the engine has been warmed up and is running.

Be sure you take notes, including notes about the orientation of any gaskets you remove, if you have any doubts about how the carburetor goes back together. Many of the parts will be replaced while installing a carburetor rebuild kit, but don't throw anything away until you know you have the proper replacement part. Some kits are applicable to more than one carburetor, so there may be parts you don't need, and that means you must be able to match the parts you do need!

Next, soak the two halves of the carburetor, along with the components you've removed, in a new container of carburetor cleaner for at least 12 hours or for the amount of time recommended on the label. Many carburetor cleaner solutions come with a parts bucket,

Most carburetors are not as complicated as they appear. If you don't think you can handle the installation of a carburetor kit, there are plenty of businesses that offer rebuilding services. With all the rust inside and out, this carburetor is in particular need of restoration.

This carburetor body required a little help from a file to straighten the float pivot arms.

so use it to turn and move the components from time to time.

Some restorers have also used a sandblasting cabinet and glass beads to scour the two halves of the unit once all the parts have been removed. You need to use care and never use sand; otherwise you can quickly ruin the brass jets that remain in place.

After complete disassembly, the body on this carburetor was cleaned in a sandblasting unit to remove all rust and corrosion.

Use a piece of coarse fishing line or soft wire to clean all fuel passages and jet openings.

You'll also need to clean the brass jets, either by removing them with a screwdriver or cleaning the passageway with a sturdy piece of nylon fishing line and an air hose by directing the air in the opposite direction of the fuel flow. Never use a wire or small drill to clean out orifices, since even a small change in the size of the hole will affect carburetor performance. If a jet is removable, make sure you have a screwdriver that fits the slot securely. Brass parts are easy to strip or damage.

Finally, inspect the carburetor fuel bowl and bowl cover for cracks or distortion and check the float for leaks, cracks, or distortion. In principle, the float bowl acts as a reservoir to hold a supply of fuel for the carburetor. It's important, however, that the fuel in the bowl remain at a consistent depth, since the fuel level regulates fuel flow to the carburetor itself. As fuel fills the bowl by gravity, the float rises on a hinge and pushes the needle valve into a seat to shut off the fuel flow. In effect, it works in much the same way as the float and valve in a toilet tank.

If the fuel level in the bowl is too low, the engine does not readily respond when accelerated and it will be difficult to maintain carburetor adjustments. If the fuel level in the bowl is too high, it can cause excessive fuel consumption and crankcase dilution. Plus, it can cause the carburetor to leak. It will be difficult to maintain carburetor adjustments.

Carburetor Reassembly

Once the carburetor has been thoroughly cleaned, it's time to put it all back together and make the necessary adjustments. Due to the popularity of Ford tractors, you have a number of choices, ranging from basic repair kits and major overhaul kits to individual parts and components that call for replacement.

It's important to inspect all moving parts and replace those that are damaged. Carefully inspect all adjusting screws, seats, inlet needles, and cages for ridges, nicks, or depressions that could affect the air-fuel mixture. If the throttle-shaft bushings or seals are worn to the point they are letting air leak into the carburetor, they're also going to affect the gas-air mixture. In some cases, the throttle shaft itself may have a groove worn into it. Some models have renewable throttle-shaft bushings and others do not. On unbushed models, you'll have to compensate by replacing the throttle shaft and/or throttle body.

In the process of reassembling the carburetor, you also need to make sure all gaskets are properly oriented; otherwise, you may block a vital orifice or passageway. When checking the float height, be sure the gasket has been positioned on the bowl half of the carburetor. The measurement specified in your service manual or kit instructions is almost always taken from the surface of the gasket to the bottom surface of the float. For 1953 and later models, this measurement should be 0.26 to 0.29 inch from the gasket to the nearest edge of the float. The float is adjusted by bending the hinge, so use caution when bending the hinge to avoid damaging the mounting bracket. Finally, when reinstalling the main jet and idle speed mixture screws, be sure to screw them all the way in and then back them out the number of turns recorded during disassembly or as instructed in your service manual.

Carburetor Adjustment

Whether you are adjusting the carburetor or readjusting the settings after overhauling the carburetor, adjustments in most cases are limited to three main locations. These are the main adjustment needle, the idle adjustment needle, and idle speed adjustment stop screw.

Before attempting to adjust the carburetor, the engine must always be at normal operating temperature as indicated on the engine temperature gauge. Keep in mind that correct carburetor adjustment cannot be obtained unless engine compression and ignition meet specifications. With that in mind, proceed as follows:

1. For the initial setting, before the engine is started, turn the idle fuel adjustment needle (clockwise) until it is seated lightly, and then back it off approximately one turn.

Replace all valve assemblies, springs jets, and needle assemblies as necessary.

Make sure all gaskets are oriented correctly when you reassemble the carburetor; otherwise you may be blocking off a vital orifice or passageway.

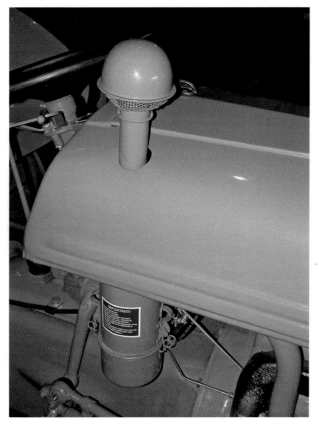

The breather and oil bath air filter are important aspects of the fuel system. If they're clogged, there won't be enough clean air to mix with the fuel in the carburetor and no amount of adjustment can cure the problem.

2. Start the engine and turn the idle fuel adjustment (clockwise) until the engine begins to roll, then back it off slowly until the engine is running smoothly.

3. With the hand throttle in the closed position, turn the idle speed adjustment screw until the engine idle speed is 450 to 475 rpm (check the Proof-Meter on models so equipped). On new engines, it may be necessary to set the idle speed slightly higher to prevent stalling.

4. The power fuel adjustment or main adjustment needle initial setting is 1 to 1 1/4 turns open (counterclockwise).

5. The final adjustment should be made in the field. With the engine running at governed speed under full load, turn the adjustment needle (clockwise) until the power picks up and the engine runs smoothly.

Diesel Systems

Unlike a number of manufacturers, Ford didn't offer diesel engines until 1957, when the company introduced the 01 Series. Models with a first number of 5, 6, or 7 could be equipped with a 134-cubic-inch gas or LP engine or a 144-cubic-inch diesel. Models with 8 or 9 as the first number came with a choice of a 172-cubic-inch gas or LP engine or a diesel engine of the same size.

Unlike gasoline, which is vaporized and ignited with a spark, diesel fuel is injected directly into the cylinder at pressures up to 2,500 pounds per square inch (psi). In fact, some of today's diesel engines utilize pumps producing up to 5,000 psi pressure at the injector. It is this high injection pressure, combined with cylinder compression, that creates the heat needed to ignite the fuel. This means that the injector pump needs to force the precise amount of fuel into each cylinder, via an injector, at exactly the right time. That's why the injection pump is generally geared to the crankshaft.

It is also the reason injection-pump testing and rebuilding is best left to a professional who has the knowledge and the equipment to work on it. One thing you can do is make sure the injector is the correct size for the tractor model and engine you're rebuilding. Any overhaul or replacement, however, requires access to complete nozzle testing equipment. In the meantime, you need to remember that cleanliness is vital when working on diesel systems. It's also important that the fuel system is purged of air whenever the fuel filters have been removed or when the fuel lines have been disconnected. The process for purging air on your tractor should be outlined in your service manual.

Oil-Bath Air Filters

For many of us, an air filter is a square or round element composed of aluminum screen and folded, paper-like material that traps dirt particles as air flows to the carburetor. Once the filter gets dirty or has been in place a certain length of time, it's replaced with a new one.

Although some vintage tractors may have that type of filter, it's more likely that the engine on your tractor has an oil-bath air filter, which was the case on nearly all Ford engines. After all, replaceable air filters didn't become a feature on most farm tractors until the 1960s.

Let's first look at how the oil-bath air filter works. As you probably noticed, the filter itself looks like it is made out of a pile of metal shavings. There's also a cup at the bottom filled with oil. When you start the engine and the air enters the air cleaner, coarse debris, such as chaff, leaves, and twigs, is filtered out by the air intake pre-cleaner screen located in the side panel above the air cleaner itself. As air enters the filter, a certain amount of oil is sucked out of the oil cup or pan and onto the metal shavings, which then filter the air as it flows through the canister.

The filter canister is designed to be just the right height and size so that the engine can pull oil up into the screen along with the air, but without pulling it into the carburetor and engine. Incoming air is drawn into the filter through a center pipe that leads to the bottom of the canister. As a result, any heavy dirt particles should fall directly into the oil cup. Lighter particles should be trapped on the oil-soaked filter surface as the air moves upward through the outer portion of the canister toward the carburetor.

Now that you understand how the filter works, it should be easier to visualize the potential problems. The first comes with using the wrong oil weight. If you add oil that is too light, it can be drawn beyond the

The oil bath air cleaner cup must be filled to the recommended level with the correct weight of oil in order to work correctly. The standard air filter on the 8N pulled air through a side inlet.

filter and into the engine. Using oil that is too heavy will have the opposite effect—not enough oil will be drawn up into the filter element, and much of the air-cleaning surface will go unused.

As inconvenient as it may sound, oil-bath air filters were designed to be cleaned and refilled daily when in use. In really dusty conditions, a farmer sometimes had to service the air cleaner a couple times a day. Naturally, the air cleaner is going to work best when the oil level is at the recommended level. An inappropriate oil level can compromose the effectiveness of the filter, but letting the oil cup fill up with sludge can be even more detrimental. Adding more oil to the cup can make it worse. When the particles-to-oil ratio gets to a certain level, the dirt will begin to hang onto the cleaning surfaces. Eventually, instead of just clean air being sucked into the intake, chunks of dirt and

The cyclone- or turbine-style air precleaners have always been a popular option on the N-Series Fords. The incoming air is swirled and the heavier dirt particles are deposited into the glass jar where they can be emptied later. The regular oil bath air cleaner doesn't need to be serviced nearly as often with the precleaner in use.

Be sure to replace any damaged hoses that connect the carburetor to the air intake. Air leaks can negatively affect the air-to-fuel mixture.

sludge are going with it. It's important to dump the old oil and wipe the oil cup out on a regular basis.

You'll recall that the air cleaner was designed to be just the right size to match engine air intake. An air cleaner that is the wrong size can mean that too much or too little oil is drawn into the filter canister. Accordingly, any replacement air filter needs to be similar in size and design, if not identical to the original. By the same token, if you make dramatic changes in the engine that are going to affect air intake, you will need to make comparable changes in the air-cleaning system.

Manifold Inspection and Repair

Just as an air leak in the carburetor can affect how smoothly your tractor runs, so can a crack in the intake manifold. When that is the case, one option is to have a local welder or machine shop make the repair. Unfortunately, most intake and exhaust manifolds are made out of one of four types of cast-iron material: white, gray, malleable, or ductile iron. To weld it, the material must be properly prepared, preheated, and welded with the appropriate method. First, however, the type of material must be identified, which involves one or more of the following tests: chemical analysis, a grinding test that identifies the types of sparks a grinding wheel gives off when in contact with the material, and a ring test that helps identify the material by the type of ringing sound it gives off when struck with a hammer.

Should you decide to try arc welding a cracked manifold yourself, it's important to use a high-content nickel/cast rod or a nickel/cadmium rod with a cast-iron-friendly flux. Try to preheat the manifold with a torch. If you try to lay a long bead of weld on a cold manifold, it could easily warp and cause a sudden stress crack somewhere else. If preheating is not possible, strike an arc and weld only an inch or so of the crack. Stop and let the heat spread to other parts of the material.

One alternative to arc welding is brazing the manifold using a brass rod melted into a prepared groove on the manifold crack. Start by locating the crack and grinding a groove along its length with a grinder. Extend the groove a half inch or so beyond the crack. Use a coarse file to remove the grinder marks from the groove. This helps remove any graphite particles that could prevent the brazing material from adhering to the iron.

Be sure to check the integrity of the intake and exhaust manifolds. Small holes in the intake manifold can sometimes be repaired with something like J-B Weld. Cracks in the exhaust manifold, however, will need to be welded by a capable welder.

As for the brazing material, it's best to select a brass rod that is high in copper content with some nickel added. Select a torch tip that has a high heat output with low gas pressure. As with arc welding, it's helpful to preheat the material to be welded so it won't crack under isolated heat stress. Once brazing has been completed, try to cool the manifold slowly by using a bed of sand, if available.

One last option when trying to repair a manifold is to use an epoxy, such as J-B Weld. This is a particularly viable option on an intake manifold that is in a relatively cool area of the engine and when the crack is not in a stress area, such as the areas around the mounting flanges. Just make sure the area is clean, free of grease and grit, and prepared according to the directions on the epoxy package.

Of course, the easiest alternative is to locate a replacement manifold at a salvage yard, flea market, or aftermarket vendor. If you have to hire someone to do the welding, finding a replacement may be the cheaper alternative, as well.

The governor on most Ford models is mounted at the front of the engine where it is driven directly off the camshaft.

Inspection of the governor should include making sure the flyweights or balls move freely. If necessary, replace the bearings, dust seal, and gasket in the process.

Make sure all linkages between the governor and the carburetor are free of binding and that they operate before reassembling the governor and reinstalling it on the engine.

Governor Overhaul

Even though it doesn't come in contact with the fuel, the governor plays an important part in the fuel-delivery system and needs to be inspected as part of your overhaul. In general, the governor uses a rotating mass applied against a spring to adjust the carburetor throttle shaft and thus regulates the engine speed around a set point established by the throttle lever position.

On virtually all Ford tractors, the rotating mass is a set of steel balls within a pair of races driven by a gear in the timing gear train. The first step in governor inspection is checking for any signs of malfunction. Symptoms can include the engine idling too fast or not idling down when the throttle lever is moved to the idle position, surging, over-revving, the engine not reaching the specified top speed, engine speed control that is erratic, and delayed reaction or sluggish response to changing load conditions or throttle movement.

Before attempting any disassembly or governor adjustments, inspect all linkages and link rods for free movement and the absence of any bends or binding. If necessary, free up and align all linkages to remove any binding. If additional internal repair or inspection is required, follow the instructions in your repair manual for governor removal, overhaul, and/or adjustment. The basics for governor overhaul include inspecting and replacing any defective bearings, seals, and drive gears. Ensure that the balls don't have any flat spots, pits, or damage. Also ensure that the races are not grooved or pitted. Repair generally calls for new bushings.

If you're not sure of your ability to overhaul or rebuild the governor as instructed in your repair manual, you might consider sending it out to one of the shops listed in the appendix that specializes in governor restoration. Special tools and gauges are often needed to replace bushings and determine the governor's accuracy. Considering the role it plays in controlling engine speed, you want to make sure it's done right. Finally, when reinstalling the governor, tune the speed adjustment as necessary to limit the engine speed to the rpm rating specified in your service manual.

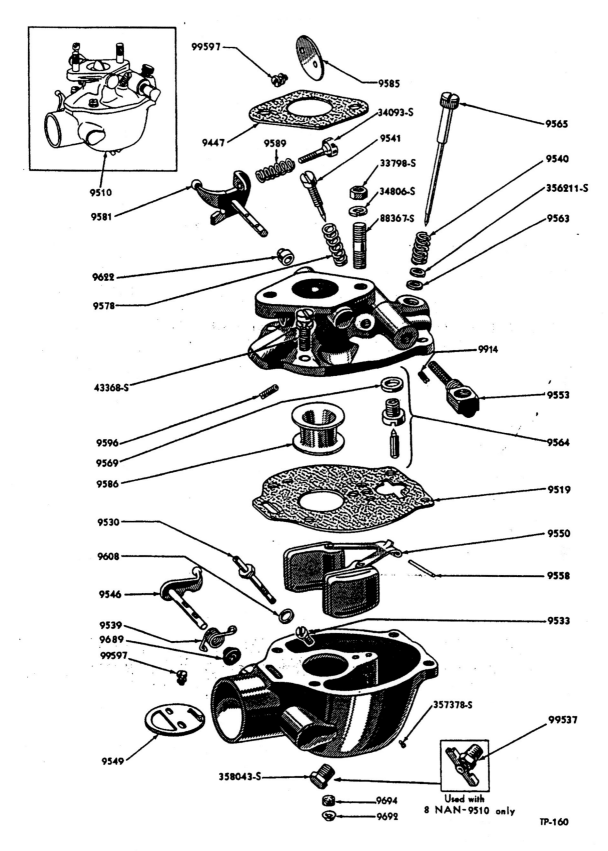

99597
9585
34093-S
9447
9589
9541
33798-S
9565
34806-S
9540
88367-S
356211-S
9510
9581
9563
9622
9578
9914
43368-S
9553
9596
9564
9569
9586
9519
9530
9550
9608
9558
9546
9533
9539
9689
99597
357378-S
99537
9549
358043-S
9694
9692
Used with
8 NAN-9510 only
TP-160

With the correct parts kit, a set of instructions, and/or an exploded-view drawing, even a novice restorer can perform minor carburetor repairs.

CHAPTER 14

Cooling System

For those used to today's thermostatically controlled, electrically driven cooling fans, the cooling system on most early-model tractors appears rather simple, and indeed it is. In most cases, it consists of a belt-driven fan, a radiator, and a water pump. Until 1943, Ford tractors didn't even use a pressurized system. On the other hand, they were far ahead of tractors built just a few years earlier that didn't even use a water pump. Some of those early models used a simple thermosyphon system that depended on physics, which meant that as water cooled in the radiator, it would sink to the bottom where it was drawn out and routed to the engine.

Cooling System Inspection and Repair

You probably had an opportunity to evaluate the cooling system to some extent when you purchased the tractor or during the troubleshooting operation. Perhaps you even had a chance to start the engine and let it run long enough to see if there were any water leaks, problems with overheating, or traces of oil in the coolant.

Unfortunately, radiator cores tend to clog up with rust, lime, or other mineral deposits and the fins plug up with weeds, seeds, and debris. In addition, the metal headers often corrode away after years of use, and the seams become moist with residual antifreeze. It's best, therefore, to start cooling system inspection and restoration at the front of the tractor, at the radiator. The first thing you should do is check the front and rear of the radiator for a buildup of bugs, seeds, weeds, and so on. A strong stream of water sprayed from the back side, or fan side, of the radiator will remove a lot of the debris.

Next, check for moisture around the radiator core and headers. These areas tend to rot out if the tractor has sat dry for a long period of time. If there is leakage, the area will be moist, and perhaps smell sweet if there is antifreeze in the system. If the leakage is minor, you can sometimes take care of the problem by adding one or two cans of radiator stop leak material.

If there is substantial leakage, it's best to remove the radiator and have it professionally serviced. Considering that you may have to remove the radiator as part of the tractor or engine restoration process, you may want to think about taking it to a professional just to have it flushed, flow tested, and checked for integrity. The other option is to simply replace the radiator assembly as part of the restoration process.

Radiator Cap

Like most tractors of the time, the early Ford 9N and 2N tractors started out with an unpressurized radiator, which meant that the radiator cap only served the purpose of keeping the water in and dirt and debris out. In 1943, during the second year of the 2N production, Ford replaced the 9N radiator that had initially been installed on the 2N with a new radiator, which was slightly smaller and pressurized to four pounds per square inch (psi). Pressurizing the radiator accomplishes two purposes. First, each pound of pressure raises the boiling point by approximately three degrees Fahrenheit, which allows the engine to operate at a higher temperature. Second, since there is now a greater difference between the water temperature and the air temperature, the radiator can operate more efficiently.

On systems equipped with a pressurized cap, check to make sure the bottom of the cap is clean and fits snugly into the filler neck. Check the rubber bottom

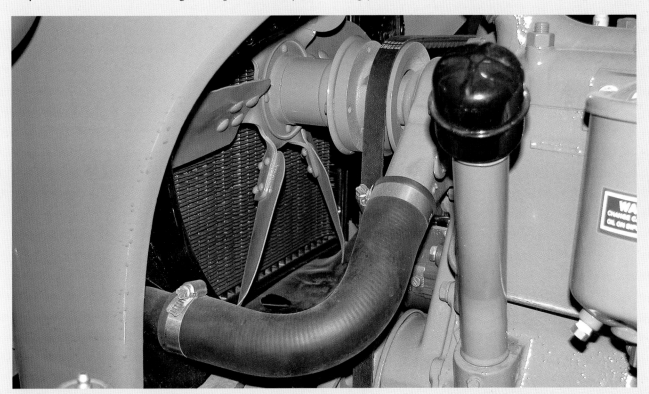

The four-blade fan became standard and the six-blade fan became optional during 1948 starting with serial number 111758.

for swelling, nicks, or cracks. Also check the filler neck for uniformity on the sealing surfaces. A warp or hairline crack will cause pressure to leak out when in use. Finally, make sure any replacement cap has the proper pressure relief rating. If the relief setting is too high, you run the risk of blowing hoses or the radiator core, especially if the core is weak in the first place.

Fan and Shroud

The fan and fan drive system on most vintage Ford tractors are pretty basic by today's standards, as there were no such things as thermostatically controlled electrical fans. Ford tractors did use a fan shroud to help ensure that air was being drawn through the radiator rather than from the side.

Fan restoration consists of little more than checking the integrity of the blades to make sure the attachment rivets are tight and the blades haven't been bent, checking the fan shaft bearings to make sure they're in good condition, and making sure the shroud hasn't been cracked or removed altogether.

Hoses

On many tractor restorations, the biggest problem with the cooling system—and many times the only problem—is the condition of the hoses. Hoses that are hard, brittle, or cracked need to be replaced. Keep an eye out for small patches of moisture on the hose surface. If holes are discovered, gently knead the area while looking for a hairline crack or pinhole. Such areas tend to leak only when the tractor is at operating temperature and under pressure, which makes them difficult to locate.

Also look for hoses that have swelled up because of oil contamination. They feel greasy and spongy when kneaded. Replace any hoses that are marginal. While you're at it, it's a good idea to change the hose clamps since dirt and grit can keep them from being sufficiently tightened to seal water.

Water Pump

The most likely problem you'll encounter with the water pump is a water leak or worn bearings. A leaking seal

Whether the cooling system is removed or left on the tractor, one of the most important steps in the cooling system's restoration is checking the integrity of the radiator.

This radiator appears to be in reusable condition; however, it will still need to be cleaned and pressure checked.

Check the upper and lower radiator hoses and replace any hose sections that are swelled because of oil contamination or if they feel greasy and spongy when kneaded.

is generally indicated by coolant leakage at the drain hole in the pump housing. Unless the impeller blades or an internal divider have been completely attacked by rust or the pump housing has cracked, you can usually rebuild the unit with new seals and bearings.

The first step in rebuilding the water pump is removing it from the tractor. Place it in a vice and drive the shaft out of the pulley. Remove the snap ring from the water pump body and press the shaft and bearing assembly out of the pump body. If you're only replacing the seal, it's important that you inspect the water pump shaft to be sure it is smooth and free from rust. If you don't, it won't be long before you're replacing seals again. If necessary, use a piece of emery cloth to smooth the shaft where it fits against the seal.

In the meantime, clean all the metal parts and inspect all components for cracks, excessive pitting, and for broken or damaged fins on the impeller. Replace any components that are severely damaged. Replace the bearing assembly if there is any end play or side play in

Until the NAA was introduced in 1953, the radiator cap was exposed above the hood on all N Series models, hence the styled design. An earlier change in the radiator cap occurred in 1943 when the radiator was pressurized.

the shaft. In some cases, it may be easiest to replace the entire water pump with a new unit, which runs around $70 or less. If you're putting the old one back together, it's a good idea to place a small amount of grease on the pump shaft to prevent damage to the water seal as the pump is being reassembled. Finally, make sure the drain hole in the bottom of the housing is kept free of dirt, grease, and paint so that any water that may leak past the seal can drain away.

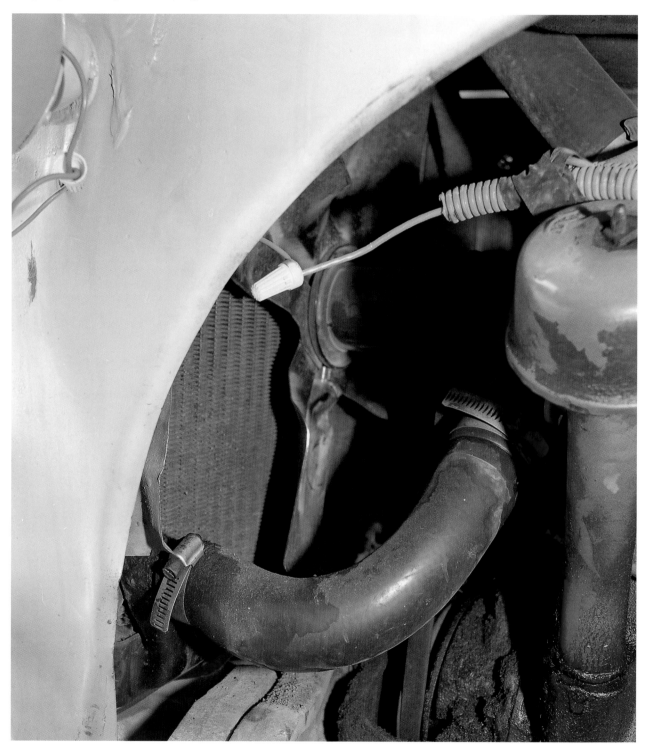

Unless the impeller or an internal divider has been destroyed by rust, you can usually rebuild a water pump with new seals and/or bearings.

Thermostat

Before you finish with the cooling system, you'll need to make sure the thermostat is operating correctly. You can tell a lot about its operation by looking into the top of the radiator with the cap removed. Never open the radiator cap when the engine is hot.

As soon as the water gets hot enough to open the thermostat, you should see water start flowing into the top of the radiator from the upper radiator hose. As a reference point, most Ford models with a non-pressurized cooling system have a 160- to 172-degree thermostat.

If you're not sure the thermostat is working correctly, you can test it by removing the thermostat and placing it in a pan of water on a stove. As the water heats up, watch for the diaphragm to open when the temperature reaches the point at which the thermostat should open. In the case of an 8N, it should start to open at 160 to 165 degrees Fahrenheit and be fully opened at 190 to 200 degrees. Considering the price of a new thermostat and the age of the tractor, you may want to replace it with a new one.

Belts

With few exceptions, all vintage tractors, including Ford models, have only one belt, which normally runs the fan/water pump and the generator. You need to make sure it is in good condition and not slipping, or the whole cooling system can suffer the consequences.

To check the belt(s), twist it around in several spots so the bottom and one side are clearly visible. Look for signs of cracking; oil soaking; hard, glazed contact surface; splitting; or fraying. Replace any belt showing these symptoms. Fortunately, the fan belt on all Ford N Series tractors and most models that followed can be replaced without removing the fan, water pump, or any other cooling components. Once you've checked the belt condition or replaced it, make sure you adjust it for the proper belt tension. A belt that is too tight can cause premature wear on the bearings, whereas a belt that is too loose can slip, squeal, or cause other problems.

If the original is too far gone, replacement water pumps are available from a number of sources.

Properly tensioned drive belts that are in good condition are essential to trouble-free engine cooling.

Chapter 15

Surface Preparation

Without a doubt, surface preparation is the single most important variable in determining the life of any paint coating that will follow later, whether you're painting your house or a vintage tractor. Even the best paint you can buy won't adhere to an excessively dirty or greasy surface or if moisture and contaminants get behind the paint film. The first step you'll need to take with any tractor is getting it clean.

You may have cleaned the tractor to some extent already. If you bought the tractor at a sale, there's a good chance the previous owner cleaned it up to make a good impression with prospective customers. Or you may have run it through the car wash on your way home.

Regardless of how much cleaning has been done to this point, the job has really just begun. The sheet metal will need to be thoroughly cleaned and degreased; and once the sheet metal has been removed, you're bound to find a lot more grease and grime than was originally evident.

The goal is to make sure every surface will hold the primer and paint you will be applying later. To handle tough, baked-on grease on the engine, frame, and powertrain, some restorers like to spray oven cleaner on the really greasy areas and let it soak before power washing the whole tractor. It is not recommended that you use gasoline or kerosene as a cleaner. There are cleaners and degreasers available at any automotive store that are safer and more effective. Keep a putty knife, screwdriver, and wire brush handy while you're cleaning to dig at the really caked on stuff.

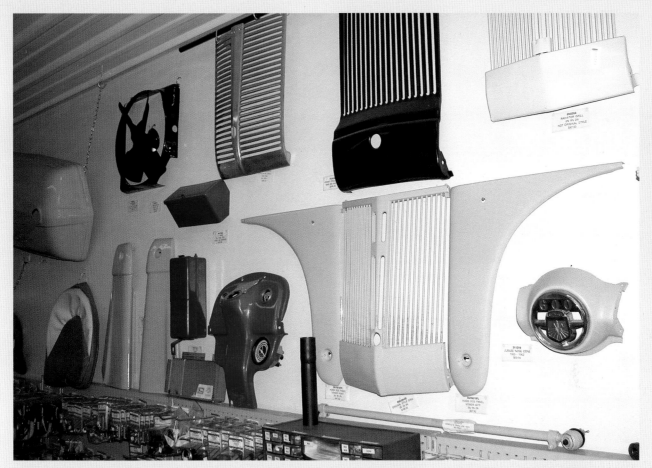

Ford restorers are fortunate that a wide variety of sheet metal components are available from aftermarket sources. They include fenders, hoods, battery boxes, and grilles.

Jim Deardorff, who owns Superior Coatings in Chillicothe, Missouri, insists that even if you plan on sandblasting the frame and drivetrain, it's important that you first remove as much grease as possible. Hitting it with a sandblaster, he insists, will only drive grease particles into the surface. That is especially true if you use too much pressure or the type of media that can pit or scratch the surface. If grease is driven into the pits or scratches instead of removed, it will only make it more difficult to apply a quality paint job. As a result, Deardorff uses a combination of stripper and media blasting on most cast-iron components.

Before he does that, Deardorff says he uses a hand sprayer to apply a coat of Dawn dishwashing detergent over the entire tractor and lets it soak overnight. It's not that Deardorff specifically endorses Dawn, but it's the only detergent he has found that rinses clean without leaving any kind of film. Don't dilute it with water, he cautions, or it will foam too much. If he uses anything to thin the Dawn concentrate, Deardorff will add 10 to 20 percent of a product called ChloroWash, which is a multi-purpose cleaner formulated to remove dirt and salts that can cause corrosion. Deardorff says ChloroWash also works well for cleaning restored tractors that have been exposed to exhaust fumes, salts, and dirt during tractor shows and events.

Once the detergent or combination has had 10 to 12 hours to soak, Deardorff uses a power washer and hot water to completely clean the project. If that isn't enough to remove the majority of the grease, he occasionally resorts to the oven cleaner.

Cast Iron Preparation

In most cases, the easiest way to finish preparing steel and cast-iron components, once you're gotten most of the grease off, is to use a sandblaster or hire someone to sandblast the components for you. This includes the frame, wheels, transmission, and rear end housing.

175

Due to the popularity of Ford tractors and the interest in tractor restoration, suppliers like N-Complete carry replacement hoods and fenders.

Your local automotive parts dealer should be able to direct you to a wide assortment of paint strippers for cleaning sheet metal down to bare metal. Many restorers say they have the best luck with aircraft remover (top).

Before you start any sandblasting, it's vital that you go over the entire tractor and look for holes that will let sand in and cause later damage. Many machines have passages to the brakes in the pinion housings. Be sure to pack these areas with heavy rags. Check to see if any of the bolts you removed during disassembly left an open hole that will let sand into the clutch or shaft areas. If so, you'll want to put bolts back in these holes.

Unless you're planning to replace the spark plugs on a gasoline engine, it's a good idea to pull the good spark plugs and replace them with old plugs or dummies when you're prepping for paint. At the very least, you'll want to remove the spark plug wires and cover the entire distributor to protect the distributor cap. The same goes for the coil. If the distributor body and shaft are to be painted, some restorers remove the cap and rotor and mask off the top of the distributor itself.

Watch out for the clutch inspection plate. It won't seal well enough to keep sand out. Most water pumps also have a vent on the bottom side that will let sand up into the bearing and shaft area. Don't count on trying to avoid these areas, because if there is a hole, sand will get into it.

Don't rely on masking tape to adequately protect an area. With enough pressure behind it, sand will go right through masking tape. Some restorers rely on multiple layers of duct tape placed over any vulnerable components or openings.

Jim Deardorff says he likes to use masking tape covered by a layer of duct tape. Masking tape by itself isn't enough, he insists. Media blasting material can tear up the plastic backing on the duct tape and make it very difficult to remove when you're finished. A layer of masking tape beneath duct tape solves this problem.

Deardorff has another tip for those who find themselves masking off a hydraulic cylinder shaft prior to sandblasting or painting. Though very few older tractors included hydraulic cylinders, you'll still find them on tractor loaders, the power steering unit, and on some of the three-point lift systems. "If you have a cylinder shaft that you need to mask off, simply run a piece of heavy fishing line along the length of the shaft before wrapping it with tape," he says. "Then, when it comes time to remove the tape, you can just pull on the fishing line and unzip the tape."

The radiator can also pose a challenge when it comes to sandblasting the tractor frame. In most cases, the best bet is to remove it from the tractor. If there is any area on the frame that really needs to be cleaned, it's probably the area under the radiator anyway. That's where the rust, caked-on dirt, and grease are prone to collect in the first place, so if you don't remove the radiator, you're going to miss a vital area.

If by chance you don't remove the radiator prior to media blasting, you should at least cover the radiator core with several layers of cardboard and seal the seams with several layers of duct tape; that is, unless you plan to replace the whole radiator core anyway.

Be sure you cover the serial number plate, as well. Depending upon the age of your tractor and the serial number, this can be a valuable component, especially if you're painting an older, vintage tractor. Wheels and cast parts can be sandblasted without much risk of damage. In fact, if you're dealing with spoke wheels, sandblasting may be the best way to get in and around the individual spokes.

You can add as many coats of paint as you want and you still won't hide the dents and wrinkles in the sheet metal on this tractor; not to mention the color is too white. In fact, a coat of paint makes dents and wrinkles show up better. It would have been better to replace the panel or spend some time on bodywork before getting to this point.

Small dents in sheet metal can often be removed with a ball-peen hammer and a mallet or large hammer to back up the piece. On stubborn dents, it may be necessary to apply heat to help shrink the metal back into place.

The last method of removing paint, and the one you're probably going to have to employ, is mechanical removal. Unfortunately, this method requires the most sweat and hard work. You'll find a wide range of weapons available at most hardware and automotive stores, but you might want to start with the

While it's not as easy as using a sandblaster, some restorers prefer to use an air-powered or electric sander to remove paint and years of accumulated rust.

basics, including wire brushes and putty knives. A wire brush or a sander that fits on an electric drill can also come in handy when removing paint and grease from powertrain and frame components.

Sheet Metal

Thanks to the huge interest in antique tractor restoration—especially in Ford N Series tractors—Ford enthusiasts have more choices today than ever before when it comes to sheet metal preparation. Due to the growing interest in the restoration hobby, vendors now offer hundreds of sheet metal parts as aftermarket reproductions. Sources like N-Complete and Carpenter both offer reproductions of nearly any sheet metal component you could ever need, including fenders, hoods, and nose pieces for 8N, 2N, and 9N models.

In addition, there are plenty of sheet metal parts available through salvage operations such as Dennis Polk Equipment or Central Plains Tractor Parts (see appendix). Finally, there are a number of businesses, including many New Holland dealerships,

To demonstrate the gentle action of his Classic Blast material on sheet metal, Jim Deardorff, owner of Superior Coatings in Chillicothe, Missouri, has been known to sandblast one-half of a soft drink can. His special blend (right) is comprised of aluminum oxide, ground black walnut shells, and his own blend of other materials, including garnet.

that sell what is commonly referred to as new-old-stock (NOS). These are old parts that have never been used, have been stored in a warehouse or stock room, and have only recently been put back into circulation. In the case of Ford tractors, there's been enough demand over the years that parts for many 50- and 60-year-old tractors are still available over the counter.

As a final note on sheet metal, you'll recall from Chapters 1 and 2, the first 600 to 700 Ford 9N models built in 1939 had aluminum hoods and grilles. The horizontal spoked grille was also cast aluminum, as were the complete steering column and dash assembly, shifter base, transmission side covers, engine timing cover, and a few other pieces. The aluminum battery/fuel cover, which is part of the hood, was not hinged, but was held in place with spring clips. It's doubtful that you would ever get your hands on one of these tractors by accident, since they are highly sought out by collectors. But should you be so lucky as to own one, do not replace any of the aluminum components. This is a case where you want to do your best to preserve the parts, even if it means taking the hood to a body shop to repair any dents, creases, or tears. Some Ford N Series collectors who have been lucky enough to find one of these models don't even bother to paint the hood and grille, as Ford did originally, but leave them unpainted and polish the components to a bright shine.

Sheet Metal Preparation

Due to the availability of so many new parts, some restorers like to replace any sheet metal parts that they can with new. That's especially true at N-Complete, where owner Tom Armstrong says he replaces any part that's been badly dented or rusted with a new component when he does a remanufacture. On the other hand, since N-Complete also sells parts, it's a matter of time and labor versus wholesale replacement cost.

For others, particularly those on a tight budget, it's more economical to strip and repair existing sheet metal components unless they are extremely rusted or wrinkled. The question that's most often debated among tractor restorers is, "How do you best go about it?"

When it comes to using a sandblaster to strip sheet metal, you'll find differing opinions. There are some restorers who sandblast all the sheet metal and

every bit of the frame prior to a restoration project, and there are others who wouldn't take a sandblast nozzle anywhere near the sheet metal, regardless of how much elbow grease it saved.

The key word is sandblasting. These days, it's more commonly referred to as media blasting, simply because there are a lot more media types than sand that can be used. That's particularly the case when you're media blasting sheet metal. Check out the media suppliers today and you'll find a wide variety of media types, including aluminum oxide, garnet, glass beads, plastic beads, wheat starch, carbon dioxide pellets, and dry ice.

Jim Seward, a tractor restorer from Wellman, Iowa, who also manages the body shop for a local General Motors dealership, is one who uses a sandblaster on everything. He insists sandblasting sheet metal is one of the quickest and most efficient methods available for removing paint and rust, providing it is done delicately. In response to people who say, "sandblasting will blow

Because the grille on a Ford N Series tractor sets out front where it is easily dented or gouged, it is often damaged beyond simple repair. Even the optional bumper failed to fully protect this grille, especially the hood emblem. Replacement grilles are fortunately available at a reasonable price.

a hole through weak metal," he says, "If the metal is so weak that you're going to blow a hole through it, it needs to be repaired anyway."

For anything but the heaviest gauge steel, make sure you or the commercial operator use fine silica sand, glass beads, or plastic. Keep plenty of distance between the nozzle and the steel to avoid warping or stretching the part. Always keep the nozzle moving.

Safety First

Although sandblasting, or media blasting, as it is more commonly called, is an effective way to remove old paint and rust, it does require a certain amount of caution and preparation. Depending upon the job and the air pressure behind it, media can be propelled at speeds up to 400 miles per hour, which means it can easily penetrate skin; hence, it's important that you protect yourself against body damage while doing any type of sandblasting. That means heavy-duty leather gloves, long sleeves, and a good-quality sandblasting hood.

It's also important that you wear a NIOSH-approved respirator to protect yourself from media particles, paint debris, and dirt and rust particles that are dislodged and floating in the air. You should be able to find all of these articles from any business that sells sandblasting equipment and media, your paint supplier, or from your local auto supply store.

If the metal gets too hot, it will have ripples that are virtually impossible to remove.

Jim Deardorff, who has stripped hundreds of cars and tractors in his career, says he has developed his own way to media blast sheet metal. A few years ago, he developed Classic Blast, a special blasting mix made up of aluminum oxide, ground black walnut shells, and his own blend of other materials, including some garnet. Using the product in a closed-top sandblast pot, which uses a vacuum to pull the media into the chamber, he says he can reduce the pressure to as little as 35 pounds and still clean fragile parts without damage. To prove it, he often demonstrates the effectiveness of his sandblast method by removing the paint from an aluminum pop can that's still filled with liquid. Since the walnut shells in the blend tend to polish the sheet metal as it assists in paint removal, Deardorff says the stripped surface is also less prone to rust than if other types of media are used. The walnut shells also soften the impact of the more aggressive material in the mix.

Chemical Stripping

Another paint removal method that is widely used by a number of restorers, particularly to remove paint from sheet metal parts, is a quality metal stripper. Unlike media blasting, the use of chemical strippers doesn't pose any risk of warping or pitting the sheet metal; yet it can remove multiple layers of paint, primer, wax, and rust. Keep in mind that chemical strippers are generally toxic and require adequate ventilation. That means you should wear a respirator and rubber gloves when using them.

Due to a ridge on the underside of the hood that easily collects moisture and dirt, a lot of Ford N Series hoods tend to rust from the inside out. By the time it gets to this point, it's often too late for body filler.

Perhaps the best option for sheet metal if you're doing the job yourself is a product called aircraft stripper. It may have been formulated at one time for aircraft sheet metal, but it's available at any paint and automotive supply store. For best results, it generally helps to scuff the old paint surface prior to any application. It doesn't matter whether you use coarse sandpaper or a rough pad, such as Scotch-Brite. The idea is to scratch the surface enough to allow the paint stripper to penetrate deeper into the paint coating.

As mentioned earlier, some restorers like to use a combination of processes, such as using a paint stripper followed by media blasting, particularly on components like the engine, transmission, and frame. Jim Deardorff is one of those people. He says he has found a water-based stripper called DoradoStrip that he likes better than any of the chemical-based strippers. Even though it contains no toxic or hazardous air pollutants, it is said to effectively lift epoxies, urethanes, and powder coatings.

It's hard to tell if it is body putty that is cracking under the paint or if it is rust working its way through from the backside. What appears to have been a nice paint job is going to waste.

At N-Complete, small parts that need to be media blasted are stripped in an enclosed unit. This is not only cleaner, but allows them to easily recycle the media blast material.

Deardorff typically applies the material to any surface he wants to strip and lets it soak overnight before washing it off the next morning with a strong stream of water. He insists most of the paint washes right off with the material.

As far as use of the stripper is concerned, it's best to read and follow the directions on the container. In most cases, however, the directions call for allowing

Jim Deardorff media blasts sheet metal by putting the material in a closed-top sandblast pot that uses a vacuum to pull the media into the chamber. That allows him to reduce the pressure to as little as 35 pounds and still clean fragile parts without damage. The key is using a large nozzle and holding it at an angle to quickly strip away material.

time for the stripper to work into the paint layer before scraping it off with a putty knife, steel wool, or a special pad. Don't be in too big of a hurry. If you start scraping the paint off too soon, you'll remove the stripper before it has a chance to work deeper. Even then, it may be necessary to apply more stripper as undercoats are exposed.

Once you've stripped away all the loose paint and exposed bare metal, it's important that you neutralize any stripper material that remains with plenty of clean water. If you haven't used it to this point, fine steel wool or a fine-grade cleaning pad works well to remove any paint particles. The material will hold enough water to help dilute the stripper at the same time.

The final step, after all paint and stripper residue have been removed, is to dry the surface and wipe it down with a quality wax and grease remover. If the surface isn't going to be coated with a filler primer or another type of primer for immediate painting, you should finish it off with a coat of epoxy primer to prevent any rust from forming on the bare surface.

If you can find someone to do it for you, another good way to strip paint from sheet metal parts is to dip them in a caustic soda bath. A lye solution has the added benefit of removing any grease that may be on a part. You may need to check around with some of the automotive repair shops or tractor or auto restorers to find someone in your area that specializes in this type of service. Don't try to do it yourself, even if you find a lye-based paint remover recipe on the Internet. Lye can burn skin and clothing just as quickly and easily as acid. It just happens to be on the other end of the pH spectrum. If you do take the parts to a professional paint stripper, it's still important that you rinse and dry each of the parts once you get them back and then coat them with an epoxy primer as soon as possible.

Repairing Sheet Metal

Once you have all the paint off, the first thing you're going to notice are all the dents, dings, scratches, and rust spots that need to be filled in or repaired. You may even have to splice in one or two pieces of sheet metal, create a new bracket, or in the worst-case scenario, fabricate a whole new sheet metal section.

Unless you're on a tight budget or enjoy seeing how far you can go on your own, it might be easier and more productive to purchase a new component from one of the many suppliers listed in the appendix. The exception, of course, would be the part on a rare model that is simply not available.

Dents and Creases

Let's start with the dents and creases. If a dent or crease is more than 3/16 to 1/4 inch deep, it's best to smooth it out with a body repairman's hammer and dolly. Do not fill it in with body putty. Bondo might be fine for automotive repairs, but the vibration that is inherent with tractor operation can cause body putty to pop right out of a deep dent and leave you with an ugly hole that will require more work and a new coat of paint.

If there aren't a lot of dents in the sheet metal, you might be able to get by with a ball-peen hammer and a mallet or large hammer to back up the piece. The thing you have to keep in mind is that the original metal was stretched as the dent was created; hence, you may have to shrink it as it is straightened. One way to do that is to heat the spot with an oxygen-acetylene torch before beating out the dent.

Another technique, particularly if you are trying to remove a sharp crease, is to drill a series of small holes (approximately 1/16 inch in diameter) along the crease. This will allow the metal to shift as it goes back into place. The holes can be filled later with epoxy or plastic putty.

Repairing Holes and Rust Areas

In some cases, you may need to cut out an old piece of metal and weld in a new piece. First, remove all the paint from the area to be worked, if you haven't already done so. Make a clean cut around the damaged area so you have removed all the bad metal and have left a clean, solid edge. It's important that you cut beyond the damage because when you take the pieces to a welder or do the work yourself, any thin, pitted surfaces will self-destruct. You'll also want to remove the section in a shape that will be easy to reproduce. A square section with clean right angles works best.

Find a scrap piece of sheet metal that is the same thickness or gauge as the original piece. The biggest mistake people make at this stage is using a slightly thicker or thinner replacement piece. You may also want to trace the hole you have created onto a piece of cardboard and make yourself a template. This will be particularly helpful when you go to cut out the new

Your local auto parts supplier can direct you to everything you'll need to fill and cover minor imperfections. Remember that body filler or Bondo should not be used to correct deep dents or creases.

piece. If necessary, bend the new piece to match the contour of the hood, grille, or fender where it is being installed. Clamp or tape the new piece into position and tack weld it in place. Finish welding around the splice and be careful not to heat the area to the point it warps or disfigures the sheet metal. You'll want to hide as much of the weld as possible. Some restorers use a series of spot welds around the patch and fill in the seam with body putty a little later. Throughout the process, be careful not to set the welder at too high a temperature and burn through the sheet metal you're trying to repair.

To complete the patch, grind the welds down to remove any high spots and fill the area with J-B Weld, body filler, or Bondo. This will also fill any rust pits and gaps that have been left. Once the filler has hardened, you can sand it down to the point where the patch is flush with the clean sheet metal, using finer sandpaper to finish the surface.

If you're dealing with rather small holes, you can often get by with putting a piece of fiberglass cloth on the back side of the cavity and filling it with Bondo, fiberglass, or body filler. It may take several thin coats before you get the hole filled to surface level. At that point, you can sand and treat it just as you would any other patch.

CHAPTER 16

Primer and Paint

Regardless of how good of a job you did on restoration and repairs to this point, the first thing people are going to notice on your restored tractor is the paint job. Small imperfections may not even be visible at this point, but rest assured, once they're covered with a coat of paint, they will show up like neon lights. Consequently, it's important to take your time and do it right. The first step is to lay down a foundation of primer, followed by multiple coats of enamel. Before you do that, it's important that you make sure the surface is clean, especially the sheet metal. If you haven't already done so, wipe down all sheet metal surfaces with a wax and grease remover solution prior to painting. Once the surface is dry, follow that with a tack rag. Try not to touch the metal any more than you have to. Even the oil on your hands can affect the way the paint adheres.

Applying the Primer and Paint

If you're like most restorers, you can't wait to get the tractor assembled and get started painting, but try to restrain yourself. You'll achieve the best results and have the easiest time painting your tractor if it is still disassembled. That means you should look at priming and painting individual sections of sheet metal, as well as the frame and engine, separately whenever possible. Most restorers also prefer to paint the wheels with the tires removed, rather than masking them, to avoid the potential for overspray on the rubber. Make sure the paint has had plenty of time to cure before remounting the tires, and be ready to touch up any blemishes.

By leaving as many parts off the tractor as possible, you also have the opportunity to paint both sides of a piece in one session. Components like the seat, grille, battery box, and so on can be hung on wire hooks and coated on all surfaces without having to let one side dry first.

The Primer Coat

Once the body and frame have been cleaned and prepared and the sheet metal has been stripped, smoothed, and filled as necessary, it's time to apply a quality coat of primer. Some restorers recommend applying a coat of etch primer immediately after the tractor frame has been cleaned, even if it won't be painted for a while. According to Gary Ledford, a paint technician with Autobody Color in St. Joseph, Missouri, bare metal can begin to rust in as little as four hours. A coat of etch primer on bare metal not only helps prevent rust, but makes it easier to clean away any grease or oil before you add additional primer coats or the paint coat.

The primer stage also gives you the opportunity to take care of a lot of the imperfections that may remain after most of the bodywork has been completed. By putting on two or three coats of primer and sanding between each coat, you can easily fill a lot of pits and crevices.

Choosing the Right Primer Type

There are a number of different types of primers that can be used to prepare, fill, or seal the surface prior to the final coat of paint. Each has its own unique role and application; for example, whereas epoxy primers protect components from new rust, urethane primers tend to form a harder finish. When choosing, you need to ensure that the primer you select is not only compatible with any paint that remains on the tractor or engine, but also with the paint you have selected to finish the project. Ledford explains that the type of primer you start with depends to some extent on the type of finish you're covering: old paint, bare metal, or cast iron.

Epoxy Primers

If you're shooting primer over bare metal or cast iron that could be exposed to the weather before you get it covered with additional primer, Ledford generally

The best resources for determining the original colors of the various components are vintage photographs found in Ford tractor literature, since other restorers have occasionally been wrong. Even though the color scheme on the 8N model is similar to the color scheme of the Golden Jubilee/NAA and Hundred Series, for example, there are minor differences: The dash on the 8N is red and not gray like on the NAA pictured here.

recommends an epoxy or self-etch-type primer. This is particularly the case with parts of the frame or cast wheels that have been sandblasted and are in no need of further work or sanding.

Epoxy is the easiest to use because it combines the qualities of a metal etch, a primer surfacer, and a primer sealer in one product. A self-etching primer, on the other hand, is basically a phosphoric-acid-type etch. Self-etching primers have to have another primer over the top of them, Ledford adds. It can't be an epoxy primer, but it can be a urethane primer. You cannot paint directly onto a self-etching primer because the paint won't adhere. That's why painters generally recommend that tractor restorers go over bare finishes with an epoxy primer since it will give you a more durable finish and etch aluminum and metal in one shot.

Epoxy primer can be used in one of two ways. It can be used as a primer-sealer, where you spray it on, wait 15 to 20 minutes, and start top coating with your color. Or it can be used as a primer-surfacer to cover minor flaws in the surface. In this case, you will want to put down two to three coats, give it 15 to 20 minutes between coats, and wait at least six hours before sanding the surface.

Finally, epoxy primer can be sprayed over the top of old lacquer paint, which was often used on older tractors, without a problem. It is a good idea, however, to seal the original lacquer to be sure the two surfaces remain compatible. It is not recommended that you ever put lacquer on top of enamel.

"We have one epoxy primer in our inventory that can go right over a partially painted surface or bare metal," Ledford explains. "Then, you can either paint

One of the requirements for a good paint job is a quality paint gun and a compressor with adequate capacity. One of the newest types of applicators is the high-volume, low-pressure (HVLP) gun, which helps conserve paint and reduce vaporization.

A number of tractor painters still prefer a siphon-type paint gun, in part because it can hold more paint or be connected to a paint pot. As long as it is a quality unit, it can do just as good a job as newer paint systems.

over it when it dries or wait up to seven days to apply a top coat. The best part is it gives you a seven-day window to finish the job before it becomes necessary to resand it."

Urethane Primers

Although urethane primers are very popular with restorers due to their hard finish, they do not include any kind of chemical agent to prevent rusting. It fact, if you put a urethane filler primer over bare metal, it soaks up the moisture and the metal will begin to rust beneath the paint. You therefore either need to ensure that the surface is completely free of rust before you apply a urethane primer, or you need to lay down a coat of epoxy primer or etching primer and put the urethane over it. If you do not, you may find rust popping through the surface four or five months down the road.

Since urethane is only a primer-surfacer, you'll also need to apply a sealer of some kind before you paint. A coat of epoxy primer over the top will serve the purpose. Plus, a coat of epoxy will serve to bridge any scratches in the urethane that have been left after sanding and leave a smooth surface for the top-coat color.

The only thing you shouldn't do with urethane is put it under a top-color coat of lacquer. Since lacquer seems to be on its way out, the use of lacquer as a top coat isn't covered in this book.

Lacquer Primers

Just like lacquer paint, lacquer primers are pretty much outdated. Although lacquer primers air dry fairly quickly, they tend to shrink for days and weeks after they have been applied. As a result, the primer can shrink for up to a month under any coat of paint that has been applied too early.

"If you use lacquer primer, it's best to let it set for at least a week, minimum, before you even do anything with it," says Ledford. "And that's under perfect drying conditions, say 70 degrees or above; otherwise, you can start to see sanding scratches show up where it pulled away under the paint." If you do use a lacquer primer, Ledford recommends putting an epoxy or urethane type primer over it before moving on to a top coat.

Filler Primers

For complete coverage of any imperfections, you might want to follow the lead of several tractor restorers and use a filler primer, heavy-bodied primer, or high-build primer on top of the etch primer or epoxy primer. No matter what you call it, a filler primer is

All Ford tractors were painted solid gray until 1948, when Ford split from Ferguson and introduced the 8N with its red and gray paint scheme.

Whether it's because the previous owners preferred the brighter colors of the 8N or wanted it to look like an 8N, you'll find more 9N and 2N tractors that are painted red and gray than only gray.

basically formulated to fill in any pits in the surface from sanding or rust even quicker than an epoxy primer alone. As one restorer put it, filler primer is little more than a liquid body filler.

Although some tractor enthusiasts use fine-grit sandpaper, such as a No. 240 grit, to smooth the surface between coats of primer, others say they apply one coat of primer over the next, once it's had time to dry. On the last sanding before painting, you'll want to use an even finer sheet, like No. 400 grit, if you're using enamel, and up to No. 600 for urethane. At the very least, you will have to sand the surface before applying a sealer and the top coat. Because it has the texture to fill pits and imperfections in the sheet metal, an unsanded primer coat would be too rough to paint over without further preparation.

It's important to note that any urethane primer will need a sealer coat before the top coat of color is applied. In general, you can apply one coat of primer every 7 to 10 minutes or when the first coat is dry to the touch. After the last coat, wait about three hours before sanding.

Some show-tractor enthusiasts have been known to apply up to 15 coats of filler primer on a sheet metal part that has had a lot of work, in order to get a glass-smooth surface. Between every 3 coats, they use long sanding boards to smooth the finish. This helps prevent high and low spots from being formed by the sander.

Another trick used by some body specialists is to switch between different colors of compatible primers so they can better identify hills and valleys in the finish. Be sure to finish with finer grades of sandpaper and ultimately end up with wet sanding paper.

One of the beneficial characteristics of a urethane filler primer is the fact that when you sand it, the material will actually reflow and close up. Urethane primers are usually 1 to 3 millimeters thick per pass, Ledford explains, noting that one of his brands averages 2.5 millimeters per pass. If you go around the tractor three times, you've got 7.5 millimeters of primer on there; whereas most new cars have about 7 millimeters total, including all primers and paints. In the end, you'll have a thicker, tougher finish that will last for years.

Sealing Primers

The final step before applying a coat of paint should be to apply a coat of sealing primer, or sealer, as it's more commonly called. This closes the surface and prepares it to accept a coat of paint. It does this in two ways. It helps minimize sand scratch swelling, which can make sand scratches more visible under the top coat. This is particularly important if you used a filler primer. If the sand marks aren't sealed, the paint solvent can cause the sand scratches to swell. As solvents evaporate, paint solids fill the voids in the surface and leave a microscopic series of hills and valleys, which results in a dull finish. In contrast, a coat of sealer provides a uniform base that, in turn, leads to uniform paint distribution and solvent evaporation.

As mentioned earlier, the sealer also acts as a barrier to protect the undercoat primers from any reaction with the top coat. Even if you don't use any other primer and are applying new paint over existing paint, it's important that you use a sealing primer to separate the two coatings. As has been mentioned more than once already, enamel and urethane paint are totally incompatible with any lacquer-based paint or primer. If there's any doubt about what kind of primer to use at any stage of the painting process, it's best to discuss it with your paint supplier or refer to the application

You'll find several different kinds of primers on the market, including filler primers and those that are self-etching. Your paint supplier can help you select the best type for your needs and application, along with the paint types that are compatible with the primer.

There's not much to mask off when you have the tractor stripped down to the point that everything is painted red or, in the case of a N9 or 2N, gray. *Dallas Mercer*

The first step in painting the tractor is applying a quality primer as soon as possible after the surface has been properly prepared. This is especially important since bare metal can begin to rust in as little as four hours. *Dallas Mercer*

guides and/or information sheets that are available for the products you plan to use. Before you apply any primer or sealer, use a tack cloth a second time to get the surface extra clean. You don't want to seal in any dirt or sanding dust.

The Color Coat

If you think all Ford tractors were gray, the first thing you need to do is brush up on your Ford tractor history. It's true that the Ford Ferguson 9N and 2N were entirely gray, but that all changed in 1948 when Ford and Ferguson parted ways and Ford introduced the 8N. It is often referred to as the "red belly" because of its red frame and lighter gray sheet metal. In the meantime, Ferguson continued with the same dark gray color on his own TE-20. As outlined in Chapters 1 and 2, which discuss Ford tractor history and model designations, later Ford models included various combinations of red and gray, followed by combinations of blue and gray.

If your goal is authenticity, it's important that you use the correct shade of gray. Don't assume the current paint job on the tractor you have is correct. It's amazing to see how many Ford 9N and 2N tractors have been repainted red and gray to look like an 8N. Perhaps it's because the 8N has become so popular in recent years or the owners thought the solid gray

color was dull and boring. The bottom line is, you're free to paint the tractor any way you want. The goal of this book is to tell you how and point out what is authentic.

If you look at suppliers, such as Dennis Carpenter or N-Complete, you'll find the two different gray paints listed as dark gray and medium gray. There's usually a cross reference to tell you which one should be used on your particular tractor; the dark gray, or vintage gray, as it is sometimes called, is for 1939 to 1947 models (9N and 2N models), while the medium gray is for 8N, NAA, and later models up through 1964. At this point, Ford went to a light gray paint that was used on tractors from 1965 on.

As for the red paint, there were two different paint colors used over the years. The Vermillion red was used from 1948 to 1957 on the 8N, 600, and 800 models. In 1958, Ford switched to a lighter shade of red, often called vintage red. This was used on the 601 and 801 models produced from 1958 to 1961. To add even more confusion, there was a Dearborn red that was primarily used on implements. Unfortunately, some vendors don't even break it down by application, year, or name. They simply list it as Ford tractor red and new tractor red and leave you to figure out which is the correct tone. John Smith, a Ford 8N enthusiast from Peoria, Illinois, insists that even the Ford red

One or more color coats should finish off the frame on this 8N owned by Chris Mercer. *Dallas Mercer*

that is sold at the Ford/New Holland dealership as the correct color is too orange for the 8N (Vermillion) red paint. The New Holland dealers sell only the Ford red that was correct for the 1958 and up tractors. It's not correct for the 8N and NAA, Smith insists, but they don't differentiate.

"It seems that everybody's Ford tractor red is different," he says. " In fact, good luck finding two restorers who can agree on the correct shades of either gray or red. I can tell you what I use, but someone else may tell you it's wrong," he admits. "I've matched several good samples of the original 8N blood red from inside the air cleaner, behind the running board brackets, etc. I tried to match it up with a ready-made formula so as to have a uniform color that I could buy off the shelf, rather than custom mix each time I needed some. What I finally came up with that is a very good match with the original paint, is DuPont Centari C8508 (single stage). It is a General Motors red from the mid-1980s. For the gray, I use PPG Delstar DAR 31657. This is listed in the old Ditzler books as Ford tractor gray, but in my opinion, it's very close to the original medium gray color."

Other sources list TISCO as a good source of colors, citing TP240 as the number for medium gray and TP310 as the code for red. The TISCO website also lists TP2888 as the part number for dark gray for 9N and 2N models. On the other hand, it lists two different reds. One is the TP240 for Ford red and the other is TP2822 for Vermillion red. Dennis Carpenter also carries TISCO paint that is already mixed and listed as the appropriate color by year and model. Other sources of paint include N-Complete, Tractor Parts Inc., and Valu-Bilt. Last but not least, you can visit any automotive paint supplier and find a match. The paint technician can either use the numbers previously listed to cross-reference a number in the catalog or use a computer-based machine called a color eye or color spectrometer to determine the color. Not every paint outlet will have one, but if you can find a professional paint store that does, it's simply a matter of finding a piece of sheet metal that hasn't faded over the years and having the technician take a color reading scan. This information is downloaded to a computer that interprets the color and displays the appropriate paint formula.

Painting a tractor is much easier if you have the room or time to spread out the parts and paint them individually. They can then be arranged for quick access during assembly.

PAINT NUMBER BY SUPPLIER

	DuPont	TISCO	PPG	Martin Senour
Modern Dark Blue	29509	N/A	12908	N/A
Ford Gray	29665	N/A	31657	N/A
Empire Blue	27863D	TP360	N/A	N/A
Industrial Yellow	N/A	TP760	N/A	N/A
Light Gray	N/A	TP330	N/A	99L3732
Medium Gray	N/A	TP240	N/A	N/A
Red	RS465	TP310	70075	99L4338

Selecting the Right Paint Type

Just as you did with the primer, you'll need to decide what kind of paint you want to use on the tractor. While some restorers prefer acrylic enamel, others opt for the new polyurethane finishes. According to Jim Seward, there are basically three types of paint in use today. As he relates, they include implement or synthetic enamel, acrylic enamel, and urethane as a single stage top coat or base coat/clear coat.

Although lacquer was often used in the past, Seward and others say it is a thing of the past for a number of reasons, including the fact that the solvent vaporizes very rapidly and does not withstand exposure to fuel spills and chemicals, as well as other types of finishes. Lacquers also tend to dry to a dull finish and must be buffed to bring out a shine. Lacquers are the most photochemically reactive, which means they fade over time when exposed to sunlight, though newer acrylic lacquers offer improved ultraviolet radiation protection.

Implement or Synthetic Enamel Paints

Jim Seward describes implement enamel paints as anything that comes in a can from the equipment dealership or farm store. This includes many of the paints available through tractor parts supply houses. Even the TISCO paints mentioned earlier are listed as industrial enamel. That doesn't mean these paints are a poor choice. There are literally hundreds of Ford tractors in the country that have been restored with paint purchased through the Ford/New Holland dealership.

"The one good thing about these is the price," Seward says. "They're a lot less expensive than either the acrylic enamel or a base coat/clear coat. Unfortunately, they don't have near as much gloss and the chemical bond often isn't as good."

Acrylic Enamel Paints

Perhaps the most popular paint type these days is acrylic enamel, since it is available in a broad range of colors, which allows it to be custom mixed to match virtually any tractor color. In addition, acrylic enamel is relatively forgiving and requires minimal surface preparation. The downside is it takes a little longer to dry and must be applied in multiple light coats to keep it from running. It also costs about twice as much as implement enamel.

According to Gary Ledford, with Autobody Color in St. Joseph, Missouri, another characteristic of acrylic enamel is that it dries from the outside in. This means that the underneath side of the coat is still porous for quite some time. As a result, if you spray back over it too soon, the new coat will work its way under the top layer and cause it to lift or wrinkle. Unlike lacquer, which air dries, enamel paints dry and adhere through a chemical process.

For that reason, both he and Seward recommend the use of a hardener, which causes the coat to dry from the inside out and allows recoats without a lift problem. The next coat can be applied as soon as the first coat is dry to the touch. In addition, an acrylic hardener will increase the gloss and provide a more durable finish. Adding a hardener has the negative effect of reducing the pot life of the mixed paint. In

If you're painting a tractor indoors, which offers better protection from dust and debris in the air, make sure you have adequate ventilation.

the case of enamel, the pot life goes from about 24 hours without hardener to about 4 hours once the hardener has been added.

Urethane Paints

Urethane paints, which are actually part of the enamel family, are becoming popular. Among the reasons for their popularity are the fast drying time compared with acrylic enamel and the durability and luster that accompany the hard finish. On the other hand, urethane paints are not available in nearly as many colors as acrylic enamels.

Ledford notes that there are basically two types of urethane in use. Perhaps the most common is single-stage urethane. Like acrylic enamels, single-stage urethanes don't need to be clear coated, although both single-stage urethanes and acrylic enamels can be clear coated for additional shine and protection. In the absence of a clear coat, at least three coats of single-stage urethane are generally recommended.

The other type of urethane finish is a base coat with a clear-coat finish, which is what most of the automotive manufacturers use on all new vehicles. In effect, less pigment can often be used to lay down a color and the gloss comes from the clear coats that go over it. As a result, base coat finishes require at least two to three coats of clear coat for both protection and shine. Ledford generally recommends three coats of base color and a minimum of two clear coats.

"The one thing about a base coat/clear coat finish is it's easier to correct mistakes than it is with a solid coating," Ledford explains. "If you get a run or some other imperfection, you can just wait for it to dry, sand out the mistake, hit the area with another light coat of color to cover the area, and clear coat the entire panel. As long as the color coat is smooth and even, you're ready to go on, since the gloss comes from the clear coat."

Ledford cautions that you need to allow enough time for the last color coat to dry completely before starting on the clear coat. Since the reducer in the mixture basically evaporates as the paint dries, the reducer needs to be completely gone before the clear coat goes on. If it is not, you can end up with what is referred to as solvent pop in the clear coat, which is essentially little bubbles formed by leftover reducer vapors trying to escape through the clear sealer.

Ledford says he has often seen tractor restorers use both types on the same tractor. Generally, they'll start with a single-stage urethane on the frame and engine, then switch to a base coat/clear coat on the sheet metal. Others use an enamel on the frame and cast-iron components and switch to an acrylic enamel or urethane for the sheet metal.

In Seward's opinion, a base coat followed by a clear coat provides the best gloss of any paint coat. It's also one of the most expensive, which means it's often reserved for museum-quality restorations.

Make sure the paint or primer is well mixed before you pour it into the paint gun reservoir. You may even want to pour it through a filter if there are any clumps in the mixture. Always wear the necessary mask and protective clothing while applying primer and paint.

A respirator approved for use with organic mists is one of the most important pieces of equipment when painting a tractor. Remember that paint fumes are not only hazardous to your health, but they are also flammable.

Unfortunately, a base coat/clear coat finish is also very susceptible to scratches.

"You wouldn't want to just take a rag to a tractor that's been collecting dust at a tractor show," he relates. "You'd see hundreds of tiny scratches in the clear coat the next time you looked across the hood in the sunlight."

A better alternative, Seward believes, is to wet sand a coat of acrylic enamel and buff it with polishing compound. "You can get nearly the same amount of gloss," he says. "It's just a lot more work and you have all the edges to contend with."

Jeff Gravert, a full-time tractor restorer from Clay Center, Nebraska, notes, "Wet sanding and buffing may take a little bit off the depth of the paint layer, but it takes out any flaws and it gets rid of any imperfections."

The one thing you won't get an argument about is the durability of a urethane finish. According to everyone who has used urethane compared to acrylic, the former is more resistant to both fading and chipping, yet it's nearly as easy to apply as acrylic enamel.

Ensuring Compatibility

As a final step in paint and primer selection, it's important that you ensure the compatibility of all the products you plan to use, including the primer, paint, reducer, hardener, and clear-coat protectant. One tractor restorer experienced the frustration of having to repaint a hood and grille three times because the paint bubbled as it dried. After several attempts to figure out the problem, he finally traced it to the hardener, which was either bad or incompatible with the paint he was using.

"We recommend that you stay within the brand that you are shooting to ensure compatibility," says Ledford. "Just like everything else, there are off-brands that will work. But we don't generally recommend them because if there is a problem, then you've got everybody passing the blame. If you're within the brand, you know everything has been tested in the lab for compatibility, and unless you've made a mistake, the company has to stand behind it." The bottom line is it's not worth the risk in terms of time and paint cost to try and save a little money on the hardener or sealer.

These sheet metal parts have had at least one coat of primer applied and are ready for the color coat.

Painting Equipment

Selecting the right paint for your tractor is one thing. Gathering the right equipment to protect yourself while completing the task is quite another. In the long run, the latter is really the most important. At the least, protective equipment should include rubber gloves, protective clothing, and an approved respirator or mask.

To be safe, use a respirator approved for organic mists, which is the type labeled for use with pesticides. While a charcoal-filter mask may be sufficient for enamel paint, urethane coatings and acrylic enamels to which a hardener has been added contain chemicals known as isocyanates, which are especially toxic. The use of urethane therefore requires a fresh-air mask and painting suit, or a charcoal mask and a fully ventilated environment.

Remember that paint, thinners, and solvents are highly flammable, particularly when atomized by an air-powered spray gun. Be sure the area is free of any open sources of ignition and keep a fire extinguisher nearby.

Make sure your air compressor and paint gun are adequate for the job. Many beginner restorers still use a siphon-type gun that siphons the paint out of a canister or cup and draws it into the air stream. If you want to spend about twice the price for a new gun, you can move up to a high-volume, low-pressure painting (HVLP) unit. This type of gun feeds the paint

These wheels and fenders have been painted with two to three coats of acrylic enamel and are ready to be mounted back on the chassis.

directly into the air stream, which tends to save paint and generate fewer vapors. Regardless of what type of paint gun you use, make sure your compressor will provide enough air capacity and that you have enough hose to move freely around the tractor.

As a final note, Jim Seward says he likes to make a paint booth around the project with drop cloth or plastic sheeting. The plastic not only keeps paint from drifting away from the area, but the plastic holds enough static electricity to attract dust and spray that could negatively affect the paint coat.

Adjust the Spray Pattern

It's important that you adjust both the spray mixture and the spray pattern before you start. One can affect the other. In general, several thin coats of paint are better than one or two thick ones. On the other hand, if you get the paint too thin, it can have a dusty appearance that reduces gloss and shine. To attain the right consistency, you'll need to add thinner or reducer. Your paint supplier will tell you that these two components do basically the same thing; they improve the spray pattern and the paint's ability to evenly coat the surface. They're usually referred to as thinners when used with lacquers and reducers when used with enamels,

including urethane products. Even though they may do the same thing, they're certainly not the same product. We can probably all remember using paint thinner to clean brushes or fix mistakes with glue or paint. Paint reducers, however, are formulated specifically for acrylic enamels and urethanes and don't offer crossover applications. Seward adds that reducers also come in different speeds to match the size of the job and the temperature.

Whatever you do, don't use gasoline in place of a reducer or thinner, even though some people have done so. It's not safe and any money you save won't be worth the risk to the quality of the end product, not to mention your own safety.

Once you have attained a mixture that sprays smoothly and evenly, adjust the nozzle to spray an oval that is approximately 3 inches by 6 inches at about a 1-foot distance. When painting large areas, spray around the edges first and finish up by filling in the center. Concentrate on moving the gun in a back-and-forth motion to produce a smooth, even coat.

As with many things in life, practice makes perfect. If you don't have much experience with painting, start by practicing on a few scrap pieces of metal. Most restorers and paint suppliers recommend at least two

Because they have the tractors custom painted off the premises, the staff at N-Complete built a set of carts to haul the remanufactured chassis between the facility and the nearby paint shop.

to three coats of paint, although some use up to five or six on sheet metal for extra durability and shine. One tractor restorer, who specializes in museum-quality restorations, applies at least seven coats of enamel on sheet metal and puts one coat on right after the other. After he finishes the last coat, he lets it cure for three or four days, then wet sands all sheet metal with No. 1200–grit sandpaper and stays clear of any edges. Finally, he applies the decals and sprays clear coat over both the paint and the decals to produce a gleaming shine. Any cast parts receive only paint to avoid a glossy, unnatural appearance.

Make sure the timing between coats is sufficient, particularly if you're using an enamel without a hardener. Most paint coatings or your paint supplier will provide some kind of guidance, so follow the recommendations.

Some restorers like to finish off the sheet metal with clear coat, while others prefer the look of hand-buffed enamel.

CHAPTER 17

Decals, Emblems, and Nameplates

When it comes to decals, the good news is they have never been easier to apply or easier to find. The interest in antique tractor restoration, coupled with advances in computer graphics technology, has seen to that.

The reproduction decal business started when a few collectors commissioned a printer to produce a set of decals they couldn't locate. Soon they found there was a demand for the product and began selling the decals to other collectors. Using modern scanning technology, decal manufacturers are now able to produce decals from drawings, literature, operating manuals, and even pencil rubbings.

The other thing that has changed is the type of decals available. At one time, almost all of the decals on the market were the water-transfer type, similar to the ones we used to apply on plastic airplane models. After soaking them in water, the backing paper was slipped off and the decal was applied and left to dry.

Don't forget about the small instructional decals that were a vital part of the original model. It's important to know which ones were used and where, since decal kits often apply to several tractor models and include extra decals.

Although the 9N and 2N didn't have any decals on the hood to identify the model, they did use water-transfer decals on certain components like the air cleaner, oil filter, and PTO. Unfortunately, water-transfer decals have a limited shelf life since they tend to crack easily. They also begin to weather and crack very quickly after they have been applied to the tractor. If your preference is for originality, though, there are still water-transfer decals available through suppliers like Dennis Carpenter. (Dennis Carpenter also has the modern, peel-back-type decals available.)

Most of the decals sold and used today are the peel-back type that are generally made by screen printing onto Mylar plastic. With this type of decal, you remove the backing paper, which protects the adhesive; carefully press the decal into position; and remove the front layer of paper that protects the letter surface.

Vinyl-cut decals are equally popular. Unlike the Mylar decals, vinyl-cut decals are sandwiched between two layers of protective paper. Since each letter or number is individually cut out of vinyl, the paper on the back protects the adhesive, while the paper on the front holds each of the letters in place as they're being applied. Unfortunately, vinyl-cut decals are often a one-shot deal without any chance for adjustment since the letters are all separate from each other.

Researching Decal Originality and Placement

Before you get started with any type of decal, it's important to have the right tools and the right information. You may think you know where all the decals go, but even experienced restorers have been fooled at times; for example, one might think that the

Although Ford didn't use a lot of decals over the years, those that are needed are available from a number of sources, including Dennis Carpenter and N-Complete, whose inventory is shown here.

Proofmeter decal would go near or on the dash near the Proofmeter. Instead, it goes under the cowl lid on models equipped with the meter.

One final warning from experienced Ford restorers is to be careful when buying a package of decals that includes logos and lettering for more than one tractor model. If there are extra decals in the package, people often feel like they need to use all of them.

Paint or Decal?

One of the cosmetic changes that occurred in 1948, when Ford introduced its own Model 8N was the Ford insignia embossed into the hood. Not only was the lettering raised, but it was painted red to contrast with the lighter gray hood. In 1950, at serial number 273178, the Ford script was also embossed into the rear fenders. At the time of manufacture, the letters in both cases were highlighted with a hard paint roller. This trend continued through the NAA models and carried well into the numbered series tractors.

Today's Ford tractor restorers have a choice on how best to apply the red coating. If you peruse the parts catalogs or websites, you find that several companies offer a painting mask for both the hood and the fenders that can be placed over the script for painting the letters. Some of those same companies, plus several others, also offer a set of die-cut decals. You can read more about die-cut vinyl decals below, but suffice to say that each letter or series is individually cut to lay right on top of the raised lettering.

Whether you use the painting mask or decal is up to you. Some claim the mask is hard to use and requires an experienced hand to make it look good. The die-cut decals don't leave much room for error either, since they need to be started right to lay correctly.

Most experienced Ford show tractor restorers feel the best way to apply the red painted highlight to the raised hood and fender script is to get a professional

 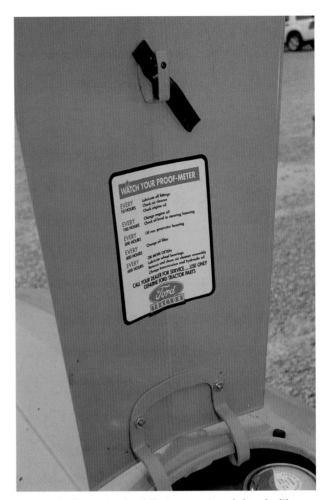

Most name and number decals intended for the hood are now made from vinyl, while instructional decals, like those pictured here, are still made from mylar and may need to be treated differently.

sign painter to hand letter it with a paintbrush. A good sign painter with a steady hand can easily do the raised lettering in just a few minutes and make it look far better than the decal or a stencil paint job. They insist the result is usually well worth the cost.

Tools and Supplies

In one respect, applying decals is no different than overhauling the engine. You need the right tools and supplies before you start. These should include a roll of paper towels; a clean, soft cotton towel; a roll of masking tape or drafting tape; and a rubber or plastic squeegee (you can find these in most craft, automotive, and wallpaper supply stores). A sponge may also be helpful. Plus, you might want to have a pair of tweezers handy for holding the edge of smaller decals. If you're using Mylar decals, you'll also need a water tray for wetting the decals before they are applied.

Surface Preparation

The surface needs to be thoroughly dry before decals can be applied. If you are applying Mylar decals to any painted surfaces, you need to be sure the paint has cured. Depending on the climate in which you live, this could be anywhere from a week to a month after the tractor has been painted. If a hardener was used in the paint, you may need to wait even longer to make sure the paint isn't going to give off gas bubbles under the decal. Unlike vinyl decals that have the ability to breathe, Mylar is impermeable to air and gas bubbles. Any bubbles that form under the decal after application will stay there. The paint surface must be smooth and absolutely clean. If there are any pits or surface imperfections, the decal may not adhere properly. Finally, make sure your hands are clean.

You need to make sure the room temperature is within a comfortable range. Decals don't do well

The first step in decal replacement is determining the correct location, which is often done by measuring the distance from a certain seam or sheet metal edge. It helps if you took these measurements before you stripped off the old decals.

when the air temperature or metal is too cold. If you're applying vinyl decals on a hot surface or under a bright sun, they can get too warm and stretch as you're trying to stick them in place and smooth them out. The shop should be between around 60 and 90 degrees Fahrenheit to ensure that the decals correctly adhere.

Decal Application

Now that everything is ready, the first step is to hold the decal in the proper location and mark the edges with a piece of tape. You should be able to see the actual decal outline, even if it does have a protective film on each side. A few pieces of tape to mark the bottom edge and a piece of tape on one or both ends will give you reference points.

At this point, it's simply a matter of peeling off the backing and applying the numbers or lettering

to the tractor. There are still a few tips that will make the job easier, depending on which type of decal you are applying.

Mylar Decals

If you're using Mylar decals, you might want to be like many veteran restorers and make sure your hands and tools are clean and wet. This will help keep the decal from sticking to surfaces it's not supposed to.

Some restorers, like Jim Seward, like to use a spray bottle filled with water and a single drop of soap to spray the metal surface. In the meantime, fill a cake pan or similar-sized container with water and another drop of soap. Run the decal through the pan of water before placing it on the metal.

"The only purpose of the soap is to break the surface tension of the water, so you don't need much,"

There are several ways to treat the raised Ford logo on the hood and fenders of most N Series models. You can purchase a decal that applies to the top of the raised letters, use a stencil to paint them, or paint them free-hand. Some end up looking better than others and some people avoided the issue and painted over the top of them.

The best paint and decal job in the world will lack something if the emblem that adorns the grille is not restored or replaced.

Seward says. "It gives the water a sheeting action, instead of beading up."

Another option used by some restorers is to use window cleaner for the same purpose. Just be sure you use a formula that does not contain ammonia, as it can damage the paint and cause it to fade in sunlight. Use the form that comes in a pump-spray bottle. An aerosol can produces too many bubbles.

It may seem that the water or liquid is used so you can remove the decal or shift it around if you make a mistake. "And you can do that," Seward continues. "The main reason you should wet a Mylar decal is so you can more easily squeeze out all the air bubbles." Remember, Mylar doesn't breathe, so if there are any air bubbles under the decal once it dries, they're real tough to get out.

Once the decal is in the exact location you want it, use the squeegee to press the decal into place and remove any water and air bubbles. Start in the center and work outward, then use a soft cloth to dry the surface and remove any adhesive left on the surface.

Vinyl Decals

Unlike Mylar decals, vinyl decals can be applied almost immediately after painting, since the material will allow air and solvents to pass through it. Keep in mind that some decal kits will contain both vinyl and Mylar decals, so you will have to treat each accordingly.

When it comes to vinyl decals, some restorers mark the position with a few pieces of tape, peel off the backing, and stick the decals in position using the tape marks as a guide. There's another method that can save time and reduce the margin of error, especially when you're working with a long decal, such as the Powermaster decal that goes along the side of the hood.

To begin, place the decal in the correct position and tack it in place with a few pieces of tape. Once you have ensured it is in the right spot, run a piece of tape across the full length of the top. This piece of tape acts as a hinge for the decal. Next, remove the pieces of tape that acted as a temporary tack and leave only the top hinge. Now, all you have to do is lift up the decal, pull off the backing, and drop it back down into position. If you're working with a long decal that has a clear dividing line, you can sometimes cut it into two pieces, separating it between letters, so it's easier to work with. To finish it off, press the decal in place, remove the top protective paper, and smooth everything with a soft, dry cloth.

Seward says another option instead of cutting the decal is to securely tape a long decal in the middle and pull off the paper toward the ends. This allows you to handle long decals one-half at a time.

Don't worry if you have a few little bubbles this time. All you have to do is set the tractor out in the sun. The pores in the vinyl will open up and allow the air to permeate through the decal and leave a smooth surface. As stated earlier, don't try to apply the vinyl decals in the sun. They may stretch.

Clear Coat or Not?

Although some restorers like to finish off the decals with a shot of clear coat, others say they never put paint or clear coat over any kind of decal. For one thing, you have to know that the decal can take it and that the protectant won't cause it to lift off the surface. Water transfer decals can't take it.

Some decals have a tendency to yellow when covered with clear coat, even if the surface is better protected. Body shop owner B. J. Rosmolen, who has a business in St. Joseph, Missouri, says he never puts clear coat over any kind of decal or appliqué, including pin stripes on an automobile, simply because it's a lot easier to replace a decal in the future than it is to restore the paint finish.

If you happen to have problems with a decal, such as a letter being gouged, you can replace a single letter. But if you covered the decal with clear coat, that gloss

New or reproduction Ford and Ferguson System emblems make all the difference on this Ford 9N restoration.

is not going to be on the new letter. Plus, you're going to have a more difficult time getting it off.

The companies that supply the vinyl for decals don't always want to warranty the product if it's sprayed with clear coat. You can find plenty of restorers who have applied clear coat over decals without any problems. In the end, it appears the choice is up to you as the restorer and your willingness to take chances in the interest of appearance.

Emblems and Nameplates

For most companies, tractor identification was limited to a decal on the side of the hood. Only later when chrome became popular on automobiles did they add a nameplate or emblem on the tractor. Being an automobile manufacturer, however, Ford did things a little differently from the start. The first Ford tractor model, the 9N, had no model or manufacturer decal at all. The only thing to identify it as a Ford was its unique style for its time and the two-piece Ford and Ferguson system emblem set on the front of the hood. Unfortunately, both emblems are in a position where they can be easily damaged while working with a loader or when the owner bumped into something in the back of the machine shed. This became an even bigger issue in 1953, when Ford introduced the cyclops medallion on the Jubilee/NAA. The good news is that reproduction emblems are readily available, which means it's easier to find new emblems than to restore the original. It will look a lot better in the end. According to a couple of websites, the Ford/Ferguson system set will run you between $25 and $50, while a Jubilee or 800 medallion will cost you $50 or more.

Only the 1953 Jubilee model used the Jubilee hood emblem that listed the Ford Motor Company anniversary dates. The 1954 NAA uses a similar but different emblem that has stars around the outside. You'll need to check the cross-reference on the website or in the catalog to make sure you've selected the correct emblem for your model before placing any order. Naturally, the price depends on how elaborate the emblem is and whether it had chrome lettering, colored plastic, etc. An alternative is to check the Internet for an emblem from a salvaged tractor or find a salvage yard yourself. Unfortunately, if the tractor has a usable emblem, the rest of the machine is probably in good enough shape that the owner doesn't want to sell it.

The NAA Golden Jubilee sported a special Cyclops emblem that appeared on 1953 models only. Naturally, the Jubilee emblem is available through restoration parts vendors.

Data Plates and Serial Numbers

For most vintage tractor restorers, the serial number plate is an important piece of the tractor. Having a tractor with a low serial number is kind of like acquiring a limited-edition painting with a low number. Vintage Ford tractors unfortunately don't carry a separate serial number plate. The serial number is stamped into the engine block on all N Series models and early NAA models. It was moved to the left side of the transmission case on later NAA models. The serial number was moved to the flat area above and behind the starter on Hundred Series and newer tractors.

The problem for collectors is that if the engine was replaced at some time in the past, you may never know if you had one of the first or last models in the series. The exception would be if you located some of the unusual features,

To finish off a restoration, some restorers like to set off the serial number, especially if it's on a unique model, like the 1,310th Model 9N built in 1939.

like the starter button on the dash, that are found only on the 1939 models. If you were to find aluminum instead of steel under the paint on the hood, you'd know you "struck gold" with one of the first 600 to 700 9N tractors built.

Whether you know everything is original or not, it's important that you treat the serial number with a little bit of care. That would include being careful with the media blasting around that area of the engine or transmission and not going too heavy on the paint so that it remains readable.

There is one plate on all N Series models you might want to preserve, assuming it is in good shape. The patent data plate lists all the patents filed by Ford for the respective models. The plate is located on the dash panel on the 9N and 2N, and it is on the side of the battery box on 8N models. Hopefully you removed the plate before stripping the paint and repainting the box or dash panel. In most cases, you can bring it back to life with a good polishing with steel wool and a quality cleaner. If it's too damaged or you want it to look a lot better, keep in mind that there are reproductions available.

CHAPTER 18

The Fruits of Your Labor

It seems that the people who restore tractors do it for a number of reasons. In the case of Ford tractors, it's often to have a reliable work tractor, since a number of Ford tractors have been in use since the day they were built. Other restorers limit their hobby to restoring a desirable model and adding it to their collection. That's not as common with Ford tractors as it is with a brand like John Deere, Allis-Chalmers, or Oliver. Those companies built several different models over the years, starting as early as the 1920s, so it's not uncommon for some tractor restorers to finish one model, only to look at the next one in the series. For them, collecting antique tractors is not much different from collecting coins or stamps; just a little more expensive.

In contrast, Ford built only one model at a time until 1954, when the company began to offer a choice of horsepower levels. That's not to say that there aren't people who collect Ford tractors. There are plenty of enthusiasts who start off with an 8N, only to decide they have to have an older 9N and a 2N, and maybe a Jubilee or an NAA. Others look for unusual models, like a propane model, a 1939 9N, or a 2N that was issued with steel wheels. And what collector wouldn't like to have one of the Select-O-Speed demonstrator tractors that were painted gold and issued to dealers in 1959 to promote the new Select-O-Speed transmission?

Other restorers see restoration as only one step in the pastime. It's a means to an end, so to speak. These people see the finished tractor as an avenue to get more involved in the growing number of clubs, tractor shows, and antique tractor events that continue to sprout up in farm country and urban areas alike.

It is hoped that the process up to this point—that of turning a pile of greasy and rusty iron into a showpiece—has been fulfilling on its own. Still, there's nothing like the friendships that can be built when you get involved with a group of collectors that share your interests, frustrations, and challenges.

Antique Tractor Shows

Each year, tractor enthusiasts put together literally hundreds of antique tractor shows throughout the United States, Canada, and Europe. While some of them are sponsored by clubs and cater to a certain brand of tractor, others welcome all tractor brands and are open to both steam- and gasoline-powered

Tractor cruises, which can cover distances of 30 to 40 miles, have become an annual highlight for a number of Ford vintage tractor owners. In fact, most tractor cruises require that the tractor be over a certain age to participate.

models. One of the biggest Ford shows is the annual Ford/Fordson Collectors Association Show, which is held in a different location each year. Various state chapters of the Ford/Fordson Collectors Association hold their own shows or at least have a contingent at the local tractor shows. There are a number of antique

Whether it's displayed at the local fair or a national show, a well-restored tractor can be a source of pride for its owner.

tractor shows that have a featured brand or tractor each year. One year it may be Ford/Fordson models and the following year it's Allis-Chalmers or Farmall. That means that someplace and sometime, Ford tractors will be the featured brand at a show near you.

In many cases, you don't even have to take a fully restored model. Go to any one of the shows, and you're sure to see at least one or two tractors sitting in the lineup that run just fine, but haven't seen a new coat of paint since they left the factory.

What you will also see are groups of men and women sitting under the closest shade tree or portable canopy, sharing stories, and catching up on each others lives since the last time they all got together. To your benefit, many of them have tips to share about how they solved a particular problem or located a certain part. You'll find that you're not alone in the challenges you face as show participants share their stories.

If you're still in the process of restoring a particular model, a tractor show will often give you the opportunity to closely inspect an identical unit and ask questions of its owner. Assuming that person has

Tractor shows are a good place to find other models like your own and pick up tips and ideas from other collectors.

restored his tractor to original condition, there's nothing like physically examining the real thing to know what yours is supposed to look like.

If those aren't reasons enough to participate in a tractor show, consider that many shows feature a swap meet or flea market where you can purchase parts for various models of antique tractors. Some of the shows also feature field demonstrations, tractor parades, and tractor games in which you can participate.

Farm Equipment Demonstrations

As the interest in antique tractors has grown, so has the interest in antique farm implements and field demonstrations—and it's easy to see why. When you've got a vintage farm tractor that purrs like a kitten, it's hard to be content just driving it in parades or showing it off to friends. There's always the urge to put it to work in a nostalgic setting.

Many antique tractor shows now feature field demonstrations as part of the agenda. While many started off with plowing demonstrations, the list of activities has grown to include such things as threshing, baling,

shelling corn, cutting silage, and so on. Some will be stationary demonstrations that use the tractor's belt pulley to power the machine. Others are in the field, where antique tractors can be seen pulling implements that are appropriately matched for the time period and power requirements.

Whether you're watching or participating, it's important to remember one thing: Farm implements built in the early part of this century were not equipped with the safety features, nor the shields and guards found on today's equipment. Carelessness could cost a finger, arm, or a life at the blink of an eye. Keep your distance from working machines. If you're operating the equipment yourself or helping a friend, never attempt to make adjustments or clear out a crop slug without first shutting off the tractor. Remember that tractors of the past were never designed for passengers. A tractor fender is not a seat!

Tractor Games

Gather a bunch of antique tractor enthusiasts together and they're bound to come up with other ways to show

The parade of colors and/or models is a customary part of many tractor shows. Remember that open platform tractors were designed for only one occupant. Never carry extra passengers on the seat, platform, or fender.

off their tractors than just a parade of equipment or a series of field demonstrations. Today, it's not unusual to see tractor shows that list such unusual activities as antique tractor square dances, slow races, and backing contests. All are designed to extend the fun associated with owning and restoring antique tractors.

A slow race, for example, tests not only your tractor-operating skills, but your mechanical skills, as well. The goal of the race is to see who can drive a certain distance in the slowest time without stopping or killing the engine. That means you have to decide which gear

Tractor restoration and tractor shows are often addictive and affect other members of the family.

to start in, how far you dare throttle the engine back, and how often to apply the brakes. The smoother the engine runs at low speeds, the better you're going to be able to challenge the competition.

If maneuvering a tractor is your forte, you can find plenty of tractor games to test your skills in that area. The barrel race, for instance, calls for participants to push a barrel, which has been padded to protect tractor finishes, through an obstacle course. Drivers with narrow-front tractors naturally tend to hold the advantage.

On the other hand, maybe you'd rather try backing. A couple of contest variations include backing a hay wagon up to a pretend loading dock or through an obstacle course. The winner in either case is the person with the fastest time. Another backing skill game requires participants to see who can back up and stop with the hitch positioned closest to an egg without breaking it. This game is designed to test your skills at hitching up an implement and your ability to line up the hitch pinholes. Just to level the playing field, the game organizers occasionally require all participants to use the same tractor.

There are other games being played by tractor clubs all over the country. The latest growing in popularity is

As the interest in antique tractors has grown, so has the interest in antique farm implements. In this case, a mounted corn picker was restored to complement a collector's Model 6000 Diesel. Note the restored front-end loader on the Model 4000 Industrial in the background.

tractor square dancing. It takes a lot of room because it is done a lot like real square dancing. A caller announces the moves to the tune of music, and the tractors drive in a circle and follow the calls.

Antique Tractor Pulls

There are several reasons antique tractor pulling has become popular with tractor enthusiasts. The first is cost. Compared to modern-day pulling tractors, which are often equipped with multiple turbochargers and high-priced tires, an antique pulling tractor looks pretty much like the original. The only difference is the extra weight racks and the wheelie bars found on some tractors.

Consequently, an antique tractor enthusiast can participate in the sport for a fraction of the cost. Since the tractors in some classes are not significantly modified, they can still be used for work around the farm or acreage. Most antique tractor pullers prefer the slow pace of antique pulls to the glitz, smoke, and noise of modern tractor pulls. Unfortunately, due to their light weight, you won't see many early Ford tractors used in antique tractor pulls. That doesn't mean, however, that a later model designed for heavier farm work couldn't be modified to compete.

In general, most antique tractor pulls are divided into four or five classes, depending upon the governing body. It used to be that pulling tractors were classified as antique if they were built in 1938 or before, while tractors produced from 1939 to 1954 were designated as classic. The dividing year had more to do with tractor history than anything else. Prior to 1939, things like the radiator, fuel tank, and steering rod were pretty much left exposed, while later-model tractors were more streamlined and typically had more power.

Today, the National Antique Tractor Pullers Association (NATPA) and United States Antique Pullers (USAP), which generate the rules followed by most sanctioned pulls, have taken both history and tractor size into consideration. They realized that fewer and fewer tractors built prior to 1939 were participating in pulls. The NATPA now has five classes, or divisions, while the USAP recognizes four.

Division I in the NATPA, for example, is designed for beginning pullers and show tractors and is used to promote stock pulling. Only tractors built in 1957 or earlier, or production models that started in 1957 are eligible. In addition, almost everything must be stock and tractors can only pull in low gear with a 2.75-mile-per-hour speed limit.

Attachments, including mid- or front-mounted cultivators, listers, and hillers, are also popular with Ford enthusiasts.

Farming demonstrations, which often include plowing, harvesting, or baling hay, have grown in popularity at antique tractor shows.

Division II is for near-stock tractors that are 1957 or older models. Only low gear is permitted, even though some tire modifications are allowed and the speed limit is increased to 3 miles per hour. By the time you get into Divisions III and IV, drivers are permitted to use any gear, and any kind of cut is allowed on tires. Division III still has a speed limit, while IV does not.

Division V is for tractors that are 1959 or older. By this stage of the game, any gear and any speed are allowed, as is turning up the engine to 130 percent over manufacturer's data. All divisions except Division I also require wheelie bars.

Meanwhile, tractors competing in USAP events generally have four classes to choose from: Super Farm Stock, Modified Stock, Pro Stock, and Super Pro Stock. Even though there are speed limits in each class, all four classes are limited to tractors that are 1958 or older models.

Keep in mind that there are dozens of tractor pulling organizations around the country, and many of them operate under their own rules and regulations. It's best to check the rules at any pull before you go to the trouble of loading up the tractor and driving any distance.

Just as with modern tractor pulls, antique tractors in each class pull a mechanical sled on which the weight increases as the sled is pulled down the track. There are basically two ways antique tractor pulls are run. One is by weight class and the other is by percentage pull. Weight classes for antique tractors generally start at 3,500 pounds and increase in 500-pound increments, usually up to 7,500 to 8,500 pounds. Determining the winner of each class is just as simple as it is in big pulls: the tractor pulling the sled the farthest wins.

Percentage pulls require a little bit of math. In this case, you generally want the tractor to be as light as you can get it, or at least at the lighter end of the class. Any frills added for cosmetic reasons are often left off. Tractors are weighed to determine their exact weight and participants attempt to pull as much weight as possible. In the end, if two tractors pull the same amount of weight the same distance, but one weighs 3,500 pounds and the other weighs 4,000 pounds, the lighter tractor would be declared the winner.

Tractor cruises, like farming demonstrations, offer the best of both worlds. It's a chance to show off a beautifully restored tractor and put it into action.

A custom-made plaque can reveal more than your source of pride. It can also answer all those questions everyone has, like "What year and model is it?" and "Where are you from?"

Appendix

Parts and Sources

Salvage and Miscellaneous Parts

Abilene Machine Parts
PO Box 129
Abilene, KS 67410
800-255-0337 or 785-655-9455
www.abilenemachine.com

Ag Tractor Supply
9301 Breagan Road
Lincoln, NE 68526
Phone: 800-944-2898 or
515-523-2363
doug@agtractorsupply.com
www.agtractorsupply.com

Alderson Tractor
22724 163rd Avenue
Sigourney, IA 52591
641-624-2275
aldersonih@iowatelecom.net
www.aldersontractor.com

Alexander Tractor Parts
301 Park Street
Winnsboro, TX 75494
903-342-3001
800-231-6876
www.alexanders.com

All Parts International, Inc. (API)
3215 West Main Avenue
Fargo, ND 58103
701-235-7503

Altenative Parts Source Inc.
7427 Boliver Road
Chittenango, NY 13037-9449
315-687-0074

Arthurs Tractors
263 Sexton Road
Indiana, PA 15701
724-349-2015
877-254-FORD (3673)
dave@arthurstractors.com
www.arthurstractors.com

Bates Corporation
12351 Elm Road
Bourbon, IN 46504
574-342-2955
800-248-2955
batescorp@batescorp.com
www.batescorp.com

Berkshire Implement Co., Inc.
U.S. 35 North
PO Box 237
Royal Center, IN 46978
219-643-3115

Bob Martin Antique Tractor Parts
5 Ogle Industrial Drive
Vevay, IN 47043
812-427-2622

Biewer's Tractor and Restoration Salvage
16242 140th Avenue S.
Barnesville, MN 56514
218-493-4696
bts@rrt.net
www.salvagetractors.com

The Brillman Company
2328 Pepper Road
Mt. Jackson, VA 22842-2445
888-274-5562
www.brillman.com

Carter & Gruenewald Co., Inc - Brooklyn
4414 State Road 92
PO Box 40
Brooklyn, WI 53521
608-455-2411
cngcoinc@mailbag.com
www.cngco.com

Carter & Gruenewald - Juda
W2898 County KS
PO Box 5
Juda, WI 53550
608-934-5201

Worthington Ag Parts (formerly Central Michigan Tractor & Parts)
2713 North U.S. Hwy. 27
St. Johns, MI 48879
800-248-9263
888-845-8456
(for store locations in the U.S.)
800-244-7662
(for store locations in Canada)
www.worthingtonagparts.com

Central Plains Tractor Parts
712 North Main Avenue
Sioux Falls, SD 57104
605-334-0021
800-234-1968

Colfax Tractor Parts
10447 Field Avenue
Colfax, IA 50054
800-284-3001
Colfaxtractor@colfaxtractorparts.com
www.tractorhouse.com

Dave Cook Tractor Parts
28800 Cook Road
Washburn, WI 54891
715-373-2092
scott@davecooktractorparts.com
www.davecooktractorparts.com

Dengler's
6687 Shurz Road
Middletown, OH 45042
513-423-4000
www.denglertractor.com

Dick Moore Repair & Salvage
1540 Joe Quick Road
New Market, AL 35761
205-828-3884

Discount Tractor Supply
PO Box 265
Franklin Grove, IL 61031
800-433-5805

Draper Tractor Parts, Inc.
1951 Draper-Brown Road
Garfield, WA 99130
509-397-2666
800-967-8185
www.drapertractor.com

Dave Geyer
1259 Rohret Road SW
Oxford, IA 52322
319-628-4257

Ellis County Tractor
1513 East Hwy. 287
Waxahachie, TX 75165
972-923-0401

Faust Bros. Repair
Rt. 1 Box 212
Pierz, MN 56364

Fresno Tractor, Inc.
2730 West Whitesbridge
Fresno, CA 93706
559 233-2174
www.fresnotractor.com

Heritage Farm Power, Inc.
PO Box 1125
Belton, MO 64012
816-322-1898
sales@tractorumbrellas.com
www.tractorumbrellas.com
Vintage tractor umbrellas

Iowa Falls Tractor Parts/ Worthington Ag Parts
10050 Hwy. 65
Iowa Falls, IA 50126-8842
641-648-467

Norman Jackson
5013 East 100 S.
Greenfield, IN 46140
317-431-4803 (cell)

John R. Lair
413 L.Q. P Ave.
Canby, MN 56220
Fenders

Mark's Tractors
2636 County Road 2300 E.
Gifford, IL 61847
217-694-4735

Antique Tractor Parts (new and used)
Martin's Farm Supply
5 Ogle Industrial Drive Lot #3
Vevay, IN 47043
812-427-2622
www.antiquetractorparts.com

Mathis Equipment and Tractor Salvage
8828 North Hwy. 63
Box 132
Cairo, MO 65239
660-295-4456

Novotny's Repair & Parts (New and used)
2631 320th Street
Chelsea, IA 52215
641-489-2271 or 641-489-2070

O.E.M. Tractor Parts
1107 East Cemetery Road
Chenoa, IL 61726
800-283-2122
www.oemtractorparts.com

Parts of the Past, Inc.
1320 Spencer Drive
Lawrence, KS 66044
785-749-5231
Many new old stock (NOS) parts

Pete's Tractor Salvage, Inc.
2163 15th Avenue NE
Anamoose, ND 58710
800-541-7383
701-465-3274

Phil's Tractor & Supply, Inc.
925 Applegate Road
Madison, WI 53713
608-274-3601
www.philstractor.com

Harold Robinson
Rt. 1, Box 161
Queen City, MO 63561
660-766-2762 (5:30–9:30 Mon–Sat. only)

Salt Lake Mechanical
2969 West 500 South
Salt Lake City, UT 84104
Specializing in 8N and 9N

South-Central Tractor Parts/ Worthington Ag Parts
Old Hwy. 61 South
Leland, MS 38756
800-247-1237

Southeast Tractor Parts
14720 Hwy 151
Jefferson, SC 29718
888-658-7171
Eric@SETractorParts.com

Steiner Tractor Parts, Inc.
1660 S. M-13
PO Box 449
Lennon, MI 48449
800-234-3280
sales@steinertractor.com
www.steinertractor.com

Surplus Tractor Parts Corp.
3215 West Main
PO Box 2125
Fargo, ND 58107
800-859-2045
701-235-7503

Taylor Equipment
3694 2 Mile Road
Sears, MI 49679
800-368-3276
231-734-5213

The Tractor Barn
6154 West Hwy. 60
Brookline, MO 65619
800-383-3678
417-881-3668

TractorHouse.Com
PO Box 85670
Lincoln, NE 68501-5670
800-307-5199
402-479-2154
feedback@tractorhouse.com
www.tractorhouse.com

Tractor Parts Unlimited
24755 Hwy. 12 East
Ethel, MS 39067
866-996-7278
www.tractorpartsunlimited.com

Tractor Works
10207 North County Road 300 W.
Jamestown, IN 46147
765-676-6292

Thorne Farm Equipment
PO Box 358
Chesnee, SC 29323
803-461-7719
803-461-7719

Tired Iron Farm
19467 C.R. 8
Bristol, IN 46507
574-848-4628

Van Noort Tractor Salvage
1003 10th Avenue
Rock Valley, IA 51247
800-831-8543

Walthill Service and Supply
PO Box 2B
103 North Tallman
Walthill, NE 68067
402-846-5450

Watertown Tractor Parts/ Worthington Ag Parts
2510 9th Ave. SW
Watertown, SD 57201
800-843-4413

Watson Farm Equipment and Tractor Parts
Ariss Rt. 2
Flora, Ontario, Canada N0B1B0
519-846-5279
519-846-0776 (Parts)

Weber's Tractor Works
201 South Lafayette
Newton, IL 62448
815-389-1493
618-783-4102 (IL)
507-434-0876 (MN)
wtw@weberstractorworks.com
www.weberstractorworks.com
Many new old stock (NOS) parts

Wengers of Myerstown
831 South College Street
PO Box 409
Myerstown, PA 17067
800-451-5240 (Tractor parts)
717-866-6656 (Machining services)
www.wengers.com

Wilson Tractor Parts Online Store
Sherwood, AR 72120
501-835-1445
www.tractorshack.com

Worthington Tractor Salvage/ Worthington Ag Parts
27170 U.S. Hwy. 59
Worthington, MN 56187
800-533-5304

Yesterday's Tractors
PO Box 160
Chicacum, WA 98325
800-853-2651
www.ytmag.com

Ford Tractor Restoration Parts

Dennis Carpenter Ford Tractor Reproductions
4140 Concord Pkwy. S.
Concord, NC 28027
704-786-8139
www.dennis-carpenter.com

Classic Ford Tractor Parts
12058 Airport Road
Staples, MN 56479
218-296-2021
jlthew@msn.com
www.classicfordtractorparts.com

Davis Tractor Parts
Ford 8N Dept
24263 Antioch Road
Andalusia, AL 36421
334-222-7214
877-610-7214
parts@davistractor.com
www.ford8Ntractorparts.com

Ford Tractor Unlimited
Tractor Parts Inc.
PO Box 2187
Glasgow, KY 42142-2187
270-651-2547
www.fordtractorpart.com

George Bradish Tractor Parts
3865 State Route 982
Latrobe, PA 15650-3914
724-539-8386
www.georgebradishtractorparts.com
1939–1964 Ford restoration and maintenance parts

Just 8N's
2505 South Post Rd.
Shelby, NC 28152
704-482-9913 or 704-482-9914
888-355-9937
just8parts@carolina.rr.com
www.just8ns.com

N-Complete
10594 East 700 N.
Wilkinson, IN 46186
765-785-2309
765-785-2314 – Technical support
877-342-2086 – Orders or catalog request
www.n-complete.com

Tractor Restoration/Painting

Ken's Body Shop
124 East Cleveland Road
Huron, OH 44839
419-433-3511
800-843-2395

Dallas Mercer
Mercer Restoration
14255 Hwy. Y
Excelsior Springs, MO 64024
816-826-6049
www.mercertractors.com

Kevin Spencer
PO Box 350
N. Clarendon, VT 05759
802-773-6687
Specializing in Ford models

Carburetors and Governors — Parts/Rebuilders

Burrey Carburetor Service
5026 Maples Road
Fort Wayne, IN 46816
206-447-6347
800-287-7390
info@burreycarb.com
www.burreycarb.com

Denny's Carb Shop
8620 North Casstown-Fletcher Rd.
Fletcher, OH 45326-9786
937-368-2304
www.dennyscarbshop.com

Link's Carburetor Repair
8708 Floyd Hwy. North
PO Box 139
Copper Hill, VA 24079
540-929-4519
540-929-4719 (after 7 p.m. EST)
laurandy@swva.net
www.swva.net/linkscarb/

McDonald Carb & Ignition
1001 Commerce Road
Jefferson, GA 30549
706-367-4179
mmcdonald_c_i@yahoo.com
www.mcdonaldcarb.com

Motec Engineering
7342 West State Road 28
Tipton, IN 46072
765-963-6628

Robert's Carburetor Repair
404 East 5th Street
PO Box 624
Spencer, IA 51301
712-262-5311
www.robertscarbrepair.com

Treadwell Carburetor Company
4870 County Highway 14
Treadwell, NY 13846
607-829-8321
carbkit@frontiernet.net
www.carbsandkits.com

Diesel Injection Pumps and Nozzles—Parts/Rebuilders

Central Fuel Injection Service Co.
2403 Murray Road
Estherville, IA 51334
712-362-4200
www.centralfuel.com

Transmission Components

Arthurs Tractors
263 Sexton Road
Indiana, PA 15701
877-254-FORD (3673)
dave@arthurstractors.com
www.arthurstractors.com
Specializing in vintage Ford tractors
and Select-O-Speed transmissions

Rich Bednarski
215 South Buffalo Road
Washington, PA 15301
724-345-3546
800-832-6350 (evenings best)

Magnetos, Starters, Generators — Parts/Rebuilders

Ed Strain
6555 44th Street N., #2006
Pinellas Park, FL 33781
800-266-1623
727-521-1597

Genesee Products
PO Box 1977
Owasso, OK 74055
918-274-8000
www.GP6.com
Electronic ignition systems

Mark's Magneto Service
321 McDonald Road
Colchester, CT 06415
860-537-0376
www.deschene.com/marksmagneto

Lightning Magneto
45685 County Hwy. 54
Ottertail, MN 56571
218-367-2819

Bill Lopoulos Magneto Parts
29 Chard Road
Tyngsboro, MA 01879
978-649-7879
blopoulos@aol.com
www.magnetoparts.com

Magneeders
8215 County Road 118
Carthage, MO 64836
417-358-7863
magneedr@ipa.net
www.magneeders.com

Shearer Equipment
7762 Cleveland Road
Wooster, OH 44691
800-431-9023
www.shearerequipment.com

Gauges

Antique Gauges, Inc.
12287 Old Skipton Rd.
Cordova, MD 21625
410-822-4963

Many of the salvage and reproduction parts sources also carry gauges.

Wiring Harnesses

Agri-Services
13899 North Road
Alden, NY 14004
716-937-6618
www.wiringharnesses.com

Several of the salvage and reproduction parts sources also carry wiring harnesses.

Seals & Gaskets

A-1 Leather Cup and Gasket Company
2103 Brennan Circle
Fort Worth, TX 76106-8318
817-626-9664

Lubbock Gasket & Supply
402 19th Street
PO Box 2154
Lubbock, TX 79408
806-763-2801
800-527-2064
www.lubbockgasket.com

Olson's Gaskets
3059 Opdal Road E.
Port Orchard, WA 98366
360-871-1207
www.olsonsgaskets.com

Wheels and Rims

Detwiler Tractor Parts
110 South Pacific
Spencer, WI 54479
715-659-4252
info@detwilertractor.com
www.detwilertractor.com

Nielsen Spoke Wheel Repair
Herb Nielsen
3921 230th Street
Estherville, IA 51334
712-867-4796

Steel Wheel Ranch
1215 Plumtree Road
Everest, KS 66424
785-548-7437

Wilson Farms
20552 Old Mansfield Road
Fredericktown, OH 43019
740-694-5071

Tires

M. E. Miller Tire Co.
17386 State Hwy. 2
Wauseon, OH 43567
419-335-7010
800-621-1955
www.millertire.com

Tucker's Tire
844 South Main Street
Dyersburg, TN 38024
731-285-8520
888-248-7146
tires4u@webtv.net
www.tuckertire.com

Several of the reproduction sources also carry tires.

Replacement Seats

Speer Cushion Co.
431 South Interocean
Holyoke, CO 80734
970-854-2911 or 970-854-2288
800-525-8156
info@speercushion.com
www.speercushion.com

Silver Seats
Darrel Darst
1857 West Outer Hwy. 61
Moscow Mills, MO 63362
636-356-4764 (nights)
636-528-4877, ext. 113 (days)

Easy Bob's Tractor Parts
3485 South State Road 19
Tipton, IN 46072
765-675-2530
info@easybobstractorparts.com
easybobstractorparts.com/index.php

Mufflers

Oren Schmidt
Rt. 1 Box 56
Homestead, IA 52236
319-662-4388

Many of the salvage and reproduction parts sources also carry mufflers.

Steering Wheels—Recovering

Minn-Kota Repair
38893 Co. Hwy. 12
Ortonville, MN 56278
320-839-3940 or 320-289-2473
www.minnkotarepair.com

Tractor Steering Wheel Recovering and Repair
1400 121st Street W.
Rosemount, MN 55068
612-455-1802

Decals

Dennis Carpenter
(See parts listings above)

N-Complete
(See parts listings above)

Restoration Equipment & Supplies

CJ Spray, Inc.
370 Airport Road, Bldg. 7
South St. Paul, MN 55075
651-455-0880
800-328-4827
www.cjspray.com
Spray systems

Jim Deardorff
Box 317
Chillicothe, MO 64601
660-646-6355
Fax: 660-646-3329
jdeardorff@yahoo.com
Classic Blast sandblasting mix made from aluminum oxide and black walnut shells

TP Tools and Equipment
7075 State Route 446
PO Box 649
Canfield, OH 44406
800-321-9260
Info Line: 330-533-3384
www.tiptools.com
Parts washers, grinders, presses, sandblasting equipment, etc.

Miscellaneous

ChlorRid International, Inc.
PO Box 908
Chandler, AZ 85244
480-821-0039
800-422-3217
www.chlor-rid.com
ChlorWash, ChlorRid, HoldBlast, and other cleaning products that remove salts and prevent flash rust

Eldorado Solutions
12780 San Fernando Road
Sylmar, CA 91342
800-531-1088
Sales and product information:
Sales@EldoradoChem.com
Technical support: TechSupport@
EldoradoChem.com
www.eldoradochem.com

International Chemical Products, Inc.
1209 Meadow Park Drive
Huntsville, AL 35803
256-650-0088
www.icpi.net
Picklex metal surface preparation
and pre-treatment chemicals

McElroy Enterprises
411 1st Avenue
Ft. Dodge, IA 50501
800-397-3669
Kreem Fuel Tank Liner

Himes Casting Repair
258 Lehr Drive
Mooresville, IN 46158
317-831-8069 or 317-831-2571
Cast iron welding, porting, and
polishing

Publications & Clubs

Tractor Manuals

Jensales Inc.
200 Main Street
Manchester, MN 56007-5000
800-443-0625 (orders)
507-826-3666
www.jensales.com

Clarence L. Goodburn Literature Sales
101 West Main
Madelia, MN 56062
507-642-3281

King's Books
PO Box 86c
Radnor, OH 43066

Yesterday's Tractors
PO Box 160
Chicacum, WA 98325
www.ytmag.com

Penton Media (formerly Intertec Publishing)
9800 Metcalf Avenue
Overland Park, KS 66212
800-262-1954
www.buypenton.com

General Magazines

Antique Power
PO Box 500
Missouri City, TX 77459
800-767-5828
888-760-8108 (subscriptions)
www.antiquepower.com

The Belt Pulley
PO Box 58
Jefferson, WI 53549
920-674-9732
www.beltpulley.com

The Hook Magazine
PO Box 16
Marshfield, MO 65706
417-468-7000
www.hookmagazine.com
Tractor pulling, including antique
and classic

Ford Publications

The N Newsletter
PO Box 275
East Corinth, VT 05040
www.n-news.com

Internet Resources

Antique Farming
www.antiquefarming.com

Antique Tractor Internet Services
www.atis.net

Antique Tractor Resource Page
www.antiquetractors.com

Fastrac – Antique Tractor Support Group and Information Site
www.adeptr.com

Ford/Fordson Collectors Association
www.ford-fordson.org

N Tractor Club
www.ntractor.club

Smith's Old Ford Tractors
www.8nford.com or
www.oldfordtractors.com

Tyler Neff's 9N Ford Page
www.my9n.com

Yesterday's Tractors
www.ytmag.com

Index

About the Author

Tharran Gaines has written about agricultural equipment since 1974, when he began his career as a technical writer for Hesston Corporation. Since then, he has written numerous repair manuals, sales brochures, news releases, and advertisements for such companies as Winnebago, Case IH, AGCO, Gleaner, Kinze, and Massey Ferguson. He has also written hundreds of magazine articles for the farm press, as well as the books *How To Restore Classic Farm Tractors*, *How To Restore Classic John Deere Tractors*, and *How To Restore Classic Farmall Tractors*, all by Voyageur Press. Tharran and his wife, Barb, live in Savannah, Missouri.